C. S. Lewis on the Final Frontier

C. S. Lewis ∾ on the Final Frontier

Science and the Supernatural
in the Space Trilogy

SANFORD SCHWARTZ

OXFORD
UNIVERSITY PRESS

2009

OXFORD
UNIVERSITY PRESS

Oxford University Press, Inc., publishes works that further
Oxford University's objective of excellence
in research, scholarship, and education.

Oxford   New York
Auckland   Cape Town   Dar es Salaam   Hong Kong   Karachi
Kuala Lumpur   Madrid   Melbourne   Mexico City   Nairobi
New Delhi   Shanghai   Taipei   Toronto

With offices in
Argentina   Austria   Brazil   Chile   Czech Republic   France   Greece
Guatemala   Hungary   Italy   Japan   Poland   Portugal   Singapore
South Korea   Switzerland   Thailand   Turkey   Ukraine   Vietnam

Copyright © 2009 by Oxford University Press, Inc.

Published by Oxford University Press, Inc.
198 Madison Avenue, New York, New York 10016

www.oup.com

Oxford is a registered trademark of Oxford University Press

Library of Congress Cataloging-in-Publication Data
Schwartz, Sanford, 1948–
C. S. Lewis on the final frontier : science and the supernatural
in the space trilogy / Sanford Schwartz.
    p.   cm.
Includes bibliographical references (p.) and index.
ISBN 978-0-19-537472-8
1. Lewis, C. S. (Clive Staples), 1898–1963. Space trilogy.
2. Lewis, C. S. (Clive Staples), 1898–1963—Philosophy.   I. Title.
PR6023.E926S55   2009
823'.912—dc22   2008032454

9 8 7 6 5 4 3 2 1

Printed in the United States of America
on acid-free paper

To my parents,
Rose and Leonard Schwartz

"that by Wisdom made the heavens . . ."
—*Psalm* 136

". . . from so simple a beginning endless forms most
beautiful and most wonderful have been, and are being,
evolved."
—*The Origin of Species*

Acknowledgments ~

In the final chapter of *Perelandra,* the king of this new and rapidly evolving paradise acknowledges that his sovereignty devolves upon him as a "gift" from others: "All is gift. . . . Through many hands, enriched with many different kinds of love and labour, the gift comes to me. It is the Law. The best fruits are plucked for each by some hand that is not his own." Many hands that are not my own have contributed to this book, and my debts are so extensive that it has become difficult to think of myself as the "author" in any conventional sense of the term. This study began and ended with my family. It was launched by my adolescent son, Nathaniel, whose childhood delight in *The Chronicles of Narnia* led him to the Space Trilogy, and his enthusiasm in turn led me back to Lewis's interplanetary romances for the first time in many years. It concluded, and indeed has been sustained all along, by my wife, Marion, who not only listened to often inchoate efforts to articulate issues and explanations but also seemed a step or two ahead of me at every turn. From them, and from the good humor and editorial assistance of my daughter Caroline, "the gift comes to me."

As a scholar of early twentieth-century modernism and as a relative latecomer to Lewis, I've depended throughout this project on the critical eye and personal support of several Lewis scholars, first and foremost Peter Schakel, who read my initial essay on *Perelandra* and encouraged me to believe that there was similar work to be done on the rest of the Trilogy. Robert Snyder, editor emeritus of *Christianity and Literature,* which published that first essay, provided excellent critical and editorial advice and offered similar encouragement to continue on. I owe an intellectual debt to Doris T. Myers, whose *C. S. Lewis in Context* (1994) departed from the prevailing image of the self-styled "dinosaur" and demonstrated the fruits of situating Lewis in the maelstrom of modern intellectual, social, and cultural life. I'm also grateful to David Downing for some sharp observations on the *Perelandra* article; to Dale Nelson for crucial biographical and bibliographical assistance at a later stage of the enterprise; to Charles Huttar for his meticulous analysis of the completed manuscript; and to Alan Jacobs for his generous reading as I neared the home stretch. A special salute to Christopher Mitchell and Marjorie Mead of the Marion E. Wade Center at Wheaton College, where most of the research for this book was conducted. Their hospitality, along with the unflagging efficiency and courtesy of their student assistants, transformed the long hours in the archives into an unforgettable pleasure.

Among the many others who have provided support along the way, I wish to thank my colleagues at Penn State, especially Philip Jenkins, Elizabeth Jenkins, Alan Stoekl, Laura Knoppers, Christopher Clausen, Mark Morrisson, and Robert Caserio. I can't say enough about the acumen of my graduate assistants—Christopher White, Jeff Pruchnic, Chad Schrock, Eric Howerton, Daniel Story, and Steve van Stempvoort—who never missed a lazy phrase, a misstep in the argument, or a critical sleight of hand. This is a much improved work as a result of their efforts and would be far better still had I been able to attend to all of their red ink. The same is true of the remarkable staff at Oxford University Press. Heartfelt thanks to my senior editor, Cynthia Read, whose high spirits kept me afloat as this manuscript passed time and again through the refiner's fire; to her assistants Meechal Hoffman and Justin Tackett; and to Christine Dahlin, Rachel Perkins, and Woody Gilmartin. Penn State provided travel support at the outset of this project and a sabbatical leave that allowed me to finish it.

Earlier versions of the chapters on *Out of the Silent Planet* and *Perelandra* appeared in *Christianity and Literature*; in *Milton and Popular Culture*, edited by Laura Lunger Knoppers and Gregory M. Colón Semenza (Palgrave); and in *C. S. Lewis: Views from Wake Forest*, edited by Robert Trexler (Zossima Press). Portions of these and other parts of the book were tested out at various gatherings: the Lewis Centennial Conference at Wheaton College (1998); annual regional meetings of the Conference on Christianity and Literature; the Guild of Episcopal Scholars; the Penn State Christian Graduate Association; the Society of the Space Between, 1914–1945; and most recently, the Lewis conference at Wake Forest Baptist Theological Seminary (2007). My sincere thanks to the many unnamed respondents who questioned, qualified, or contradicted my presentations, but whose attentiveness and passion for Lewis kept alive my desire to keep going.

Contents ～

Abbreviations ~

Page numbers throughout refer to the Scribner trade paperback editions of the Space Trilogy (2003). For those reading different editions, see Appendix B: Tables for Converting Page References to Chapter Numbers. Appendix B also contains similar conversion tables for longer apologetical works—*Mere Christianity, Miracles, The Problem of Pain*—and for "The Dark Tower."

AM	*The Abolition of Man*
AMR	*All My Road Before Me*
CR	*Christian Reflections*
D	*Dymer*
DI	*The Discarded Image*
DT	*The Dark Tower and Other Stories*
ELSC	*English Literature in the Sixteenth Century Excluding Drama*
GD	*The Great Divorce*
GID	*God in the Dock: Essays on Theology and Ethics*
GO	*A Grief Observed*
L	*Letters* [3-volume set; *L* I, *L* II, or *L* III]
LM	*Letters to Malcolm*
M	*Miracles*
MC	*Mere Christianity*
OS	*On Stories and Other Essays on Literature*
OSP	*Out of the Silent Planet*
P	*Perelandra*
PP	*The Problem of Pain*

C. S. Lewis on the Final Frontier

Introduction ∼

Darwin in Deep Heaven

> Supposition . . . presupposes that the actual or real
> fact is not the whole of reality. It implies that there are
> other spheres, or other provinces of the same sphere, all
> connected in a wider universe.
> —F. H. Bradley, *Essays on Truth and Reality*

> In the mind of the fallen Archon under whom our
> planet groans, the memory of Deep Heaven and the
> gods with whom he once consorted is still alive. Nay,
> in the very matter of our world, the traces of the
> celestial commonwealth are not quite lost.
> —C. S. Lewis, *Perelandra*

Before there was *Narnia* there were the interplanetary romances,
commonly known as the "Space" or "Ransom" Trilogy. C. S.
Lewis's unlikely hero, Elwin Ransom—a Cambridge philologist
turned cosmic warrior—may never attain the superstar status of the
Pevensie children or see his tales transformed by the magic of the
marketplace into a lucrative corporate franchise. The series in which
he stars—*Out of the Silent Planet* (1938), *Perelandra* (1943), and *That
Hideous Strength* (1945)—occupies a respectable niche in the annals of
modern science fiction. But at the start of the new millennium, the
Space Trilogy owes much of its resilient shelf life to the reflective glow
of *The Chronicles of Narnia* (1950–1956) and to its author's enduring

reputation as the preeminent religious apologist of our times. When Ransom first appeared on the scene, Clive Staples Lewis was a forty-ish academic unknown beyond the lecture halls of Oxford and the compact company of scholars acquainted with *The Allegory of Love* (1936), his first major study of Medieval and Renaissance literature. By the time of Ransom's final farewell in 1945, Lewis was a household name in Britain and something of a celebrity in the rest of the English-speaking world. His fame was fueled by a daunting mélange of fiction, lively and inventive apologetics, engaging literary criticism (not yet an oxymoron), and above all, by the four series of immensely popular radio broadcasts (1941–1944)—later assembled into *Mere Christianity* (1952)—which unexpectedly captured the pulse of an embattled nation. In the decade following Ransom's debut, there appeared in rapid succession *The Problem of Pain* (1940), the much-admired *Screwtape Letters* (1942), *Broadcast Talks* (1942, the print version of the first and second radio series), *A Preface to 'Paradise Lost'* (1942), *Christian Behaviour* (1943, the third set of radio talks), *Perelandra* (1943), *The Abolition of Man* (1943), *Beyond Personality* (1944, the final set of broadcasts), *That Hideous Strength* (1945), *The Great Divorce* (1946), and *Miracles* (1947), in addition to some notable essays and other writings. By the close of these *anni mirabili* Elwin Ransom had been dispatched to his celestial resting place, but his creator was sitting on the cover of *Time* magazine (September 8, 1947, with his head slightly angled toward the protective wing of a dove on one side, his more visible ear slyly exposed to a pitch-forked tempter on the other). *The Lion, the Witch and the Wardrobe*—first of the *Narnia* chronicles—was still a distant gleam on the horizon.

Lewis's fighting philologist was conceived in an atmosphere of looming international crisis, and however far he travels from his own planet, the issues surrounding the causes, conduct, and consequences of the Second World War are never far from the surface. Ransom's first adventure, *Out of the Silent Planet,* was published in September 1938, three weeks prior to Neville Chamberlain's infamous appeasement of Hitler at Munich, and it is no accident that most of the novel takes place on the planet named for the god of war. Abducted seemingly by chance and taken to Mars (Malacandra) by a pair of cosmic imperialists, Ransom spends the first part of the narrative struggling with the terrors, real and imaginary, that threaten to engulf him. Lewis's peace-loving protagonist is not a committed pacifist, as were many in the thirties, but Ransom's experience on Mars seems calculated to restore confidence in his own courage, which has never recovered from the traumas of the First World War, and to promote "the *good* element in the martial spirit, the discipline and freedom from anxiety" (*L* II, 702, 1/31/46), which will be required for the all-but-inevitable struggle ahead. Twelve months later hostilities commenced, and by the time of Ransom's next appearance in *Perelandra,* the war had been raging for nearly four years, its outcome still in doubt. In his new role, a more self-assured Ransom travels to a freshly minted creation on Venus (Perelandra) and primes himself for a Christlike battle of wits with the powers of evil, echoing Milton's elaboration of the biblical temptation in the wilderness in *Paradise Regained.* But Lewis turns the tables on his hero, who discovers that words and wisdom will not suffice and slowly progresses toward the horrifying realization that he has been called upon to engage in hand-to-hand combat with the Evil One himself. The author's decision to resolve the conflict in this manner—an open attempt to justify, if not sanctify, the recourse to arms—remains a disturbing aspect of the novel even to sympathetic readers who assent to the position it supports. So does the blood-soaked resolution of Ransom's last adventure, *That Hideous Strength,* which appeared in print one week prior to the cataclysmic events at Hiroshima and Nagasaki and portrays the rise and fall of a totalitarian conspiracy on our own planet. Once again, few of Lewis's readers dispute the justice of the cause, but many never fail to wince at the level of divinely sanctioned violence visited on the architects of the New Leviathan. In light of such scenes, Lewis is often accused of harboring an anachronistic (if not boyishly sadistic) ideal of Christian knighthood scandalously out of place in the modern world. But whether or not we are satisfied by Lewis's management of the moral and religious issues he raises in these war-torn novels, Elwin Ransom's three-volume transformation from terrified victim to anointed guardian of the planet bears the unmistakable imprint of the violent conditions of the time.

It is not physical but ideological warfare, however, that dominates the Space Trilogy and ultimately encompasses the war itself. Proceeding from Mars and Venus to the final showdown on our own planet, each new installment examines another facet of the seemingly impassable conflict between Christian tradition and the evolutionary or "developmental" tendencies of modern thought. In his contemporaneous essays Lewis states repeatedly that his target is not the biological theory of evolution, which he regards as a "genuine scientific hypothesis" ("Funeral of a Great Myth," *CR* 83), but the more deep-seated conceptual paradigm, well established by the time of Darwin's monumental *Origin of Species* (1859), which transferred the focal point of creation from a transcendent God to the progressive development of Man. For the most part Lewis is less concerned with the prospect of subhuman ancestry than with a conceptual apparatus that consigns other human beings to subhuman status, or summons up an "evolutionary imperative" to legitimate the suspension of time-honored ethical norms. These issues were increasingly acute in the early twentieth century, when projects for the "transformation of humanity" turned from speculative fictions into real-life legislative agendas for the improvement of the species, and at their most extreme, into lethal crusades to secure the future of the evolutionary process itself. Seen from this vantage point the war against Nazi aggression was not simply a conflict between rival nations in a traditionally fractious continent but a struggle over the very way in which we conceive of human nature and its relations to the rest of the natural order. The outcome of the war drastically altered the political map of the planet, but in setting Ransom's final battle in postwar England, Lewis makes it clear that the ideological issues at stake in the conflict would not disappear with the demise of fascism. Indeed, they are very much with us today. The capacity for the biotechnical transformation of humanity—driven by the extraordinary developments in genetic, robotic, information, and nanotechnologies—increases on an almost daily basis, and even if (for now) we in the West are somewhat less haunted by the specter of state-enforced eugenics, it seems as though the major concerns of the Space Trilogy are becoming ever more ominous as we move further into the twenty-first century.

The following chapters are designed to accompany readers through each of Elwin Ransom's adventures and to offer some reflections on the series as a whole, including the unfinished story posthumously published as *The Dark Tower* (see Appendix A). They draw liberally on earlier full-length studies of the Trilogy—by Martha Sammons (1980), David Downing (1992), and Jared Lobdell (2004)—and on the vast stream of other commentary that shows no sign of exhaustion nearly a half-century after the author's death.[1] This excursion through the Space Trilogy, however, proceeds from three distinctive premises, which account for the organization of its individual chapters and for their prevailing points of view. The first premise issues from the observation that the three novels share the same internal configuration (outlined below), and this common structure sheds light not only on each individual novel but also on the relationships between them. The second premise, which requires some historical reconstruction, calls attention to significant changes in the representation of the modern evolutionary model as the series proceeds from one novel to the next. Each of the three books examines the dire consequences of the developmental paradigm, but over the course of the Trilogy the paradigm itself develops, or in a sense ascends, from the "materialist" assumptions of the first story to the presumably higher "organic" or "vitalist" level of the sequel, and then mutates once again into a "spiritual" principle in the finale. The third premise, which issues from the second, is grounded in the perception that each of the providentially governed communities with which Ransom is associated—the "unfallen" Mars and Venus in the first two novels, and their terrestrial counterpart, the manor of St. Anne's, in the finale—is constructed

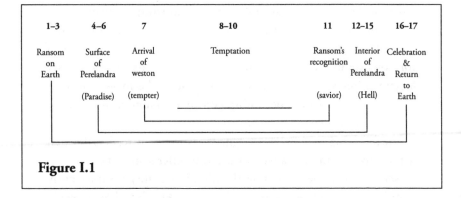

1–3	4–6	7	8–10	11	12–15	16–17
Ransom on Earth	Surface of Perelandra	Arrival of weston	Temptation	Ransom's recognition	Interior of Perelandra	Celebration & Return to Earth
	(Paradise)	(tempter)		(savior)	(Hell)	

Figure I.1

not as the polar opposite but the transfiguration or "working-up" (*RP* 112) of the specific phase of the evolutionary model to which it stands opposed. As we shall see, this final and most complex premise, which is also more consistent with Lewis's Augustinian view that "bad things are good things perverted" (*PPL* 66), entails a significant departure from the traditional approach to these novels. Taken together, these three working tenets suggest that the Space Trilogy, which began with no evident master plan and developed gradually over a period of years, is a more integrated and systematically organized series than is generally assumed. More important, they indicate that contrary to Lewis's self-styled image as an intellectual "dinosaur" stranded in the modern world ("*De Descriptione Temporum*" *SLE* 13), the Space Trilogy and its author are at once deeply engaged with the modern intellectual revolution and eager to explore some of the pioneering insights that arose in its wake.

Structure

Ransom's three adventures share a precise internal symmetry. Scholars have long known that the seventeen chapters of *Perelandra* form a tightly knit unit. Although there are no formal indicators other than chapter numbers, the first part of the novel (chapters 1–7) may be divided into three discrete sections, which proceed toward a climactic center—the temptation scene (chapters 8–10)—followed by another seven-chapter sequence (chapters 11–17) that mirrors the tripartite division of the first seven chapters. On an initial reading we cannot discern this pattern until well into the second half of the novel (if we do so at all), but from a bird's eye view what emerges is a structure comprised of a central core (chapters 8–10) surrounded by a balanced series of frames: This "ring" structure, in which the later sections of the work circle back to the beginning, is by no means unique to Lewis.[2] But if we keep this formation in mind as we read the novel, we will catch some of the notable shifts in focus as we progress from section to section; and once we've crossed the central divide (chapters 8–10) we can appreciate the significant and often extensive network of references through which each successive section in the second half echoes and answers to its counterpart in the first.

No such scholarly consensus exists on the other two novels, which also lack any structural markers other than chapter numbers (though the chapters have titles in the final book). One of the working principles of this study is that *Out of the Silent Planet* and *That Hideous Strength* possess the same internal configuration as *Perelandra,* and conceiving them in this manner yields equally rewarding results. Hence each of the following chapters is divided into segments that reflect the section-by-section development of the novel it examines (see the figures on pp. 28, 66, and 98). This arrangement enables us to follow the narrative through its various twists and turns in each individual volume and to identify some striking similarities in the corresponding sections of consecutive volumes. Many of these correspondences will be identified along the way, but in the conclusion we will examine a compelling instance of this multivolume symmetry: at the identical point in all three novels the previously passive protagonist is placed in a situation that requires personal decision, a commitment to violent action, and a reckoning with the prospect of death. As we shall see, these closely related scenes also form a distinctive progression that reveals the larger design of the series as it unfolds from one novel to the next.

Sequence

Each volume of the Space Trilogy may be read on its own, but Lewis establishes a clear line of continuity and progression over the course of the series. The continuity rests primarily on the conflict between Elwin Ransom and his two ruthless foes—the physicist Weston and the venture capitalist Devine—who are first introduced in *Out of the Silent Planet* and then resurface in the sequels: Weston in *Perelandra* and Devine (now Lord Feverstone) in *That Hideous Strength*. The sense of progression is most apparent in the gradual transformation of Elwin Ransom, but the less evident changes that occur in his enemies, or more important, in the things they represent, bring to the fore a significant but neglected aspect of the Trilogy. In the opening volume, Ransom's kidnappers are associated with the popular "materialist" view of "orthodox Darwinism" ("Is Theology Poetry?" *WG* 136)—the infamous "struggle for existence"— especially as it appears in H. G. Wells's dramatic portrayal of this conflict on an interplanetary scale in *The War of the Worlds* and elsewhere (see p. 4). In Lewis's novel the two terrestrial villains use the presumption of their own evolutionary superiority to justify the conquest, displacement, or even the extermination of other rational beings, whether they are members of other species, as they are on Mars, or "inferior" members of our own species here on earth. In *Perelandra*, Ransom once again encounters Weston, but this time the physicist claims that he has been converted from the crude materialism of the previous book. As a result of his reading in modern "biological philosophy" (*P* 78), Weston now espouses the developmental vision of "creative" or "emergent" evolution, the former associated with the celebrated philosopher Henri Bergson (*Creative Evolution*, 1907), the latter with a subsequent movement among British thinkers who modified the Darwinian paradigm to allow more room for novelty, discontinuity, and creative development in the evolutionary process (see p. 5). At first glance, Weston's conversion may seem a distinction without a difference, since the encounter between Ransom and Weston (or rather the Satanic Un-man who gradually takes possession of Weston's mind) rapidly descends, as it does in the first book, into a mortal conflict between Christian tradition and evolutionary naturalism. Nevertheless, as Lewis tells us, "the Bergsonian critique of orthodox Darwinism is not easy to answer" ("Is Theology Poetry?" *WG* 136), and the passage from the "materialist" (or "mechanistic") view of "orthodox Darwinism" to the "organic" (or "vitalist") view of creative/emergent evolution plays a constitutive role in the development of the Trilogy. As we shall see, the distinction between these two conceptions of the evolutionary process illuminates some of the notable differences between the "unfallen" worlds of Mars and Venus, and as the ostensible "middle way" between "materialist" and "religious" points of view, Bergson's new "vitalist" or "Life-Force philosophy" (*MC* 26) sets the stage for the third formulation of the evolutionary model in the final volume of the series.

In *That Hideous Strength* Ransom remains on his own planet to battle Devine and his seemingly scientific institution—the National Institute of Co-ordinated Experiments (N.I.C.E.)—whose leaders are actually conspiring with demonic powers to seize control of the evolutionary process and bring about the self-transformation of man into "God almighty . . . a being made by man—who will finally ascend to the throne of the universe. And rule forever" (*THS* 176). As paradoxical as it seems, the modern developmental paradigm as it appears in *That Hideous Strength* is no longer confined within the bounds of its own naturalistic moorings. As the titular allusion to the Tower of Babel suggests, the N.I.C.E. transports us beyond both the "material" (Wellsian) and the "organic" (Bergsonian) realms to the "spiritual" (Babelian) plane of the supernatural "New Man, the man who will not die, the artificial man, free from nature" (*THS* 174). Strangely enough, as we progress through the Trilogy we are also progressing to seemingly higher forms of the evolutionary model itself as they ascend (and in a sense return) to the transcendent heights of the religious worldview that the new developmental cosmology had presumably left behind.

Other Worlds

In a postwar discussion of his avowed literary model, David Lindsay's *A Voyage to Arcturus* (1920), Lewis informs us that "no merely physical strangeness or merely spatial distance will realize that idea of otherness which is what we are always trying to grasp in a story about voyaging through space: you must go into another dimension . . . you must draw on the only real 'other world' we know, that of the spirit" ("On Stories" *OS* 12).[3] It is well known that Lewis endows his "other worlds" on Mars and Venus with attributes drawn from the "medieval model" of the cosmos—"the heavens which declared the glory" (*OSP* 34)—and populates them with unfallen rational creatures free from the fears and temptations that plague our own wayward species. The singular focus on the medieval model, however, deflects attention from the surprising similarities between the "unfallen" worlds of Mars and Venus and the seemingly antithetical "evolutionary model" propounded by the terrestrial invaders. As we shall see, certain features of Lewis's Malacandra suggest that this spiritually uncorrupted planet should be viewed not as the polar opposite but as the transfiguration or "up-grading" (*RP* 118) of the Wellsian war between the species, while the distinctive temporal dynamism of the new Eden on Perelandra may be seen as a sanctified version of Bergson's own creative evolution. In accord with his Augustinian view that "bad things are good things perverted," Lewis transforms first the "materialist" and then the "vitalist" views of evolution into "unfallen" worlds that make their terrestrial counterparts appear as parodic distortions of unspoiled and divinely created originals. Seen from this perspective, the distinction between the "Wellsianity" ("Is Theology Poetry?" *WG* 123) of *Out of the Silent Planet* and the "Bergsianity" (my term) of *Perelandra* illuminates not only the changing character of the evil powers in the two "interstellar romances" but also some of the most salient differences between the imaginary worlds that Lewis envisions on Mars and Venus before returning to earth in the final volume of the series.

On an initial reading, *Out of the Silent Planet* seems to present a relationship of sheer antithesis between Christian and modern "developmental" points of view, the first objectified in the "unfallen" world of Malacandra, the second in Weston's self-defined mission to perpetuate his "race" by extending the Darwinian "struggle for existence" from our planet to other sectors of the universe. It is significant, however, that Lewis portrays the Malacandrans not as untried innocents but as courageous and disciplined rational beings who have endured and triumphed over an environmental catastrophe—the result of a failed invasion by the "evil one" who corrupted the earth—that permanently damaged the surface of their planet but ultimately failed to turn the ensuing condition of scarcity into a relentless war between the species. The Martians also engage in the ritual of the hunt, a form of divinely sanctioned violence in which rational and irrational creatures participate in a mutually uplifting struggle that manifests the enduring kinship between them (see p. 6). Such similarities to the terrestrial struggle between the species suggest that, in transporting us to an "unfallen" world, Lewis is not simply repudiating but rather transfiguring or "up-grading" (*RP* 116) the Wellsian vision of Nature "red in tooth and claw" into an "archetype," or "original," that simultaneously preserves and "takes up" (*RP* 116) some of the defining features of the evolutionary conflict itself. Elsewhere in his writings Lewis posits a similar relationship of "copy" to "original" in his discussion of the undeniable "cruelty and wastefulness" of Nature, which he claims "may yet be derived from a principle which is good and fair, may indeed be a depraved and blurred copy of it—the pathological form which it would take in a *spoiled* Nature"

(*M* 189–190).[4] In his novel, the relationship between spoiled copy and original principle is evident not only in the martial discipline of the Malacandrans but also in the striking contrast between our situation on earth, where a single rational species lords it over other animals and even competes ferociously with other members of its own kind, and the circumstances of life on Mars, where three rational species—each with its own distinctive anatomy and temperament—live separately but companionably in mutual acknowledgment of their shared rationality. In chapter after chapter, Elwin Ransom's honest but misdirected attempt to identify the hierarchy among the three talking species turns on the tension between terrestrial conditions and the interspecies brotherhood on Mars. In this respect, the Martian cosmopolis, in which reason transcends biological difference, is a composite entity—a spiritually uncorrupted planet akin to our visions of the earthly paradise, and at the same time a "sublimation" (*RP* 112) of the terrestrial "struggle for existence" into a "principle" that simultaneously transfigures the Wellsian "biocentric" view of evolutionary strife and exposes its one-sided view of the natural order. Moreover, to conceive the Darwinian conflict as the "blurred copy" of an uncorrupted "original" is not only more consistent with Lewis's Platonic/Augustinian theology but also takes us closer to some of his demonstrably modern concerns. Far from simply turning back the clock to a premodern conception of the "heavens," Lewis's appropriation of Wells's evolutionary naturalism builds on the modern preoccupation with order of the "species"—their origins, development, and modes of relationship—while it simultaneously transfigures Wells's own use of interplanetary conflict to explore the spiritual affliction that produces perpetual strife within our own self-divided species and troubles our relations to the other species with whom we share the earth.[5]

Perelandra offers a compelling illustration of the "taking up" of the evolutionary model into an imagined archetype. In this second interplanetary struggle, Weston's shift from materialist "Wellsianity" to "creative evolution" is reflected in the dynamic (and remarkably

Bergsonian) character of the new world that Ransom discovers on Venus.[6] In a dramatic departure from traditional views of the earthly paradise, Lewis presents the prelapsarian order as a state of continuous flux, a "universe of shifting slopes" (*P* 34), and he portrays its crowning achievement—its Adam and Eve—as dynamic creatures who are fast learners and seem to develop with every passing moment. Instead of an immutable condition that precedes the fall into time and change, Lewis's new Eden is a world of perpetual movement in which the one prohibition—its Tree of the Knowledge of Good and Evil—is to avoid habitation of the "Fixed Land." This feature of the novel rarely receives the attention it deserves: when it is not simply taken for granted or chalked up as a clever conceit, it is attributed either to the "floating islands" that appear in extant scientific accounts of Venus's atmosphere, or to hints of an evolving Eden in Milton's *Paradise Lost*. These are significant sources, but the shift from Being to Becoming on Lewis's mobile paradise is so pronounced—and the psychological, spiritual, and cosmological implications of this "inversion of Platonism" explored in such exacting detail—that a more far-reaching alternative suggests itself: the new world on Perelandra is a Christianized "working-up" of "creative evolution" itself.[7] In other words, on the basis of his encounter with Bergson and others who followed him, Lewis shows how the fertile but flawed reconception of time in creative/emergent evolution may be "taken up" (*RP* 115) onto a higher plane and synthesized with the traditional conception of a transcendent Creator in whose image we are made. Just as *Out of the Silent Planet* at once censures and sublimates Wells's "orthodox Darwinism," *Perelandra* simultaneously rejects and raises Bergson's more affirmative "organic" theory of evolutionary process, reversing its naturalization of the supernatural and reshaping its model of cosmic progress into a Christian vision of Becoming.

Seen from this perspective, the first two novels of the Space Trilogy form a coherent set. In each instance the journey "into another dimension" involves the "up-grading" (*RP* 112) of one version of the developmental paradigm into its imagined archetype. But what happens to this process, we might ask, in *That Hideous Strength,* which takes place on our own planet and depicts the techno-magical sublimation of the evolutionary model onto the "spiritual" plane of the "New Man, the man who will not die"? Lewis has abandoned the literary prototype of the cosmic voyages, but in shifting from "interstellar romances" to the terrestrial "spiritual shockers" of Charles Williams, he is turning to a fictional "formula" ("The Novels of Charles Williams" *OS* 22) in which the process of imaginary transfiguration to an original informing "principle" continues to play a fundamental part. The Faustian necromancers of Williams's thrillers are the stuff of Gothic fiction, but at the same time Williams raises Gothic terror to a higher dimension, ingeniously using its revenants, doppelgangers, and other spectral resources to "haunt" his modern protagonists and restore the palpable presence of the divine Omnipotence—the "dreadful goodness" (*Descent into Hell* 16)—that creates and sustains the ordinary world we inhabit. In a manner that we will later explore in some detail, Lewis follows Williams in the double use of the Gothic to portray the Faustian aspirations of the N.I.C.E. and simultaneously to reaffirm (in a peculiar mixture of Arthurian and Gothic romance) a traditional conception of the supernatural. As in the "up-gradings" of Wells on Mars and Bergson on Venus, the construction of a beatific "original" at the manor of St. Anne's, like the very form of the novel itself, retains many of the defining elements of the Gothic—above all, its trademark "mixture of the realistic and the supernatural" (*L* II, 682, 12/6/45)—that ultimately reduces the hideous power of the N.I.C.E. to a distorted Gothic double.

If Lewis constructs his imaginary worlds by "taking up" the very things he is putting down, then we must reconsider the terms of engagement that have traditionally informed the interpretation of this series. Ever since its publication, the Space Trilogy has been read primarily in terms of a sharply defined struggle between religious and naturalistic points of view, the first associated with the "discarded image" of premodern cosmology, the second with the modern developmental paradigm that has supplanted it.[8] There is much to support this approach, but it also obscures the more complex process of Lewis's world-building, which would be better served by conceiving the conflict in these novels not as a clash between antithetical principles but as a relationship between "archetype" and distorted "copy." In one sense, Lewis's creation of pristine "originals" out of warped reproductions is merely a skillful adaptation of an age-old polemical maneuver. As the critic Northrop Frye (1976) once described it, the Augustinian strategy of transforming the ideological enemy into a distorted derivative or demonic double reflects "the revolutionary and dialectical element in Christian belief, which is constantly polarizing its truth against the falsehoods of the heathen, but, like other revolutionary doctrines, feels most secure when the dark side takes the form of a heresy that closely resembles itself" (*The Secular Scripture* 142). Lewis employs this strategy to reduce the opposition to a parodic imitation, but at the same time his imagined archetypes bear witness to an irreducible element of receptivity to the very "falsehoods" he is exposing. Lewis's Malacandra is not only an "unfallen" planet that reflects the traditional conception of the "heavens"; it is also a transfiguration of the evolutionary model into the site of a modern exploration of the means through which we establish the most basic distinctions between ourselves and other beings—and in particular, the process that makes it possible for certain human beings to relegate other members of their own kind to inferior or subhuman status. Similarly, the emergent Eden on Perelandra, which is virtually inconceivable in the absence of creative evolution, establishes the grounds of compatibility between Christian orthodoxy and a distinctively modern conception of time and temporal process. As for the conclusion of the series, critics have long regarded *That Hideous Strength* as a "Charles Williams novel by C. S. Lewis" (Green and Hooper, *C. S. Lewis: A Biography* 205). Nevertheless, the tendency of critics to conceive the rival powers in terms of a sheer antithesis between religious and naturalistic worldviews, or medieval romance and modern realism, covers up Lewis's ambitious attempt, inspired by Williams's example, to employ the modern Gothic mix of "the Probable and the Marvellous" ("The Novels of Charles Williams" *OS* 21) in the service of "a better school of prose story" ("On Stories" *OS* 17), which would not revert to medieval romance but reactivate the powers of enchantment cast aside by the practitioners of modern realism. In this respect, Lewis's work should be viewed not as a casual dismissal of the modern imaginary but as a searching exploration of its possibilities. With an appropriate adjustment of our optic, we may begin to see his Space Trilogy less as the irreconcilable struggle between an old-fashioned Christian humanism and a newfangled heresy and more as the effort of a modern Christian writer to sustain and enrich the former through critical engagement with the latter.

I ～

Out of the Silent Planet

Cosmic Anthropology: Race and Reason on Planet Mars

> The most useful and least advanced of all human
> knowledge seems to me to be that of man. . . . For how
> can the source of inequality among men be known
> unless one begins by knowing men themselves?
> —Jean-Jacques Rousseau, *Discourse on the Origin and*
> *Foundations of Inequality among Men*

> Something is wrong in your head, *hnau* from
> Thulcandra. There is too much blood in it.
> —Oyarsa of Malacandra to Weston,
> *Out of the Silent Planet*

In his first venture into science fiction, *Out of the Silent Planet* (1938), C. S. Lewis presents an encounter between a trio of interplanetary travelers and the rational inhabitants of an alien planet. The fact that Malacandra (Mars) has three rational species, none with bodies identical to our own, gives rise to considerable mayhem. The two villainous earthlings, Devine and Weston, regard the most anthropomorphic Martian species—the *sorns*—as ignorant "primitives" or "brutes," and they shoot the seal-like *hrossa* as if they were mere beasts. The third earthling, Elwin Ransom, whom the villains have abducted in the mistaken belief that the *sorns* are demanding a sacrificial victim, labors under a different set of illusions. Incited by H. G. Wells and other architects of modern science fiction, Ransom initially envisions the aliens as monstrous bestial predators, and although these preconceptions are soon dispelled, he continues to assume that one of the alien species must dominate (and may well feed upon) the other two. This misapprehension of other rational beings as savages, beasts, or ghastly monstrosities suggests that Lewis is concerned with the modern "biocentric" vision of the "struggle for existence" and its effects on the relations between the different peoples who inhabit the earth and on our imaginary apprehension of life beyond our own world. If nothing else, the peace and equality among the three Martian species, who live separately but never seek to subordinate one another, involve the transfiguration of the terrestrial vision of relentless evolutionary strife into a harmonious community that participates in the beneficent rationality of the cosmic order. As we shall see, the Martians have not been immune to the perils that plague terrestrial existence. As a result of an ancient invasion by the fallen archangel who still reigns over Earth, they have learned to compensate for the irreparable physical damage to the surface of their planet. In the process they also acquired the discipline and courage to overcome the insecurity—and above all the fear of death—that impels the mistrust and violence of life on our own "silent" planet. Moreover, at least one of these rational species exercises these martial virtues in the ritual of the hunt—a form of violence that expresses the ancient kinship—a union of enmity and love— between rational and irrational creatures and enhances the joy of life through the very risk of death. In this respect the imaginary world of Malacandra is a composite entity—an "unfallen" planet akin to our own visions of the terrestrial paradise, but also a "raising up" of the evolutionary struggle for existence into an "original," or "archetype," which simultaneously transfigures the "biocentric" view of universal strife and parodies its one-sided character.

One of the functions of Lewis's fictional collision between terrestrial expectations and extraterrestrial reality is to challenge the evolutionary paradigm of nineteenth-century anthropology, which continues to distort our relations to one another and to the rest of the natural order. At the same time, Lewis's most remarkable invention—a planet that possesses three rational species—provides a corrective or "cosmic" rationality ("*De Futilitate*" *CR* 68) that sets the stage for constructive reflection on the order of terrestrial creation. Thus, in the transit from Earth to Mars, the reader of the novel must keep in mind several distinct but related spheres of reference. At the literal level, Lewis draws on the age-old speculative tradition of the "plurality of worlds" to establish that rationality is not merely a "biological" phenomenon unique to our own species but rather a "spiritual" endowment that transcends its embodiment in any single species. Would we regard one another differently, and treat the rest of the animal kingdom more compassionately, if rationality was distributed among several species and we could behold "reason in an inhuman form" (66)?[1] At another level, the unity of the three Martian species underscores the opposite situation here on Earth—the propensity of a single rational species to split into factions that regard each other as inherently inferior to themselves or even as creatures of a different species. More concretely, the openly imperial ambitions of Devine and Weston, compounded by their failure to acknowledge the rationality of the Malacandrans, recalls the long and violent history of Western imperialism and the presumption of rational superiority that has colored Western relations to other peoples of the earth. Finally, as a result of the fact that two of the alien rational species resemble nonhuman animals on our own planet, the novel at yet another level raises issues concerning our problematic relations to the beasts: the persistent confusion and moral quandaries over animal sentience, cognition, and consciousness; the (mis)use of the traditional distinction between rational and nonrational beings to rationalize our indifference and cruelty to other species; and, in light of our presumptive status as the one rational species on the planet, the tendency to forget that we ourselves are embodied creatures inescapably bound to the animal kingdom. In this deceptively simple novel, all three sets of relationships—humans and aliens, humans and other humans, humans and nonrational animals—intersect at various points in the text. Lewis tells the story of first contact between ourselves and other rational species, but woven into this cosmic drama is the distressing record of contact with other members of our own species and with the other creatures with whom we share our planet.[2]

Lewis's exploration of our troubled reckonings with human, animal, and extraterrestrial Otherness is at once a meditation on the perennial problems of our fallen state and a critique of the naturalistic orientation of modern thought, particularly in the wake of the Darwinian revolution.[3] Unfortunately, the focus on the spiritual dimensions of the novel has led many readers to overlook Lewis's portrayal of the political and social crises of his own time. In the actions of his two villains, Lewis presents not only a timeless satire on human corruption but also an exposé of European imperialism and the ideological apparatus employed to legitimate it. Moreover, as Devine and Weston tout their own racial supremacy and openly pursue the domination, displacement, or elimination of presumably inferior peoples, it becomes increasingly clear that Lewis is linking the violent legacy of traditional imperialism to the new ideology of militant racism, especially virulent after the Nazi rise to power, which would soon lead to global warfare on an unprecedented scale and a genocidal campaign of unimaginable savagery. In a similar manner, Lewis uses his benign but timorous hero at once to satirize the naturalistic nightmares of H. G. Wells and to address the fears of his contemporaries as international tensions mounted and the prospect of war seemed ever more certain. It is therefore no accident that the events of this novel take place on the planet most closely associated with martial virtue. Ransom's progressive reorientation from his terrifying Wellsian illusions to his recognition of the beneficent character of the universe beyond his own "silent planet" will go hand in hand with the restoration of his courage. In this respect, Lewis's attempt to reawaken his readers to the presence of a rationally ordered and divinely governed creation—the "discarded image" obscured by the modern naturalistic worldview—is closely tied to his immediate efforts to speak to the perilous conditions of his time and prepare a frightened people for the inevitable struggle ahead.

I

In an introductory note to his novel, Lewis apologizes for "certain slighting references" to Wells's science fiction and proceeds to honor his most influential predecessor. Lewis makes no secret of his dependence on Wells, and scholars have demonstrated the extent of his debt to seminal works such as *The Time Machine* (1895), *The Island of Doctor Moreau* (1896), *The War of the Worlds* (1898), and especially *The First Men in the Moon* (1901), upon which he drew extensively for the plot, characters, and incidental details of his novel. Nevertheless, as a result of these "slighting references," which play a significant role in the novel, it is not surprising that most readers regard Wells primarily as a foil for Lewis's own assault on evolutionary naturalism and his reassertion of a Christian worldview. But this tendency to emphasize points of contrast between the two authors conceals some of the most significant affiliations between them. Lewis may reject the assumptions of Wells's evolutionary naturalism, but in his use of alien encounter to explore our problematic relations to each other and to nonhuman animals, he is a resourceful disciple of his literary master.[4]

In one of his most compelling works of science fiction, *The War of the Worlds,* Wells describes the invasion of Earth by predatory superintelligent Martians with "minds that are to our minds as ours are to those of the beasts that perish" (52). His narrator, an educated Englishman, sympathetically records the plight of his people, but at the same time he dispassionately situates the extraterrestrial invasion in the naturalistic context of the terrestrial "struggle for existence," coolly reminding his readers that to the Martians we are "at least as alien and lowly as are the monkeys and lemurs to us." From this vantage point, Wells's Martians are treating us no differently from the way we have treated other inhabitants of our own planet:

And before we judge of them too harshly, we must remember what ruthless and utter destruction our own species has wrought, not only upon animals, such as the vanished bison and the dodo, but upon its own inferior races. The Tasmanians, in spite of their human likeness, were entirely swept out of existence in a war of extermination waged by European immigrants, in the space of fifty years. Are we such apostles of mercy as to complain if the Martians warred in the same spirit? (55)

In the very process of asking us to suspend moral judgment upon the Martians (who seem to possess no ethical faculty in any case), the narrator frowns on the actions of our own species. Furthermore, while directing attention to our cold-hearted brutality toward other members of our own kind, the narrator's reference to the "human likeness" of the Tasmanians exposes the way we rationalize our aggression by consigning the Other to less-than-human status.

By his own account, Wells regarded *The War of the Worlds* as an attempt to unsettle the modern West from complacency and self-deceptive pride in its own ascendancy. After all, the aliens have targeted the most powerful nation on earth and easily brush aside its most sophisticated weaponry. If in the end the seemingly invincible Martians are themselves swept away by simple bacteria, the unlikely defeat of a mighty invader by humble microbes (appearing soon after the rout of a well-equipped Italian army at the hands of Ethiopian tribesman) serves as a cautionary tale to the imperial powers that currently rule the earth. In this sense, *The War of the Worlds,* like *Heart of Darkness* and other turn-of-the-century fiction, displays a certain uneasiness over the very success of Western civilization. The novel registers the diffuse but widespread undercurrent of anxiety over Western technological superiority—its apparent "empire over matter" (52)—and its present hegemony over the other peoples of the planet. The imaginary Martian invasion of imperial England seems to express the fear of recompense in kind for the violence and indifference at the heart of our domination of the globe.[5]

Similar issues attend Lewis's most immediate source, *The First Men in the Moon,* which depicts the lunar expedition of two earthlings—the businessman Bedford and the scientist Cavor—and their discovery of the vast subterranean kingdom of the Selenites. This novel, like *The War of the Worlds,* focuses more on our fear than our hostility toward the unknown Other, especially after the rather hapless terrestrial intruders are discovered and pursued by the aliens. But the issue of human aggression is never far from the surface: the bankrupt Bedford comforts himself with dreams of colonial exploitation of the Selenites, and in his climactic meeting with the "Grand Lunar" of this physically variable but instinctually unified species, Cavor makes the fatal mistake of describing the fractiousness of our own species and the lethal threat we pose to other species. In this sense Bedford and Cavor, who are the direct ancestors of Devine and Weston, exhibit by turns the fear and aggression that accompany the imperial adventure.

Lewis at once simplifies and complicates Wells's scenario by reducing the businessman-scientist duo to ruthless predators, while vesting their more humane attributes, and their fears of the mysterious Other, in his hero Ransom. In his portrait of an alien world that "so closely resembled the unattained ideals of that far-divided species Man" (*OSP* 75), Lewis also attempts to turn the tables on Wells by suggesting that the latter's evolutionary naturalism, which places conflict between species at the center of the "struggle for existence," may be symptomatic of the very fears and suspicions he wishes to overcome.[6] In addition, Lewis's critique of what might be called "biocentric" thinking—the collapse of the "spiritual" into the "biological" realm, the reduction of rationality to a purely naturalistic phenomenon, and the concomitant elevation of "blood" and "race" to the highest value—introduces a new and historically ominous dimension to the social issues that Wells addresses. Nevertheless, as significant as these differences may be, Lewis appropriated not only the external trappings but also much of the substance of Wells's fiction. Like his predecessor, Lewis relates interplanetary conflict to the anguished conditions of life on our own planet, and, though he occupies a different point on the modern political spectrum, he is equally critical of the militant nationalism, imperialism, and racism that Wells railed against throughout his career. Perhaps a somewhat more sympathetic assessment of Wells's influence would enable us to see that Lewis was not so dismissing as transfiguring his predecessor's evolutionary naturalism and attempting to rethink, from his own Christian perspective, the modern problem of relations between (and divisions within) the species.

II

The relatively simple linear plot of *Out of the Silent Planet* belies the complexity of its themes, which issue from the mismatch between terrestrial expectations and the realities of the alien world. In the opening section (see the figure on p. 28) Elwin Ransom, a Cambridge philologist on a walking tour of the countryside, is approached by a cottager concerned that her son Harry, "being a little simple" (11), has not returned home. We soon learn that the boy works for Devine and Weston, who are planning to exploit and conquer the red planet— the former out of sheer greed, the latter out of a distorted view of human destiny. The two partners have already been to Mars and met the *sorns,* whom they regard as savage tribesmen, and as a result of this misapprehension they believe that the aliens are demanding a terrestrial victim as a sacrifice to their gods. After Ransom's intrusion foils their plans to hand over the "feebleminded" Harry, the villains decide to sacrifice Ransom himself, and under the guise of hospitality they snare him with the help of a loaded drink.[7] As a prisoner on their spaceship (chapters 3–6), Ransom discovers the reason for his captivity, and his initial anxieties approach the level of uncontrollable terror as images of cannibalistic savagery combine with Wellsian fantasies of ravenous arthropod monstrosities. Hence the villains and the hero travel to Mars with different but related misconceptions of its inhabitants. The arrogant imperial dreams of the entrepreneur and the scientist seem remote from the nightmarish literary illusions of their victim; but taken together, these misapprehensions encompass the various domains of the modern imaginary—practical, intellectual, and aesthetic, respectively—and evoke the immemorial complex of fear and aggression that haunts our relations to the menacing Other. Moreover, in their misguided belief that the Martians are demanding a sacrificial victim, Devine and Weston are at once projecting onto the aliens the barbarity within themselves and engaging in the very forms of violence they attribute to the primitive Other. The chain of sacrificial substitutions—first the dog whom they have already sacrificed to scientific experimentation, then the allegedly subhuman child, and finally one's own acknowledged peer—exhibits not only the reversion to human sacrifice but also the slippery slope through which the distinction between inviolate and disposable beings reveals its arbitrary, mutable, and increasingly treacherous character.

Devine and Weston offer a satirical portrait of Western imperialism and its ideological supports. With their pith helmets and khakis they are the fictional heirs to the boundless imperial ambition expressed in Cecil Rhodes's notorious (and most likely apocryphal) assertion, "these stars . . . these vast worlds which we can never reach! I would annex the planets if I could" (Millin 1933, 138). The cynical Devine, a veteran of the "public school" system that operated as a training ground for future servants of the Empire, makes no pretense about his motives. Harboring no illusions of high-minded colonial service, he informs us that his approach to the "native question" on Mars will not be complicated by "the white man's burden" (OSP 32) or similar notions that conceal (and occasionally constrain) the real aims of imperial conquest back on earth.[8] The scientist Weston is a more complicated case. Although his ruthless evolutionary ethics makes him equally prepared to exploit or exterminate the aliens, Weston is impelled by a seemingly impersonal ideal of human progress and regards his venture into space as a necessary step in the development of the species. In his letters, Lewis associates "Westonism" with the "dream of interplanetary colonization," and he attributes the genesis

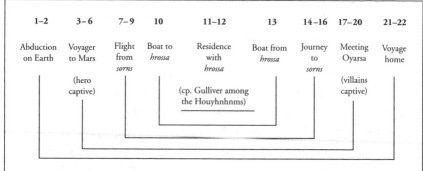

Figure 1.1

The reader of the novel proceeds in linear fashion from Ransom's abduction to Mars to his gradual transformation as he progresses from the *hrossa* to the *sorns,* and finally to the climactic meeting with Oyarsa. From a bird's-eye view, the text possesses a central core (chapters 11–12) surrounded by a series of symmetrical frames. The two-chapter account of the *hrossa* in the center of the novel is preceded by the episode (chapter 10) in which Ransom enters the boat that will bring him to the *hrossa* and followed by the episode (chapter 13) in which he joins the boating expedition that takes him from the *hrossan* settlement to the next stage of his travels. Together, chapters 10 and 13 frame the central chapters and are framed in turn by chapters 7–9 and 14–16, the first triad depicting Ransom's flight *from* the *sorns* after his arrival on Mars and the second recounting his journey *to* the *sorns.* These chapters are surrounded by another symmetrical set: chapters 3–6, which take place on the spaceship and depict Ransom's captivity and anticipatory fears of the aliens; and chapters 17–20, which are set in Meldilorn, the spiritual center of Malacandra, and reintroduce Devine and Weston, now in captivity, while completing the process of Ransom's spiritual emancipation. Finally, the opening section on earth (chapters 1–2) and the concluding section on the return to earth (chapters 21–22, plus the postscript) form the outer frame of the novel.

of the novel to his "realisation that thousands of people, in one form or another, depend upon some hope of perpetuating and improving the human species for the whole meaning of the universe—that a 'scientific' hope of defeating death is a real rival to Christianity" (*L* II, 262, 8/9/39; see also *L* II, 236–37, 12/28/38; *Letters of C.S. Lewis* [1966] 368, 8/42). But as Lewis indicates in other writings of the period, the "Westonism" that appears in the scientific speculations of J. B. S. Haldane or the novels of Olaf Stapledon should be conceived as the most recent fruit of a more fundamental change that has been taking place over the course of several centuries—the transposition of the principal locus of Being from a transcendent God to an immanent power that realizes itself in the dynamic development of Man. As it took shape in the early nineteenth century, the new paradigm of "'Evolution' or 'Development' or 'Emergence'" ("Funeral of a Great Myth" *CR* 83) may have found sublime expression in Hegel and Romantics such as Keats and Shelley, but as the century wore on and it became further entangled with European capitalism and overseas expansion, this momentous turn in Western thought began to assume a darker form. The appearance of Darwin's *Origin of Species* (1859) gave additional impetus to this process by accelerating the tendency, already well under way prior to Darwin, to think of differences within the human species in terms of a ladder of ascent from the "primitive" to the most "civilized." As it filtered back into social thought, Darwinian theory seemed to provide a biological rationale not only for an unregulated capitalism that encouraged "survival of the fittest" at home but also for the political, economic, and social domination of "undeveloped" peoples abroad.[9]

Weston's cosmic imperialism expresses all these elements of the nineteenth-century developmental paradigm—or "Wellsianity," as Lewis sometimes called it ("Is Theology Poetry?" *WG* 123)—and adds a few more recent touches as well. Devine regards young Harry as little more than a "savage" and bribes him with alcohol to keep him pacified. Weston shares the view that Harry is more like a "preparation" than a "human," but he takes the crucial step beyond the evolutionary anthropology of the imperial era into the insidious ideologies of the twentieth century: "'The boy was ideal. . . . Incapable of serving humanity and only too likely to propagate idiocy. He was the sort of boy who in a civilized community would be automatically handed over to a state laboratory for experimental purposes'" (*OSP* 21). It is tempting to associate Weston's remark with his later, more blatantly transparent assertions of the supremacy of his "race" and its right to interplanetary *Lebensraum* (134–139). But if it is uncertain whether Lewis at this time was aware of the emerging atrocities of Nazi "racial hygiene," we should remember that for several decades prior to Hitler's accession to power in 1933, the "science" of eugenics was promoted vigorously by many intellectuals, conservatives and progressives alike, not only in Great Britain, where it first appeared, but also in the United States and elsewhere in the Western world. Indeed, Weston's reference to the propagation of "idiocy" calls to mind the one legislative success of the British eugenics movement, the Mental Deficiency Act of 1913, which limited the rights of the "feebleminded" by permitting (under certain conditions) their detainment and segregation from the rest of the population. Thus the modern developmental paradigm, which underwrote the "guns and gospel" imperialism of the late nineteenth century, finds its fulfillment in the noxious mix of racism and eugenics that sanctions, in the name of progress, the most savage treatment of those we have deemed less human than ourselves.[10]

III

If Devine and Weston embody an imperial contempt for the Other, Ransom carries within him the fears, and the underlying sense of insecurity and vulnerability, that fuel the impulse to exercise control over other beings. One of the most prominent aspects of the novel is its concern with the debilitating effects of fear and the courage required to contain it. Throughout his voyage in space (chapters 3–6),

Ransom is besieged by a multitude of terrors that threaten to overwhelm him. Sometimes his emotions are tied to specific objects; at other times "he did not even know what he was afraid of: the fear itself possessed his whole mind, a formless, infinite misgiving" (27). After he lands on Mars, Ransom's sighting and subsequent flight from the dreaded *sorns* (chapters 7–9) bring him close to the point of panic and raise the specter of madness and suicide. In his struggle to retain possession of his faculties, the hero begins to understand how fear has distorted his perception and dimmed his reason. But even as he adjusts to his unfamiliar surroundings and realizes that most of his apprehensions have been unfounded, his fearful imagination resurfaces with each successive phase of his adventure.

Many of Ransom's terrors are tied to fantasies of extraterrestrial life inspired by his reading of modern science fiction:

> He had read his H. G. Wells and others. His universe was peopled with horrors such as ancient and mediæval mythology could hardly rival. No insect-like, vermiculate or crustacean Abominable, no twitching feelings, rasping wings, slimy coils, curling tentacles, no monstrous union of superhuman intelligence and insatiable cruelty seemed to him anything but likely on an alien world. . . . He saw in imagination various incompatible monstrosities—bulbous eyes, grinning jaws, horns, stings, mandibles. Loathing of insects, loathing of snakes, loathing of things that squashed and squelched, all played their horrible symphonies over his nerves. But the reality would be worse: it would be an extra-terrestrial Otherness—something one had never thought of, never could have thought of. (37)

It is significant that these extraterrestrial nightmares are based on the fear and loathing of certain types of creatures on our own planet. Whereas Devine and Weston express the hubris that reflects our increasing control over the rest of creation, Ransom manifests the ancient and enduring fear of living things that are proximate and ubiquitous but alien and threatening to our very existence. Paradoxically, this fear may be intensified, as it is in Wells's portrait of alien invasion, by a naturalistic worldview that conceives the relations between the species in terms of a ceaseless struggle for existence. But whatever its origin and historical mutations, this estrangement between man and other creatures reflects an elemental insecurity that accounts for our proclivity to transform the animal Other into a terrifying monstrosity, and consequently for the self-serving habit of disregarding the often brutal excesses of our dominion over the "irrational" beasts. Therefore, when our imagination is given free rein to envision an encounter with extraterrestrial life, it is no surprise that we conjure up bestial figures that express our most primitive fears and that these beasts of the modern imagination continue to disturb our ever-expanding hegemony over the rest of creation.

Ransom's fright is also tied to the social and political situation of the thirties. Just as Weston's actions point beyond traditional imperialism to fascist racism, Ransom's ordeal extends beyond its direct reference to Wellsian fantasy to the pervasive fear and confusion of his contemporaries over the growing threat of Nazi aggression. Although this element of the novel seems to have escaped the attention of its contemporary reviewers, the opposition between a humane but frightened protagonist and a ruthlessly belligerent enemy—a common scenario in the literature of the thirties—could not be more pronounced.[11] The narrator reminds us that Ransom has seen action in World War I, and, as with many of his generation, the terrible experience of the trenches has left him unsure of his courage and horrified by the prospect of another war:

> The bellicose mood was a very rare one with Ransom. Like many men of his own age, he rather underestimated than overestimated his own courage; the gap between boyhood's dreams and his actual experience of the War had been startling, and his subsequent view of his own unheroic qualities had perhaps swung too far in the opposite direction. (38)

Over the course of the novel Lewis probes the mind of his apprehensive hero but also begins to provide him with the resources, at once physical and spiritual, to overcome the crippling effects of fear. It is worth noting that Lewis's own participation in the Great War left him physically impaired and haunted by memories and nightmares related to the horrors he had witnessed at the front. But as frightful as the war had been, Lewis was opposed to the widespread pacifist movement of the thirties, and despite private attestations of his dread of another war, he joined the debate over pacifism and publicly defended the traditional doctrine of the "just war."[12] There are no explicit references to the pacifist debate in *Out of the Silent Planet*, but in the progress of his hero, Lewis addresses the collective trauma of his own generation and attempts to instill, as he later put it in a discussion of Mars in Gustav Holst's *The Planets*, "the *good* element in the martial spirit, the discipline and freedom from anxiety" (*L* II, 702, 2/15/46). Such are the virtues that will be required to face the impending terrestrial ordeal.

IV

In order to face the real enemy, Ransom must first confront the illusory ones that deform his understanding and consume him with fright. His saving grace is that his fear of the Other is offset by the good will and open-mindedness that gradually transform his thoughts, perceptions, and feelings. The process begins on the trip to Mars as he sheds his Wellsian terror of outer space and finds himself "drawn by an irresistible attraction" (*OSP* 33) to the celestial beauty around him:

> A nightmare, long engendered in the modern mind by the mythology that follows in the wake of science, was falling off him. He had read of "Space": at the back of his thinking for years had lurked the dismal fancy of the black, cold vacuity, the utter deadness, which was supposed to separate

the worlds. . . . He had thought it barren: he saw now that it was the womb of worlds, whose blazing and innumerable offspring looked down nightly even upon the earth with so many eyes—and here, with how many more! No: Space was the wrong name. Older thinkers had been wiser when they named it simply the heavens—the heavens which declared the glory. . . . (34)

In this pivotal passage Lewis launches his critique of Wells and his (re)turn from the modern conception of "Space" as mere extension to an earlier vision of a resplendent universe infused with the presence of its divine creator. Nevertheless, we should remember that this revelatory moment does not issue in any instant or wholesale transformation of the hero. Moreover, this vision of cosmic glory prematurely disposes of the enduring elements of anxiety and doubt that attend our earthbound contemplation of the heavens. Lewis's recognition of the latter point is evident in an essay that praises Wells for his rendering of Bedford's chilling encounter with "'the infinite and final Night of space'" ("On Stories" *OS* 9). Bedford's dread of the cosmic void may reflect some questionable modern assumptions about the universe, but, like "the silence of the eternal spaces" (*M* 84) that terrified the devout Pascal in the seventeenth century, his state of mind on the lunar surface elicits a primitive stratum of fear that links the mystery and vastness of the universe to the implacable insecurities of terrestrial life. In his portrait of Ransom, Lewis acknowledges this intractable element of fear in the human heart, but he also endows his hero with a receptivity to "otherness" ("On Stories" *OS* 12) that mitigates the terror of infinite space and reveals that our fears are at least in part a function of our own distraught imaginations. At the same time, Ransom's brief glimpse of the heavens initiates the progressive change in perspective that slowly transforms our planet from the imperial center to the barbaric periphery of the cosmos, while simultaneously turning the extraterrestrial Other from an object of suspicion into a welcome rational copresence in a divinely ordered universe.[13]

Not long after he lands on Malacandra, Ransom catches sight of the *sorns,* and tearing loose from Devine and Weston, he flees into the Martian forests. For days he struggles with the terrors that threaten to consume him, but he also finds some comfort in the beauty of the Martian landscape and sustenance in its edible plants. The decisive turn in his fortunes occurs when he sees a large seal-like creature and discovers that it is speaking to him. Lewis lingers over the crucial moment of recognition as "two so far-divided species stared each into the other's face":

> Ransom rose to his knees. The creature leaped back, watching him intently, and then became motionless again. Then it came a pace nearer, and Ransom jumped up and retreated, but not far; curiosity held him. He summoned up his courage and advanced, holding out his hand; the beast misunderstood the gesture. It backed into the shallows of the lake and he could see the muscles tightened under its sleek pelt, ready for sudden movement. But there it stopped; it, too, was in the grip of curiosity. Neither dared let the other approach, yet each repeatedly felt the impulse to do so himself, and yielded to it. It was foolish, frightening, ecstatic and unbearable all in one moment. It was more than curiosity. It was like a courtship—like the meeting of the first man and the first woman in the world; it was like something beyond that; so natural is the contact of sexes, so limited the strangeness, so shallow the reticence, so mild the repugnance to be overcome, compared with the first tingling intercourse of two different, but rational, species. (*OSP* 56–57)

The meeting between two different rational species has no terrestrial counterpart, but the comparison to the courtship between the sexes, reminiscent of the meeting of Adam and Eve in *Paradise Lost,* evokes the complex of desire and mutual recognition that sometimes outweighs the suspicions that distance us from those we perceive as different from ourselves. At the minimum, the ambivalence of this

encounter—the "thrill of mingled attraction and repulsion" (57)—
suggests that no instinct confines us to an exclusive attachment to
our own kind and that our relations to strangers are not entirely
at the mercy of our fears. Somewhat more hopefully, the tension
between curiosity and suspicion indicates that we are often inspired
by the "shy, ineluctable fascination of unlike for unlike" (61) as we
look for signs of reciprocity that enable us to set aside the insecurities
that breed enmity and violence. Implicit in the fictional encounter
between human and *hrossa* is a vision of social harmony that transcends the divisions between peoples as well as the barrier between
species.[14] If the Miltonic image of "the meeting of the first man and
the first woman" is not entirely adequate to this vision, as the narrator himself maintains, the chapter's final vision of verbal commu-
nication between the species, "as though Paradise had never been
lost and earliest dreams were true" (59), indicates that we are never
entirely reconciled either to the cultural alienation that separates us
from other persons or to the biological gap that has established a
seemingly insuperable limit to relations between the species.

What ensues from this crucial encounter is a progressive shift in
Ransom's perspective. The change is signaled topographically by
the discovery that he is not on the surface of the planet and surrounded by high mountains but rather in a deep canyon looking
upward toward the uninhabited surface. This spatial reorientation
sets the stage for the more momentous change that takes place as
he becomes further acquainted with the *hrossa* (chapters 11–12). As
an observer steeped in nineteenth-century developmental assumptions, Ransom initially identifies *hrossan* culture as "old stone age"
(67), despite the poetic sophistication of its populace and other evidence to the contrary. In accord with his residual sense of Western
superiority, he responds to questions about his origins by offering
"a childish version of the truth in order to adapt it to the supposed
ignorance of his audience" (68).[15] But Ransom soon discovers that
the *hrossa* know a great deal more than he supposes, and when it

comes to spiritual matters "he found himself being treated as if *he* were the savage and being given a first sketch of civilized religion" (69). This centrally situated section, which recalls Gulliver's life among the Houyhnhnms, makes up the Swiftean core of the novel. Here Ransom has the opportunity to observe a community of unfallen rational beings whose temperament and manners "so closely resembled the unattained ideals of that far-divided species Man whose instincts were so deplorably different" (75). Realizing that "it was not they, but his own species, that were the puzzle" (75), he continues to shift away from the anthropocentric orientation of our own species toward a recognition of the rational intelligence (cf. Jonathan Swift's "universal reason") that transcends the narrow and self-aggrandizing perspective of a single fallen species.[16] At this point, however, Ransom still has a long way to go. On the basis of terrestrial experience, he finds it difficult to believe that the three rational species coexist in a condition of equality and persists in the assumption that one must dominate the others. His failure to grasp that the three species—referred to collectively as *hnau*—submit to the common rule of a higher being is underscored by his recurrent inability to detect the presence of the angelic *eldila,* who are immediately evident to the *hrossa* and their children. Ransom's perception will continue to sharpen, but before he departs from the *hrossa* and ascends to higher reaches of awareness, he will clear away another obstacle to his transformation by testing his uncertain courage in an adventure that turns risk and danger into the very spice of life.

V

Somewhat surprisingly, Ransom's life among the peaceful *hrossa* concludes with a violent episode that pits man against beast—the hunt for an ancient sea creature, the *hnakra* (chapter 13).[17] The *hrossa* conceive their relationship to the *hnakra* in terms that resemble a totemic kinship. They long to hunt and kill the *hnakra* as it longs to kill them, but they regard the sea-beast as at once "our enemy" and "our beloved":

> We feel in our hearts his joy as he looks down from the mountain of water in the north where he was born; we leap with him when he jumps the falls; and when winter comes, and the lake smokes higher than our heads, it is with his eyes that we see it and know that his roaming time is come. We hang images of him in houses, and the sign of all the *hrossa* is a *hnakra*. In him the spirit of the valley lives; and our young play at being *hnéraki* as soon as they can splash in the shallows. . . . I do not think the forest would be so bright, nor the water so warm, nor love so sweet, if there were no danger in the lakes. (76)

The *hrossa,* like the other rational species, have no fear of death, but the mortal danger associated with the pursuit of the *hnakra* seems to heighten the joys of life on this side of the grave. In this instance we are asked to consider a form of violence between man and beast that originates not from fear or indifference but from a primordial bond that transcends the division between rational and irrational animals and manifests their mutual respect and common destiny as finite beings. Ransom shares the *hrossa's* excitement at the prospect of the hunt. Despite his fears and the ominous warning of an *eldil,* he joins the expedition and delights in "his new-found manhood" (81) when he proves equal to the challenge. As it turns out, the victory over the *hnakra* comes at a heavy price. While Ransom and his *hrossan* comrades have been hunting the *hnakra,* Devine and Weston have been hunting for Ransom himself. Spotting him on the shore just after he slays the *hnakra,* Ransom's pursuers shoot and kill his *hrossan* friend (whom they perceive as a violent beast and hence a threat to Ransom, who must be kept alive for sacrifice to the *sorns*). In the aftermath of this sequence, Ransom sees that his own exuberance, which prompted him to ignore the *eldil's* command to refrain from the hunt, has led to the death of his closest companion, and in sorrow he heeds the angelic summons to proceed to the supreme *eldil,* the Oyarsa of Malacandra.

It is difficult to sort out the various strands of the hunting scene and its seemingly conflicting implications. The main difficulty is that the unfallen rational *hrossa* are engaged in a form of violence that cannot be dismissed as the consequence of an unnatural rupture of creation's original order. Translated into terrestrial terms, the relationship between *hrossa* and *hnakra* elicits memories (or fantasies) of an ancient kinship between man and beast that acknowledges our common animal ancestry and a shared instinct for mutual challenge. Whether or not this state reflects a lapse from a primordial condition that precedes the institution of violence between the species, the ritual of the hunt, which plays a prominent role in medieval and Renaissance literature, is associated not only with a life-enhancing kinship between man and beast (a viewpoint that may not be shared by our prey) but also with the cultivation of martial skills that would be perilous to abandon in a world that often requires the virtues of St. George.[18] In this respect the hunting expedition serves as the means through which Lewis's hero restores his sense of physical well-being and prepares himself for the conflict that awaits his return to earth. At the same time, the prohibition against Ransom's participation in the hunt suggests that unlike the Martians we were not fashioned for this type of violence, and the tragic outcome of Ransom's impassioned act of disobedience indicates that as fallen creatures we must remain wary of the passions incited by this or any other form of violence. At the end of this complex chapter, Ransom asks for pardon from his dying friend, who has no fear of death and hails his terrestrial companion as heroic *hnakra*-slayer. But if Lewis is training his hero for future warfare, the Adamic drama of disobedience and death that accompanies the restoration of Ransom's martial prowess reminds us that the recourse to arms should be regarded as at best a tragic necessity of life in a violent world.

VI

After his departure from the *hrossa,* Ransom once more finds himself alone in the Martian woods. In the symmetrical structure of the novel, the hero's solitary journey to the *sorns* (chapters 14–16) recalls the account of his earlier flight through the forest (chapters 7–9) but with a significant difference. While he remains frightened of the *sorns,* Ransom is now marching *toward* the object of fear and possesses the requisite "confidence in himself and in the world" (87) to accomplish his mission. Moreover, as soon as he reaches his destination, Ransom realizes that his fears have been misdirected. The *sorns* are far less gregarious than the *hrossa,* but they are no more violent, and as the most contemplative of the three rational species they enhance Ransom's knowledge of the physical, social, and spiritual conditions of their planet. The *sorns* also delve further into the differences between our world and their own by focusing on the fact that Malacandra has more than one rational species. As a satire on the human condition, *Out of the Silent Planet* might have succeeded reasonably well if the alien world contained merely a single unfallen rational species possessing either human form or, like Swift's Houyhnhnms, the form of another terrestrial species. But the presence of three rational species, each resembling a particular kind of animal life on our own planet, not only adds a new dimension to the traditional utopian formula but also constitutes the speculative center of the novel.[19]

During his stay with the *hrossa,* Ransom's efforts to fathom the relations between the species focus exclusively on the issue of domination. The basis for his thinking is the terrestrial struggle for existence, reinforced by his "imaginative training" in Wells's science fiction:

> Were the *hrossa* . . . the dominant species on Malacandra, and the *sorns,* despite their more man-like shape, merely a semi-intelligent kind of cattle? . . . On the other hand, the *hrossa* might be the domestic animals of the *sorns,* in which case the

latter would be superintelligent. His whole imaginative training somehow encouraged him to associate superhuman intelligence with monstrosity of form and ruthlessness of will. (60)

Although the *hrossa* inform him that all three species submit to the lordship of the supernatural Oyarsa, Ransom continues to search for "the real master" (70) among them. He supposes that the *hrossa* may be deceived and "were after all under the thumb of the *sorns,* superior to their masters in all the qualities that human beings value, but intellectually inferior to them and dependent on them" (86). From a terrestrial perspective such conjectures are quite reasonable (see note 13). Like the relations between Eloi and Morlocks in Wells's *The Time Machine,* they are a plausible extrapolation of common assumptions about the evolutionary process and the perpetual struggle for mastery that characterizes relations within our own species. Even as his other illusions begin to evaporate, Ransom's preconceptions about the Martian order of species are so entrenched that they survive his dawning recognition that the ruthless conditions of our own planet are a singular aberration from the universal norm. In this way Lewis prepares us for Ransom's experience with the *sorns,* which lays to rest any lingering doubts about the equality of the three Martian species and establishes a new perspective on the sorrows of our own species.

The import of this new perspective becomes apparent during Ransom's conversations with his reflective Martian hosts. The latter are particularly intrigued by the fact that the earth has only a single rational species, a condition that "must have far-reaching effects in the narrowing of sympathies and even of thought" (102). As one of the company describes it, "'Your thought must be at the mercy of your blood . . . for you cannot compare it with thought that floats on a different blood'" (102–103). The narrator does not relate the rest of this discussion, leaving us to ponder its crucial if at first misleading implications. Initially it sounds as if our terrestrial woes proceed from an accident of circumstance or, worse yet, from a flaw in the original design of creation. But few if any readers are likely to conclude that Lewis is attributing our tendency to behave like spoiled children to a prior act of divine miscalculation. A more likely interpretation is that Lewis is challenging the modern biocentric tendency to confuse the spiritual and organic realms by reducing the former to a function of the latter. As embodied creatures our "thought" is never dissociated from our "blood," but unless we recognize that rationality is an essential part of the spiritual endowment through which we participate in an order that transcends the natural, we will continue to employ our distinctive gifts in a way that betrays their original purpose and deforms our relations to the world around us.

The *sorns* have little acquaintance with terrestrial conditions, but their observation that our "thought" must be at the mercy of our "blood" also evokes the atmosphere of distrust and hostility that pervades relations within our own species, particularly at a moment when "blood" had become the very basis for "the narrowing of sympathies and even of thought." Once again, the problem is not a structural deficiency in the natural order but the process of false "speciation" through which a fallen creature denies its kinship to others of its own kind. If, as the *sorns* imply, this impulse to self-division is related to the very absence of other rational species on our own planet, there is still very little in our history to indicate that we would treat these other species, especially if they were less powerful than ourselves, any better than we treat other sectors of our own species. In this sense, the harmonious relations of the several kinds of Martians, who are far more different in appearance than we are to one another, bear painful witness to the ceaseless strife and divisiveness within our own kind. Lewis suggests that this unhappy situation has been intensified rather than alleviated by the modern reduction of rationality to a naturalistic and exclusively anthropomorphic function. By denying that our rationality is related to an order of being that transcends our own species, we blind ourselves to that element of our nature through which we transcend our differences; and as a result of this shift from "spiritual" to "biological" kinship ("Religion and Rocketry" *WLN* 91), we end up turning minor variations into essential distinctions based on impassable differences of "blood."

The primary effect of Ransom's conversation with the *sorns* is to reestablish a conception of rationality that transcends its distinctive embodiment in the human species or in any single subset of the species. Paradoxically, the acknowledgment of a universal community of reason that is not limited to our own kind also involves the admission of our own animal nature and therefore of our kinship with the beasts. It is no accident that Ransom first identifies himself to the *sorns* with the words ironically reminiscent of Descartes' "*Cogito, ergo sum*"), "'The animal I am is called Man'" (92).[20] The encounter with "reason in an inhuman form" (*OSP* 66) heightens Ransom's awareness of his own body as it appears in the eyes of a rational creature with a different form of embodiment. The narrator later returns to this issue when his protagonist attends a gathering of the three species and is startled by its level of mirth and humor, as if "the comic spirit arose chiefly from the meeting of the different kinds of *hnau*" (116). He analyzes this phenomenon in the concluding "Postscript":

> Each of them is to the others *both* what a man is to us *and*
> what an animal is to us. They can talk to each other, they can
> cooperate, they have the same ethics; to that extent a *sorn*
> and a *hross* meet like two men. But then each finds the other
> different, funny, attractive as an animal is attractive. Some
> instinct starved in us, which we try to soothe by treating
> irrational creatures almost as if they were rational, is really
> satisfied in Malacandra. They don't need pets. (154)

Readers are sometimes troubled by this passage, which suggests either a flaw in the design of terrestrial creation (the absence of other rational species, which produces a misplaced affection for the beasts) or, from a point of view different from Ransom's own, a lapse on the part of the Malacandrans (the lack of feeling for nonrational animals that we express in our fondness for pets). But in light of Ransom's encounter with other rational species, it requires only a minor adjustment of perspective to read these lines not as a wish to reinforce the already troublesome estrangement between rational and nonrational creatures but as a recognition of our own animal status and its significance for our relations to other living things, human as well as nonhuman. As Ransom describes it, the instinct satisfied in Malacandra is akin to our amusement in observing certain differences in gesture, custom, and sensibility in our visits to unfamiliar places. The pleasure derives from the simultaneous recognition of identity and difference—the identity that involves the awareness of others as centers of consciousness like ourselves, which prevents us from reducing them to mere objects, and the difference that marks them as embodied creatures with features, habits, and sentiments somewhat dissimilar to our own. Perhaps if we are as self-aware as Ransom when he introduces himself to the *sorns* as "the animal . . . called Man," it may dawn on us that we appear as odd and amusing to others as they seem to us. When we see with the eyes of the Other, we are conscious of ourselves not simply as subjects but also as objects, as centers of experience who are also creatures with bodies. As for our relations to the beasts, the admission that we are animal as well as rational offsets the gnostic tendency of our species (intensified in modern thought by the Cartesian dissociation between spirit and matter, mind and body) to view ourselves primarily as knowing subjects who stand apart from the rest of creation. The recognition that we are embodied creatures who remain inextricably bound to the animal kingdom takes us a step closer to reclaiming the deeper kinship expressed in our love of pets, our fantasies of talking beasts, or our remembrances (real or imagined) of a primordial intimacy with species other than our own.[21]

VII

The various elements of the novel come together in the climactic episode (chapters 17–20) on the island sanctuary of Meldilorn. Here Ransom completes the process that began with his glimpse of the "heavens." When he arrives on the island, Ransom examines a series of sculptured stone monoliths that finally reveal to him that Malacandra is the planet Mars. He also meets the last of the rational species, the *pfifltriggi*, and for the first time he can see "as much as he ever would see" (109) the supernatural *eldila*, for whom "light is instead of blood" (118). This opening sequence culminates in his long-anticipated appearance before the planet's Oyarsa. From the Martian ruler he learns of the ancient conflict between their two planets—the story of the rebellion of the once magnificent Oyarsa of Thulcandra (Earth); the latter's attempt to extend his rule to Malacandra, which damaged the surface of the planet and forced its inhabitants to live below it; the failure of his invasion and the retreat to his own world, where "he lies to this hour, and we know no more of that planet: it is silent" (120).

Ransom's encounter with Oyarsa raises once again the persistent problem of fear. The hero has been gaining in self-confidence ever since the hunting expedition, but as he approaches Meldilorn his apprehension increases, and Oyarsa's opening line, "'What are you so afraid of, Ransom of Thulcandra?'" (118), launches a new phase in the novel's exploration of the blinding effects of fear. Since we have shared Ransom's point of view from the outset, we sense his surprise upon learning that his presence on Malacandra is not the result of a chance encounter. The plot strains credibility at this point, but in the final and most sudden shift in his orientation Ransom discovers that Oyarsa has summoned him to Malacandra (via Devine and Weston) and that the *eldila* have been protecting him throughout his journey:

> "You began to be afraid of me before you set foot in my world. And you have spent all your time then in flying from me. My servants saw your fear when you were in your ship in heaven. They saw that your own kind treated you ill, though they could not understand their speech. Then to deliver you out of the hands of those two I stirred up a *hnakra* to try if you would come to me of your own will. . . . After that I sent

my *eldil* to fetch you, but still you would not come. And in the end your own kind have chased you to me. . . ." (119)

Attributing Ransom's unresponsiveness to his fears, Oyarsa learns that Devine and Weston never apprised their captive of the real origin of his adventure. Whether or not Oyarsa's judgment of Ransom is circumscribed by his limited acquaintance with the ways of fallen creatures, his focus on martial virtue is not misplaced. As we soon discover, the chief *eldil* possesses a profound understanding of the power of fear and sees that its dominion extends beyond the terror-prone Ransom to his ostensibly bold and aggressive enemies.

Ransom's appearance before Oyarsa is interrupted by the entry of Devine and Weston, who have been captured and escorted to Meldilorn with the bodies of the *hrossa* they have slain. Somewhat disconcertingly, the two of them remain obstinate and seemingly fearless even in captivity. In contrast to Ransom, Devine and Weston "clearly thought that they had good reason to fear, though neither was by any means lacking in courage" (125). Still regarding Oyarsa as little more than a savage chieftain, Weston adopts the condescending stance of the colonial adventurer, employing "the most orthodox rules for frightening and then conciliating primitive races" (127). His efforts to intimidate the natives—"Pouff! Bang!" (126)—or to seduce them with trinkets—"Pretty, pretty! See! See!" (127)—seem ridiculous in this context, and they meet with resounding laughter on the part of the Malacandran assembly. The comic spirit of this moment concludes with Oyarsa's pronouncement, "Something is wrong in your head, *hnau* from Thulcandra. There is too much blood in it" (129), followed by the command to submerge the physicist's head in cold water. If at one level we can smile at this sequence, Oyarsa's reference to "blood" also has a less literal meaning and more dire connotations, which come to the fore after Weston returns from the treatment that has presumably brought him to his senses.

In his last appearance before Oyarsa, Weston's old-fashioned colonialism mutates into a cosmic version of modern racism that echoes the most militant forms of fascism. As he braces himself for the final confrontation, Weston remains as undaunted as ever, "a brave man suffering in a great cause, and rather eager than reluctant to face the worst or even to provoke it" (132). In his truculent manner the physicist asserts the supremacy of his "race" and sets forth the iron law of evolutionary ethics—"the right of the higher over the lower" (134)—that justifies the elimination of lesser forms of existence if they impede the relentless development of "Life," which is "greater than any system of morality" and ruthlessly crushes the "obstacles" and "failures" that stand in the way of its progress. As the self-appointed emissary of the highest form of life, Weston leaves no doubt about his willingness to sacrifice himself (and anyone else) to the advancement of his species as it "presses forward to that interplanetary leap which will, perhaps, place her [Life] for ever beyond the reach of death" (135). As it appears in the text, Weston's bombastic address is cleverly broken into a series of discrete sections so that Ransom can "translate" each one in turn. Ostensibly designed to cross the barrier between languages, Ransom's "translation" presents Weston's ideology in terms that unmask its shameless self-aggrandizement and render it at once shocking and virtually beyond comprehension to rational beings unacquainted with the misuse of reason to sanction naked aggression.[22]

Oyarsa acknowledges Weston's bravery as well as the selfless devotion with which he pursues his irrational cause. With Augustinian insight, he sees that the physicist's obsession, like that of his less selfless counterparts back on earth, is a perversion of the natural "love of kindred" (137), which has been elevated into an object of idolatry and pursued to the exclusion of all other virtues. At the same time the Martian ruler exposes the essential element of fear that lies at the heart of Weston's crusade. According to Oyarsa, it was fear that clouded Weston's comprehension of their initial meeting: "'When you first came here, I sent for you, meaning you nothing but honour. The darkness in your own mind filled you with fear. Because you thought I meant evil to you, you went as a beast goes against a beast of some other kind, and snared this Ransom. You would give him up to the evil you feared'" (133). Oyarsa goes on to attribute Weston's fixation on the perpetuation of his "race" to the unshakable fear of death that plagues our species. In response to Weston's declaration that the goal of his cosmic imperialism is to "make man live all the time," Oyarsa begins to ponder the terror that once came close to overwhelming his own planet. During the ancient war with his terrestrial counterpart, Oyarsa witnessed the trauma of his own *hnau,* who were in danger of becoming "'as your people are now—wise enough to see the death of their kind approaching but not wise enough to endure it'" (138). But in their retreat from the surface of the planet, the stoic Malacandrans also left behind their fears "'and with fear, murder and rebellion. The weakest of my people do not fear death. It is the Bent One, the lord of your world, who wastes your lives and befouls them with flying from what you know will overtake you in the end. If you were subjects of Maleldil you would have peace'" (138–139). Weston and his kind are admittedly brave and prepared for self-sacrifice, but their courage, which has been pressed into the service of ends that turn martial virtue into a monstrous vice, is ultimately an expression of the very fear and insecurity it is meant to overcome.

After announcing his decision to send the remorseless duo back to Earth, Oyarsa turns his attention to Ransom, who is granted the choice of remaining on Mars or returning to his own planet with his original captors. Given his recently acquired distaste for his own species, it is significant that Ransom appeals to the same virtue that underlies Weston's fanatical racism—"love of our own kind"—and decides to return home. In his parting speech, Oyarsa returns once more to the problem of fear with which their acquaintance began: "'You are guilty of no evil, Ransom of Thulcandra, except a little fearfulness.'" Reminding Ransom that Devine and Weston "may yet do much evil" (142), Oyarsa admonishes him to maintain vigilance and exercise his new-found courage to stand up to their aggression. Although racial violence has been successfully checked on Malacandra, it will require patience, fortitude, and confidence in the final triumph of Maleldil to subdue the powers that threaten to conquer the earth. In the end, Ransom survives the trial of the return voyage and savors once again the familiar sensations of his native planet, but there is a something of a sting to the bracing "pint of bitter" (149) that greets his arrival home.

VIII

After the launch of Sputnik in 1957, Lewis returned to the issue of extraterrestrial intelligence he had explored in the Space Trilogy.[23] Unlike his earlier letters, which focus on the conflict between naturalistic and religious worldviews, the post-Sputnik essays are far more explicit in establishing the connections between our hypothetical encounters with rational aliens and our troubled ties to others on our own planet. Considering the previous record of our species, Lewis is relieved to hear that we are unlikely to meet another rational species anytime soon:

> This thought is welcome to me because, to be frank, I have no pleasure in looking forward to a meeting between humanity and any alien rational species. I observe how the white man has hitherto treated the black, and how, even among civilized men, the stronger have treated the weaker. If we encounter in the depth of space a race, however innocent and amiable, which is technologically weaker than ourselves, I do not doubt that the same revolting story will be repeated. We shall enslave, deceive, exploit or exterminate; at the very least we shall corrupt it with our vices and infect it with our diseases. . . . We are not yet fit to visit other worlds. We have filled our own with massacre, torture, syphilis, famine, dust bowls and with all that is hideous to ear or eye. Must we go to infect new realms? ("The Seeing Eye" *CR* 173)

In retrospect, Lewis claims that it was reflections of this sort that first motivated him to reverse the tendency of his literary predecessors, who "almost automatically represented the inhabitants of other worlds as monsters and the terrestrial invaders as good" (173).[24] As in the letters of the thirties and forties, Lewis still identifies the impulse behind this cosmic imperialism with the modern "'scientific' hope of defeating death," but in situating "Westonism" within the context of the colonialism, racism, and global exploitation with which it has been entwined for the past two centuries, he now comes closer to articulating the more complex network of relations between extra-terrestrial, human, and animal Others implicit in the novel he completed more than two decades before.

In these later pieces, Lewis also directs more attention to the failures of "recognition" (172) that afflict not only his villains but also his well-intentioned hero. As we have seen, Ransom's perceptions of the alien Other are not instantly transformed by his initial cosmic revelation, which replaces Wells's naturalistic conception of "Space" with the spiritual conception of the "heavens." In fact, it takes Ransom most of the novel to overcome his misconceptions of the Martians and the fear and suspicion that provoke them. For a fallen species that often fails to acknowledge other members of its own kind, the question of whether a particular species of extraterrestrial animal possesses a "rational soul" might not be so easy to decide. In one instance, we may be foolish enough to misidentify some clever talking creatures who are, "from the theological point of view, really only animals, capable of pursuing or enjoying only natural ends" ("Religion and Rocketry" *WLN* 85). In another instance we may fail to discern our essential kinship with beings who are "genuinely spiritual, whose powers of manufacture and abstract thought were so humble that we should mistake them for mere animals. God shield them from us!" (86). "Much depends on the seeing eye" ("The Seeing Eye" *CR* 171), and since our detecting apparatus has proven so fallible and vulnerable to our capacity for self-deception, we have little reason to think that we will fare any better in our interplanetary exploits than we have on our own planet.

In the spirit of the extract from Rousseau's *Second Discourse* with which this chapter began, Ransom's confusion over the nature of extraterrestrial species compels us to consider the enigma of our own species. Rousseau, who stood at the crossroads between traditional and modern worldviews, challenged Enlightenment pretensions to knowledge of human nature by examining the prevailing (and often contradictory) assumptions about humankind in the original "state of nature" from a proto-anthropological perspective. Anticipating the modern problem of "recognition," Rousseau exposes the ethnocentric prejudices that led explorers and missionaries of his own day to relegate various "species of anthropomorphic animals" (207) to subhuman status.[25] Revealing how even philosophers are prone to attribute to human nature the accidental accretions of their own particular culture, Rousseau's analysis of the conceptual confusions over our own essential attributes goes so far as to lead him to speculate whether rationality itself, at least in its present constitution, should be regarded as an original and therefore defining characteristic of our species. Lewis, who saw himself poised at another crossroads at the far end of the Enlightenment epoch, engages in a similar search for knowledge of humankind by journeying to "another dimension" ("On Stories" OS 12) where the problem of identifying the nature of the alien leads to perplexity over the origins of our own self-divided species—"What was the history of Man?" (OSP 75)—and hence to crucial questions about human nature itself.

Lewis, like Rousseau, also challenges the prevailing view of human origins and development among the philosophers and scientists of his own era. But as a witness to what he considered the disastrous results of the naturalistic reduction of reason in the modern centuries, Lewis departs from Rousseau's hypothetical reconstruction of the "state of nature" by attempting to restore the concept of the "rational soul" as an original spiritual attribute that has been corrupted by its own misuse. In this respect he follows the lead of another speculative history of human nature, G. K. Chesterton's *The Everlasting Man* (1925), which calls into question the modern image of "primitive" man and the story of human evolution as it appears in Wells's *The Outline of History: Being a Plain History of Life and Mankind* (1920).

In a manner akin to Rousseau's critique of European ethnocentrism, Chesterton demonstrates that the same "primitive" arts and artifacts that modern scientists associate with subrational humanity might well have been produced by creatures with minds as rational as our own. Like Chesterton, who proposes that we reexamine the modern account of the origins and progress of our species from the sobering vantage point of another planet, Lewis demonstrates the need for a new and less self-centered "cosmic" or "corrective" anthropology, which is at once wary of our own provincial rationality, cognizant of our aptitude for misrecognition of the Other, and most of all, confident of the power of transcendent Reason to correct "human imperfections of Reason" (*"De Futilitate" CR* 68), and in so doing, restore us to our senses.

II ⁓

Perelandra

Paradise Reframed: Keeping
Time on Planet Venus

> And from these corporal nutriments perhaps
> Your bodies may at last turn all to spirit,
> Improved by tract of time, and winged ascend
> Ethereal, as we, or may at choice
> Here or in heavenly paradises dwell . . .
> —John Milton, *Paradise Lost,*
> V 496–500

> I believe the waves of time will often change for us
> henceforward. We are coming to have it in our own
> choice whether we shall be above them and see many
> waves together or whether we shall reach them one by
> one as we used to.
> —Tor of Perelandra to Ransom,
> *Perelandra*

In his second voyage into the "heavens," a more confident Elwin Ransom travels to the new and physically unscathed creation on the planet Venus (Perelandra). As in the previous novel, Lewis seems to present an impassable conflict between Christianity and the evolutionary or "developmental" tendencies of modern thought. Ransom again encounters the physicist Weston, who in the interval since their confrontation on Malacandra claims to have repudiated his former ways and is now a disciple of "creative" or "emergent" evolution.[1] It is tempting to disregard this alleged change of heart, especially since the Satanic Un-man, who is gradually taking possession of Weston's mind, proceeds to tempt the New Eve with a popular version of this modern "biological philosophy." But what has been overlooked in this new confrontation between religious and naturalistic points of view is that some of the most distinctive features of the new Eden are themselves derived from the Adversary's own philosophy. As we saw in the Introduction, Lewis departs from traditional views of the earthly paradise by presenting the prelapsarian order as a state of continuous flux (in the lower levels of the creation) and perpetual development (in the new Adam and Eve). It is therefore no accident that the single prohibition in this dynamic paradise—its Tree of the Knowledge of Good and Evil—is to avoid settling on the "Fixed Land." Far more than a mere conceit, the new world on Perelandra embodies the transfiguration or "uplifting" of Bergson's "creative evolution": its critique of "mechanistic" science; its radical reformulation of the concept of time; its reconstruction of evolutionary theory on the basis of "organic" (or "vitalistic") principles; and its ingenious if ultimately inadequate attempt to resolve the antinomy between religious and materialist points of view. Out of his encounter with H. G. Wells's mechanistic view of the evolutionary "struggle for existence," Lewis had previously constructed an imaginary universe in which rationality transcends biological differences and the various species dwell together harmoniously in a divinely ordered cosmos. Similarly, in his encounter with Bergson's vitalistic view of a dynamically evolving universe, Lewis envisions a world in which Becoming is the originary principle and the Creator, who "never repeated Himself" (*P* 123), has endowed the creation with the potential for perpetually new and spontaneous development. In this respect, it is insufficient to consider *Perelandra* solely in terms of the opposition between "Religious" and "Materialist" viewpoints; we must also take into account the highly influential "In-between view" (*MC* 26) of Bergson and the "Life-Force philosophy" he inspired.

At first glance it seems strange, if not contradictory, to think of Lewis constructing his new Eden according to a blueprint provided by the opposing side. But such a view of *Perelandra* is less perplex-ing if we consider Lewis's contemporaneous study of Milton, *A Pref-ace to 'Paradise Lost'* (1942). In this highly influential work, Lewis overturns the Romantic reading of Milton as "of the Devil's party without knowing it" by reducing Satan from an exalted tragic hero to a parody of the God against whom he has rebelled.[2] Invoking the Augustinian notion that evil has no substantial existence and should be regarded merely as a defection from the good, Lewis shows that Milton's fallen archangel should be regarded not as an authentic hero but as a warped imitation of his Creator. The same logic, which pre-supposes that God "has no opposite" (*L* II, 121, 9/12/33), may ac-count for the otherwise baffling situation in *Perelandra,* where Lewis presents creative evolution as a dangerous distortion of the divinely ordained and beneficent temporal dynamism of his own imaginary paradise. Armed with Augustine's view that "what we call bad things are good things perverted" (*PPL* 66), Lewis took the Platonic step of conceiving an "original," or an "archetype," which "raises" crea-tive evolution to a higher level and simultaneously reduces it into a misshapen derivative. Put somewhat differently, just as Bergson transfigured a "mechanistic" theory of evolution still entangled in the static categories of traditional metaphysics into a new principle of Becoming, so Lewis transfigures Bergson's "vitalistic" naturalism, re-jecting his reduction of the divine to an immanent creative impetus but reworking his radical reformulation of the concept of time into a Christian vision of perpetual cosmic development.

I

In order to understand Lewis's complex response to Bergson, we must consider the character and distinctive appeal of "vitalism," which occupied a strategic position in the ideological warfare of the late nineteenth and early twentieth centuries. Strictly speaking, the vital-ist controversy was the province of biologists, who debated whether organic processes are reducible to the same kind of mechanistic laws as those that govern physics and chemistry. At the same time, however, a more momentous battle over vitalism was being waged in philosophy and the human sciences, where the assumptions and procedures of positivism—the use of mechanistic forms of explanation to account for the experience and actions of human beings—had penetrated virtually every field of inquiry. Late nineteenth-century vitalism (or *Lebensphilosophie* [Life-philosophy]) developed in opposition to the triumph of positivism. Whereas the positivist applies the procedures of the physical sciences to the study of human thought, feeling, and action, the vitalist maintains that the organic nature of "life" is irreducible to mechanistic explanation, and that the methods appropriate to the investigation of the physical world lead only to a distorted understanding of human nature. This insistence on the irreducible phenomenon of "life" and the primacy of "lived experience" plays a prominent role in the works of Bergson, Nietzsche, Dilthey, and many of their contemporaries, who at once recall the Romantics in the early nineteenth century and anticipate the work of Heidegger, Sartre, Merleau-Ponty, and others in the following century.

Seen from another vantage point, vitalism occupied the middle ground between naturalism and spiritualism, the two antithetical poles of nineteenth- and early twentieth-century intellectual life, and it elicited enthusiasm and enmity on both sides of the ideological divide. The vitalist quarrel with positivism was especially attractive to those who regarded naturalistic explanation as an assault on the sanctity of the human spirit. To this group, vitalism appeared to dispel the specter of mechanistic determinism and provide new grounds for affirming the moral freedom of the individual. At the same time, vitalist notions could also be employed in the opposite direction against religious orthodoxy and the metaphysics that was used to sustain it. In defiance of a tradition that privileged Being over Becoming, unity over multiplicity, and essence over existence, vitalists celebrated the creative and multiform power of "life" that spontaneously gives rise to new forms of expression and ceaselessly strives to overcome the obstacles that impede its realization. This type of vitalism was often attractive to secular progressives, who were themselves not always hospitable to positivism and welcomed a philosophy that sanctioned the dismantling of anachronistic institutions.

Thus, "Life-Force philosophy," as Lewis sometimes called it, lent itself to cultural values at both ends of the ideological spectrum. There was in effect a vitalism of the Right and a vitalism of the Left, the first a modified form of spiritualism (or at least a repudiation of positivism), the second a more dynamic form of naturalism. This peculiar position between opposing ideologies accounts for the ambiguity of vitalism as a cultural phenomenon. It also accounts for the conflicting responses to highly complex figures such as Nietzsche and Bergson, whom both conservatives and progressives could regard as either friend or foe. In Bergson's case, the conflict was introduced by a single major development in the author's own work. Bergson regarded his own career as the gradual unfolding of a single insight into the nature of time—first as the distinguishing feature of human experience (*durée réelle,* or "real duration"), and later as a fundamental condition of all existence (*élan vital*)—but this development, as we shall see, produced dissension among his early supporters and significantly shifted the character of his appeal.[3]

On the basis of his first two books, *Time and Free Will* (1889) and *Matter and Memory* (1896), Bergson established a major reputation as a critic of positivism, demonstrating that the mechanistic procedures designed to explore the physical world are insufficient for the study of mental life. In *Time and Free Will,* Bergson distinguishes sharply between physical and psychological realms and attacks the various schools of psychology that rely on the methods of physical science and thereby obscure the distinctive qualities of consciousness. For instance, the influential school of association psychology, which employs a model derived from the laws of mechanics, pictures the mind as a collection of discrete impersonal elements or "atoms"—such as fear and desire, or love and hate—that are juxtaposed side by side as if they were so many objects spread out in space. Once the mind is conceived in this manner, the associationist approaches consciousness in the same way that the physicist approaches matter. Adopting the scientific assumption that the same causes always produce the same effects, the associationist concludes that from any existing state of psychic elements we can calculate the course of future action—in other words, we can reduce the moral life to a system of laws as determinate as the laws of mechanics. Bergson grants that this type of analysis may apply to our superficial mental states, which reflect our practical transactions with the external world. But at a deeper level, our psychic life is not a mirror image of the spatial world of discrete and self-same objects but rather a process in which the individual elements of consciousness "cease to stand in juxtaposition and begin to permeate and melt into one another, and each [is] tinged with the colouring of all the others" (164). Moreover, since we are endowed with memory, which preserves the past into the present and makes possible their mutual interpenetration, consciousness is not a sequence of discrete isolatable moments but rather a seamless continuity—"a constant state of becoming" (200) in which each moment flows into all of the others in a manner distinctive to each individual. For Bergson, this "succession without distinction" is the essential feature of consciousness as it exists in "real duration" (*durée réelle*). The principal assumption of mechanics—that identical causes will always produce identical effects—cannot be translated to the psychological realm, since identical conditions never reappear on the stage of consciousness "and the same feeling, by the mere fact of being repeated, is a new feeling" (200). The mind that develops in real duration is irreducible to a determinate calculus, which means that our thoughts and actions are free to the extent that they issue from a unique personality that develops and changes over time. Simply stated, "to act freely is to recover possession of oneself, and to get back into pure duration" (231–32).

In an intellectual milieu still dominated by positivism, Bergson's early works appealed to many younger intellectuals who flocked to his lectures at the Collège de France and referred to him as the "liberator"—the philosopher who redeemed Western thought from the nineteenth century's "religion of science." His young English publicist, T. E. Hulme, expressed a widespread sentiment when he stated that Bergson brought "relief" to an entire generation by dispelling "the nightmare of determinism" (Hulme, *Speculations* 173). But soon after the turn of the century, Bergson's thought began to develop along lines that would alienate many of his early admirers. In *Introduction to Metaphysics* (1903), he veers away from the sharp division between physical and psychological processes and begins to extend the idea of real duration from the human mind to the external world itself. Whereas *Time and Free Will* presents the outer world as a collection of stable material objects, *Introduction to Metaphysics* conceives it as a process of perpetual becoming. In this famous "inversion of Platonism," Bergson maintains that the reality given to us in immediate experience is dynamic rather than static—a shifting flux rather than a system of unchanging forms. His principal distinction now lies in the division between the intellect, which organizes the flow of experience into useful but static concepts, and the faculty of intuition, which reverses this tendency of the intellect and restores us to the mobile reality of the surrounding universe.

The implications of this turn in Bergson's thought became explicit a few years later with the appearance of *Creative Evolution* (1907). In this wide-ranging and enormously influential work, Bergson simultaneously dismantles the Darwinian theory of evolution and proposes an alternative view in which real duration provides a model through which to reconceive the development of life itself. Tracing the problems of nineteenth-century positivism back to the origins of Western philosophy, Bergson claims that by its very nature the rational intellect reduces time to a function of space, and as a consequence of this spatialization of the temporal, it treats the past and the future as calculable functions of the present. The intellect is an ingenious instrument for organizing and arranging the existing products of creation, but its inability to comprehend processes involving true novelty and unforeseeable change accounts not only for the problems of traditional metaphysics but also for the failures of modern scientific theories of evolution. By definition, the mechanistic theories of Darwin and his successors explain future states on the basis of antecedent conditions, while teleological theories, which assume that antecedent conditions are merely stages in the realization of "a programme previously arranged" (*Creative Evolution* 39), are simply mechanistic theories in reverse. Bergson departs from both of these conceptions by postulating the existence of a creative spiritual impetus—the *élan vital*—which spontaneously produces novel forms of life and thereby raises creation to new and previously unpredictable levels of development. While acknowledging the speculative character of the *élan vital*, Bergson marshals a formidable array of scientific evidence to demonstrate that the creative impetus accounts for many biological facts which previous theories distort or ignore. To complete the argument, he also suggests that the future of the human species, and perhaps of the evolutionary process itself, may lie not in the further development of the rational intellect as we know it but in the creative interaction between the intellect and the still emergent faculty of intuition. This interaction, which is already bringing us to a recognition of the dynamic character of the human psyche and the surrounding universe, may have the capacity to advance the natural order to a higher though as yet indefinable stage of self-realization.

Creative Evolution was a hugely popular success, and its author soon became an international celebrity. The basis of Bergson's remarkable appeal lay in his synthesis of opposing points of view. Under his spell the presumably unbridgeable gap between religious and naturalistic viewpoints appeared to dissolve into mere illusion. Bergson achieved this feat by simultaneously spiritualizing biology and naturalizing the spiritual. After reading his book one could believe that the Darwinian theory is essentially a consequence of the mechanistic nature of intellect, and that the *élan vital* makes far more sense of the entire evolutionary process. One could also view the traditional metaphysical conception of God as a product of the intellect, which leads us to identify reality with stasis rather than dynamic process, and reconceive the Divine as a creative spirit that realizes itself progressively in the natural order. As it turned out, this middle way between naturalism and spiritualism achieved a considerable if momentary following, but it also provoked a good deal of criticism. At one end of the ideological spectrum, Bergson's emphasis on dynamic and open-ended change endeared him to many progressives, including George Bernard Shaw, who incorporated Bergson into his own vision of evolutionary development, and the young Walter Lippmann, who adapted Bergson's metaphysics to the politics of the progressive era, declaring that we must discard the notion of government as a static mechanism and reconstruct it along vitalist lines as "a process of continual creation, an unceasing invention of forms to meet constantly changing needs" (Lippmann 1913, 13). And yet for every progressive who applauded Bergson's idea of spontaneous development, there was another who dismissed the *élan vital* as a pseudo-mystical confection and bristled at his deprecation of the rational intellect. On the other side of the ideological spectrum, many French Catholics continued to applaud his work, but others, who had been inspired by his early studies of the psyche, were far less receptive to his evolutionary cosmology and his account of ancient and medieval philosophy. Sympathetic critics such as Charles Péguy praised Bergson for restoring the distinction between the mechanistic realm of matter and the vital realm of human existence, but also attacked him for collapsing the distinction between the vital and the spiritual realms. From their perspective, *Creative Evolution* denied the transcendence of God by reducing the Divine to an immanent life force that realizes itself through the course of evolutionary progress. Bergson continued to inspire many Catholic intellectuals, particularly those who believed that the Church must eventually come to terms with modernity. But by suggesting that the *élan vital* may be equated with God, Bergson had entered into a fatal collision course with Rome, which eventually placed his works on the Index of Prohibited Books. Hence the Bergsonian synthesis proved to be an unstable compound, and as a means of reconciling opposing points of view it was often treated as a suspicious compromise by representatives of both sides. To make matters worse, with the outbreak of World War I the cultural climate of Europe began to change dramatically, and by the time the war was over the ethos that could support either the notion of an immanent spiritual force or the idea of unlimited progress had seriously eroded. Bergson would remain an imposing presence during the postwar decade, but the extraordinary vogue of Bergsonism had begun its steady descent.

II

Ironically, C. S. Lewis's fascination with Bergson began while he was recovering from his battlefront wounds in spring 1918, and the young scholar continued reading Bergson intermittently in the years that followed.[4] As we might expect, after his conversion in the early thirties Lewis assumed the more critical stance reminiscent of Péguy and other French Catholics. While affirming Bergson's separation of the vital and mechanistic realms, he rejected the virtual equation between the vital and the spiritual. According to the older Lewis, creative evolution is a "modern form of nature religion" ("The Grand Miracle" *GD* 86). Its distinctive appeal lies in its "In-between view," which promises to deliver us from the "Material" while diluting the "Religious" into an emotionally uplifting but ethically undemanding sense of "striving" or "purposiveness" in the natural universe (*MC* 26). (In *Perelandra*, Lewis would explore the darker implications of this ethical deficiency in his portrayal of Weston, for whom evolutionary advancement is the supreme end that justifies any means of achieving it.) But even as he dissected the temptations and dangers of "Life-Force philosophy," Lewis continued to treat Bergson himself with considerable if qualified respect. He admired the Bergsonian critique of "orthodox Darwinism" and repeatedly distinguished the philosopher's own works from its various popularizations by Shaw and others.[5] In his autobiography, *Surprised by Joy* (1956), Lewis is quite open in his praise as he recalls his initial response to Bergson in 1918:

> The other momentous experience was that of reading Bergson in a Convalescent Camp on Salisbury Plain. Intellectually this taught me to avoid the snares that lurk about the word *Nothing*. But it also had a revolutionary effect on my emotional outlook. Hitherto my whole bent had been toward things pale, remote, and evanescent; the water-color world of Morris, the leafy recesses of Malory, the twilight of Yeats. The word "life" had for me pretty much the same associations it had for Shelley in *The Triumph of Life*. I would not have understood what Goethe meant by *des Lebens goldnes Baum*. Bergson showed me. He did not abolish my old loves, but he gave me a new one. From him I first learned to relish energy, fertility, and urgency; the resource, the triumphs, and even the insolence, of things that grow. I became capable of appreciating artists who would, I believe, have meant nothing to me before; all the resonant, dogmatic, flaming, unanswerable people like Beethoven, Titian (in his mythological pictures), Goethe, Dunbar, Pindar, Christopher Wren, and the more exultant Psalms. (198)

Bergson may have naturalized the supernatural, but for the young agnostic caught between a dreamy late romanticism and the horror of the trenches, Bergson's way of infusing nature with spirit appears to have worked like a charm. Seen from this perspective, *Perelandra* is Lewis's own paean to "the resource, the triumphs, and even the insolence, of things that grow"—a celebration of the vital realm that reaches its highest expression in the *"animal rationale"* (P 178) who presides over the rest of creation. However much he criticizes Bergson and those he inspired, Lewis constructs his own version of creative evolution by endowing his imaginary world with a principle of dynamic change in which even the evolutionary lapses, including the spiritual catastrophe that has overtaken our own fallen planet, are transfigured into something new and more marvelous by the redeeming act of God.

Far less obvious than the tonic effect of Bergson's vitalism is his lesson on "the snares that lurk about the word *Nothing.*" In his autobiography, Lewis goes on to explain the significance of this discovery:

> Finally, there was of course Bergson. Somehow or other (for it does not seem very clear when I reopen his books today) I found in him a refutation of the old haunting idea, Schopenhauer's idea, that the universe "might not have existed." In other words one divine attribute, that of necessary existence, rose above my horizon. It was still, and long after, attached to the wrong subject; to the universe, not to God. But the mere attribute was itself of immense potency. When once one has dropped the absurd notion that reality is an arbitrary alternative to "nothing," one gives up being a pessimist (or even an optimist). . . . It was perhaps the nearest thing to a religious experience which I had had since my prep-school days. It ended (I hope forever) any idea of a treaty or compromise with reality. (*SJ* 204–205)

Lewis may have forgotten the details, but his memory didn't betray him. In a long and challenging section of *Creative Evolution*, Bergson argues that concepts such as "nothingness" are actually complex derivatives proceeding from the negation of the original plenitude of creation. Whereas ancient philosophers and modern scientists share the assumption that "Nothing" is prior to "Being"—chaos precedes cosmos, void is anterior to the emergence of things—Bergson demonstrates that each of these negative terms issues from, and depends upon, the positive term it supposedly precedes. The same relation holds for other oppositions such as absence/presence, emptiness/fullness, and disorder/order. Somewhat surprisingly, it also pertains to the distinction between possibility and actuality: in line with his emphasis on unforeseeable development, Bergson reverses the assumption that the possible precedes the actual and shows that possibility may be regarded as the retrospective effect of a new actuality (*The Creative Mind* 91–106). In the case of "Nothingness," the negative term is the final result of a complicated process that develops from the temporal structure of human consciousness, which allows us to feel disappointment in the present by comparing it to the recollected past or the anticipated future (*Creative Evolution* 272–98; cp. *P,* chapter 5, discussed below). Lewis welcomed Bergson's solid appreciation of the actual over "what might be" or "what might have been," just as he found satisfaction in the Bergsonian plenum that upholds the priority of Being (as opposed to "Nothingness") and presence, and consigns their opposites to a secondary and derivative position.

In *Perelandra* Lewis merges Bergson's notion of "Nothingness" with his own Augustinian view that grants ontological status only to the Good and relegates evil to a privative notion that is parasitic upon it. As we shall see, just as Lewis ascends much higher than Bergson with his reaffirmation of divine transcendence, his Augustinian sense of sin leads him much deeper into the darkness of negation. Nevertheless, in a manner akin to Bergson's treatment of "Nothingness," Lewis considers the problem of evil in relation to the difficulties inherent in the temporal experience of a free agent. Thus he draws on Bergson not only for his celebration of creative development but also for his critical examination of the trials of temporality that plague our own world— the limitations of our fragile finitude in a world of ceaseless change; the insecurities that lead us to fixate on the past or attempt to control the future; and ultimately, the temptation to deny our time-bound condition and thereby defect from the developing stream of actual life into self-deceptive fictions and the eternal darkness of the "Nothing."

III

The first two chapters of *Perelandra* take place on Earth (see the figure on p. 66) and set the stage for the new temporal order that Ransom encounters on Venus. As the narrator (identified as "Lewis")

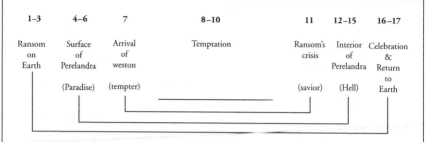

1–3	4–6	7	8–10	11	12–15	16–17
Ransom on Earth	Surface of Perelandra	Arrival of weston	Temptation	Ransom's crisis	Interior of Perelandra	Celebration & Return to Earth
	(Paradise)	(tempter)		(savior)	(Hell)	

Figure 2.1

Perelandra, like *Out of the Silent Planet*, was published with no structural indicators other than chapter numbers. But as Lewis scholars have pointed out, chapter 11 begins to reveal the structural symmetry of the novel's seventeen untitled chapters. The temptation scene in the center of the novel (chapters 8–10) is preceded by the chapter in which Weston gradually discloses his diabolical identity (chapter 7) and followed by the one in which Ransom gradually comprehends his own identity and the character of his mission (chapter 11). Together, these two chapters frame the central core and are surrounded in turn by chapters 3–6 and 12–15: the first tetrad portraying the Edenic surface of Perelandra and the second bringing us into its hellish underworld. The opening chapters on earth (1–2) and the finale on the Holy Mountain of Perelandra (chapters 16–17) make up the outer borders of the novel. Notice that each arm of the inner frame (chapters 7 and 11) consists of a single chapter, as it does in *Out of the Silent Planet* (chapters 10 and 13) and in *That Hideous Strength* (chapters 7 and 11). In each novel, the chapters of the inner frame not only serve as the entry and exit to the central section, but also bear considerable thematic weight. In each case, the scene that follows the central section depicts a crisis in the spiritual journey of the protagonist—Ransom's participation in the Martian hunt, which leads to the death of his friend and departure from the *hrossa;* Ransom's realization of the mission, at once horrifying and salvific, that he has been called upon to fulfill on Venus; and in the finale, Jane and Mark Studdock's terrestrial confrontation with the imminent prospect of death.

disembarks from his train and apprehensively begins his walk to Ransom's cottage, he is acutely aware of the distressing effects of time—the transition from daylight to darkness, the decay of an abandoned industrial site, the gloom of an empty house with a single unboarded window "staring like the eye of a dead fish" (*P* 13). Anticipating Ransom's own temptation to resist the flow of time, the narrator is repeatedly assailed by "the impulse to retreat" (15) and must rely on "the rational part of my mind" (13) to maintain his resolve to go on. The emphasis on time shifts to the cosmic level when we meet Ransom and the supernatural *eldil* who is sponsoring his mission. The veteran of *Out of the Silent Planet* wishes to return to Mars—the planet he visited in the first book of the trilogy—but he knows that he "can never, never get back" (20). Maleldil's universe is changing continuously and irreversibly, and Ransom has been called to assume an as yet undefined role in what may be "a whole new phase in the life of the Solar System" (20). The presence of the *eldil* underscores the predicament of our time-bound condition. When the narrator expresses his concern that they have kept the *eldil* "waiting," Ransom informs him that unlike humans, who possess "a sense of cumulative duration," the angelic *eldila* are exempt from the travails of creatures who grow weary or restless over time: "'You might as well say that a tree in a wood was waiting, or the sunlight waiting on the side of a hill'" (26). Even the progression of the narrative calls attention to the dynamics of time. As Ransom prepares for his voyage, the relatively slow-paced narration, which has lingered over the uncertainties of the impending future, suddenly races forward to the hero's return a year later. Perhaps this is merely a convenient device for casting the ensuing narrative in the form of a tale told retrospectively to a circle of friends. But coming as abruptly as it does, this fast-forward in time also conveys a compound sense of time traversed (Ransom casually resumes conversation as if he had never gone), of time reversed (the "new Ransom" looks ten years younger than he appeared the year before), and of time transcended, since like the *eldila* we've been relieved of the burden of waiting.

IV

The sense of time, change, and movement shifts once more when Ransom lands on the watery surface of Venus (chapter 3). As he rides the ocean waves, the hero finds himself in the midst of a confusing though surprisingly pleasurable flux. Inspired by scientific accounts of Venus's "floating islands," Lewis depicts a "universe of shifting slopes" that never ceases to change and offers the observer no still point of orientation:

> It looked exactly as though you were in a well-wooded valley with a river at the bottom of it. But while you watched, that seeming river did the impossible. It thrust itself up so that the land on either side sloped downwards from it; and then up farther still and shouldered half the landscape out of sight beyond its ridge; and became a huge greeny-gold hog's back of water hanging in the sky and threatening to engulf your own land, which was now concave and reeled backwards to the next roller, and rushing upwards, became convex again. (45)

Such passages are not merely a display of their author's powers of description. Lewis is also inverting the traditional conception of paradise as an immutable state that precedes the lapse into time and change. Just as Bergson and others were challenging the traditional relationship between Being and Becoming, Lewis presents his new Eden as a world of continuous movement in which the one proscription is to avoid settling on the Fixed Land. Lewis's portrayal of paradise as a perpetual flux is also a means of examining the human predicament in our own world, where temporal progression is distorted by insecurity and the specter of death.

These issues begin to surface when Ransom notices that he wants to repeat the experience of tasting the wondrous fruit of Perelandra:

> This itch to have things over again, as if life were a film that could be unrolled twice or even made to work back-

wards . . . was it possibly the root of all evil? No: of course the love of money was called that. But money itself—perhaps one valued it chiefly as a defence against chance, a security for being able to have things over again, a means of arresting the unrolling of the film. (43)

Ransom understands the implications of his urge to immobilize the flux: our desire to overcome the temporal conditions of our existence and assume control of our own destiny is the very basis of our fallen state. Echoing the narrator's "impulse to retreat" in the opening chapter, Ransom's impulse to substitute the past for the present also anticipates the Un-man's attempt to ruin the new Eden by exploiting the temptation to replace "what is" with seductive fictions of "what might be."

As long as Ransom's experience is confined to the vegetable and lower animal life of Perelandra, the surface of the planet appears as a ceaseless but directionless flux, more akin to the cyclical stream of Heraclitus than to the developmental views of Bergson and his successors.[6] But the situation begins to change when Ransom meets the Green Lady—the Eve of this mobile Eden. Physically, the Queen of Perelandra manifests the perpetual novelty of Maleldil's creative activity: she possesses human form, though as Ransom soon realizes, she is the progenitrix of a new and independent species. Spiritually, she is even more remarkable. Unlike her earthly counterparts who feel the compulsion to repeat, the woman simply accepts "the unrolling of the film" and finds it difficult to imagine why anyone would wish to do otherwise. In this pristine state, the Lady possesses a kind of intuitive wisdom, but as it turns out she is also a fast learner who grows "older" with each new conversation. Not surprisingly, her development involves an emerging awareness of the modalities of time, as her worldly-wise tutor tries to enlighten her on the quandaries of recollection and anticipation. But even as she learns to take account of past and future within the unfolding present, the woman also reveals what it would be like to possess a mind at peace with the progression of time. When

Ransom remarks that one cannot become much "older" in a single night, the new Eve responds with Bergsonian insight into our propensity to reduce time to a function of space: "'I see it now,' she said. 'You think times have lengths. A night is always a night whatever you do in it, as from this tree to that is always so many paces whether you take them quickly or slowly. I suppose that is true in a way. But the waves do not always come at equal distances" (52). The Lady also lives in harmony with duration at the cosmic level. In response to Ransom's lament that Maleldil no longer brings forth rational creatures with nonhuman form of the kind he met on Mars—"Are they to be swept away? Are they only rubbish in the Deep Heaven?" (54)—she offers a refreshing corrective that sanctifies each moment of the creative process:

> "I do not know what *rubbish* means," she answered, "nor
> what you are saying. You do not mean they are worse because
> they come early in the history and do not come again? They
> are their own part of the history and not another. We are on
> this side of the wave and they on the far side. All is new." (54)

From this vantage point, cosmic progression entails no loss. Untouched by our impulse to transform the qualitative into the quantitative and measure one moment against another, the Green Lady rejoices in the distinctive character of each phase of the creation as it unfolds in time. Along with Ransom, we are just beginning to learn that it is our own troubled condition which makes the passage of time such a difficult burden to bear.

While the Lady unfolds the temporal logic of her unspoiled world, Ransom attempts to press on her the perils of time in our own world. In a revealing moment, Ransom foreshadows the Un-man's temptation by launching into a Bergsonian account of the origins of negation in recollection and anticipation: "'But even you,' he said, 'when you first saw me, I know now you were expecting and hoping that I was the King [her husband]. When you found I was not, your face changed. Was *that* event not unwelcome? Did you not wish it to be otherwise?'"(59). When the Lady responds, "'You make me grow older more quickly than I can bear,'" Ransom begins to understand the fragile character of free agency in a time-bound world where nothing prevents us from wandering off into the "otherwise":

> It was suddenly borne in upon him that her purity and peace were not, as they had seemed, things settled and inevitable like the purity and peace of an animal—that they were alive and therefore breakable, a balance maintained by a mind and therefore, at least in theory, able to be lost. There is no reason why a man on a smooth road should lose his balance on a bicycle; but he could. There was no reason why she should step out of her happiness into the psychology of our own race; but neither was there any wall between to prevent her doing so. (59)[7]

Ransom has every reason to feel terrified by this "sense of precariousness" (59). He has ruptured the pristine "unrolling of the film" and has generated the self-consciousness that is the precondition of our freedom and therefore of the fallibility inherent in it. But once again the Lady surprises him with her reply. Instead of shattering her innocence, the birth of self-consciousness engenders the joyous realization that she is a free agent who willingly assumes her place in Maleldil's creation. She now understands how recollection and expectation can entice us into making "the real fruit taste insipid by thinking of the other," or into sensing disappointment in "finding a stranger when you wanted your husband" (60). But at the same time she realizes that in affirming the actual and the present, "it is I, I myself, who turn from the good expected to the given good. Out of my own heart I do it. One can conceive a heart which did not: which clung to the good it had first thought of and turned the good which was given it into no good" (60). The awakening of self-consciousness entails no necessary rupture of the primordial unity with the will of Maleldil, suggesting that it is our own fallen state that leads us to associate the passage from innocence to experience with a lapse from an original state of purity.

For the Green Lady, the dawning sense of freedom is not so much terrifying as "a delight with terror in it!" (60). She is awed but excited by the recognition that "He made me so separate from Himself. . . . The world is so much larger than I thought. I thought we went along paths—but it seems there are no paths. The going itself is the path" (60). While the Queen of this new world continues to delight in the challenge of this freedom, her visitor from an unhappier world grows increasingly sullen, and when she asks him why he is wrinkling his brow and shrugging his shoulders, his evasive reply that these gestures "mean nothing" (61) is at once a lie (which in shame he emends to "nothing I could explain to you") and an acknowledgment of the impassable difference between her present condition and his own. As the conversation ends, we appear to have reached a state of irresolvable tension between innocence and experience, between the ennobling freedom for which we were meant and the dejection of a creature whose fragile freedom has ended up in woeful acquaintance with all "the snares that lurk about the word *Nothing*" (*SJ* 198).

All of these issues are compressed into the ban on the Fixed Land. If acceptance of temporal progression is the defining feature of the paradisal state, the archetypal transgression lies in the attempt "to make sure—to be able on one day to command where I should be the next. . . . to put in our power what times should roll towards us" (*P* 179). Translated into the terms of our own world, the Fixed Land is a kind of surrogate eternity—a false haven of security that offers an idolatrous escape from the disappointments and terrors of an uncertain world. It is a flight from the present that expresses our desire for an eternal present that can never roll into the past because it has already foreclosed on the future. Not surprisingly, it is during their visit to the Fixed Land that Ransom and the Lady catch sight of the diabolical Weston. In his effort to alert the Lady to the imminent danger, Ransom tries to explain the archetypal rebellion of Lucifer, which he describes in terms of "'clinging to the old good instead of taking the good that came'"(71). But in her innocent wisdom the new Eve simply replies that "'the old good would cease to be a good at all if he did that,'"and looks for further clarification. When Ransom tells her that "there is no time to explain," the Lady's response—"No time? What has happened to the time?" (71)—at once reveals the vulnerability of her condition and characterizes the imminent threat to her world of pure duration.

V

When Weston arrives on the Fixed Land (chapter 7), he claims that he is a different man from the crude materialist of *Out of the Silent Planet*. As a result of his encounter with "biological philosophy," he is now an emissary of the new gospel of "emergent evolution" (78).[8] At this point, Lewis turns from his "Beatific" transfiguration of creative evolution to the more familiar "Miserific" (96) version presented by his villain. Weston's doctrine bears only a rough resemblance to the sophisticated views of Bergson, Alexander, Morgan, or even to the more popular adaptations of Shaw and others. But Lewis employs Weston's self-serving vulgarization to bring to light the dangerous assumptions behind "biological philosophy": by positing a scale of evolutionary progress and placing humanity at its forefront, the developmental paradigm can turn into a means of rationalizing our own worst impulses. In Weston's hands, it degenerates into little more than an excuse to pursue the "fixed idea" (77) of interplanetary conquest, while closer to home his real-world counterparts twist this type of thinking into pseudo-scientific theories that justify the domination of one sector of humanity—whether class, nation, or race—over another. In this respect, modern "biological philosophy" is merely another manifestation of a disastrous turn in Western thought—the transfer of the "vortex of self-thinking, self-originating activity" (79) from a transcendent God to an immanent power that realizes itself in the dynamic development of Man. Behind the various promethean visions from Blake and Shelley to Nietzsche and Bergson resides the temptation to deny our dependent condition and assume the sovereignty traditionally reserved for the gods. From this perspective, the theory of "creative" or "emergent" evolution is ultimately an expression of our desire to usurp control over the conditions of our existence. It is a parody of true temporality, a theory of cosmic progression that paradoxically reveals our inability to accept the inexorable flow of time.

The Un-man's temptation, which occupies the three central chapters of the novel (chapters 8–10), hinges on this paradox. The Un-man tries to seduce the Lady with a vision of development that at once resembles and distorts the beneficent dynamism of Maleldil's universe. The process begins with an attempt to disrupt the Lady's acceptance of "what is" by enticing her into inventing stories of "what might be" (89). By associating "what is" with static repetition and "what might be" with dynamic change, the Un-man reverses the primordial relationship between flux and fixity. It also tries to persuade its victim that Maleldil secretly wishes her to violate his interdict, since He longs "to see His creature become fully itself, to stand up in its own reason and its own courage even against Him" (101). In terrestrial terms, this ploy to corrupt the Lady's imagination is a readily identifiable (and at times rather clever) version of the Romantic myth of creative rebellion. As envisioned by Shaw in *Back to Methuselah* and elsewhere, the initial act of disobedience ignites the spark that liberates the species from its inherited dependency and propels its march toward the realization of its higher destiny. But from the outset of this section, the Green Lady discerns that the Un-man's unwavering fixation on the same topic belies his emphasis on change and progress: "'I am wondering,' said the woman's voice, 'whether all the people of your world have the habit of talking about the same thing more than once. I have said already that we are forbidden to dwell on the Fixed Land. Why do you not either talk of something else or stop talking?'" (89). Knowing that "to walk out of His will is to walk into nowhere" (100), the Lady proves remarkably resilient in countering the tempter's efforts to dislodge her from the actual into the abyss of infinite possibility. Ransom sees the Un-man's distortion as well, but as one of our own kind he also knows how readily we are seduced into imagining that our freedom lies not in voluntary obedience but in the assertion of our own autonomy. In the final phase of temptation, the element of repetition and sameness subsumes the Un-man's vision of dynamic development as it settles into the routine of relating countless stories of courageous, self-sacrificing women. As Ransom soon realizes, the Un-man is attempting to lure the woman into envisioning herself as a tragic heroine enacting "a grand rôle in the drama of her world" (113). At first this promotion of an "external and, as it were, dramatic conception of the self" (118) may seem like an inexplicable shift in tactics, but it recalls and exploits the initial awakening into self-consciousness when the Green Lady first senses the danger of "stepping out of life into the Alongside and looking at oneself living as if one were not alive" (52). In an effort to incite this pathological form of self-consciousness, the Un-man hands the Lady a mirror with which "to walk alongside oneself as if one were a second person and to delight in one's own beauty" (117). To the still unfallen Queen of Perelandra, this bifurcation of the self into spectator and actor is a strange and confusing phenomenon—an unnatural process of self-alienation in which the individual is no longer simply living one's life but observing oneself perform a pre-scripted role. Whereas for fallen beings such as ourselves, who are rarely exempt from some degree of self-dramatization, it is more a matter of remaining aware of an ever-present temptation and reminding ourselves of the ease with which we can be subsumed into our self-constructed fictions.[9]

Appropriately, the terminal development of this dissociation between consciousness and action lies in the tempter himself, or more precisely, in the Un-man's possession of Weston's body. As the tormented physicist realizes in his occasional moments of self-possession, the process of dissociation has reached the point where "he does all my thinking for me" (111). When the Un-man assumes full control, Weston's body merely executes the actions it is directed to perform. Ransom notices the frightful disjunction between the demonic spirit and the body it inhabits. The actions of the latter seem inorganic and "mechanised" (110), as if they were an "imitation of living motions" manipulated by some "external force" (105). In Bergsonian terms, the Un-man represents the reduction of humanity from the vital to the mechanistic realm, the devolution from a condition of flexible responsiveness and continuous development to a desiccated state of repetition and interminable sameness.[10] In line with its mechanistic character the Un-man requires no sleep, and Ransom begins to suspect that its chance of victory over the woman lies as much in its capacity for relentless and monotonous repetition as in the theatrical self-image it is attempting to instill. Ransom is painfully aware of the enervating power of this repetition, which identifies itself in the Un-man's ceaseless and self-canceling solicitation of his name:

> "Ransom," it said.
> "Well?" said Ransom.
> "Nothing," said the Un-man.
> * * *
> "Ransom," it said again.
> "What is it?" said Ransom sharply.
> "Nothing," it answered. (105)

In this unnerving repetition we have reached the end-game where the process initially launched by stepping outside the actual into the Alongside discloses itself in the (non)identity of the Un-man and the deadly "Nothing" which is nothing other than the voiding of what is.

VI

In contrast to the Un-man's repetition and sameness, Maleldil never repeats Himself, and in His presence Ransom begins a process of self-clarification that gradually reveals the terrifying singularity of his mission (chapter 11).[11] Like the Lady, he must struggle against his own version of the "external" and "dramatic" conception of the self. Ironically, while the Un-man tempts the new Eve with "a grand rôle in the drama of the world," Ransom's tempter—his own "voluble self" who serves as the skeptical critic within him—protests against his dawning realization that "he himself was the miracle" (120). In the stillness and darkness associated with Maleldil's presence, Ransom is overwhelmed by the recognition of how much depends on his own actions:

If the issue lay in Maleldil's hands, Ransom and the Lady *were* those hands. The fate of a world really depended on how they behaved in the next few hours. The thing was irreducibly, nakedly real. They could, if they chose, decline to save the innocence of this new race, and if they declined its innocence would not be saved. It rested with no other creature in all time or all space. . . . Thus, and not otherwise, the world was made. Either something or nothing must depend on individual choices. And if something, who could set bounds to it? A stone may determine the course of a river. He was that stone at this horrible moment which had become the centre of the whole universe. (120–121)

As he continues to clarify his mission, Ransom also comes face to face with the seemingly absurd and terrifying recognition that he has not been called to re-enact the more familiar scenario of a purely spiritual struggle but rather to engage in direct physical combat with the Un-man.[12] In terrestrial terms the emerging story makes little sense: "If the Lady were to be kept in obedience only by the forcible removal of the Tempter, what was the use of that? . . . Did Maleldil suggest that our own world might have been saved if the elephant had accidentally trodden on the serpent a moment before Eve was about to yield? Was it as easy and as un-moral as all that? The thing was patently absurd!" (122–123). But in the presence of Maleldil he knows that parallels between Eden and Perelandra are limited and misleading. The new world is "not a mere repetition" of the old: "the same wave never came twice. . . . nothing was a copy or model of anything else" (123). Slowly the impulse to escape the reality of the present by comparing it to the past gives way "to the here and the now, and to the growing certainty of what was here and now demanded. . . . only the actual was real: and every actual situation was new" (124).

Ransom resigns himself to the stark singularity of his assignment, but still finding the task as impossible as it is necessary, he discovers within the apparent accident of his own name the one divinely sanctioned repetition that places his mission within a larger design: "'My name also is Ransom,' said the Voice" (126). In this utterance, he finds the assurance that "if he were not the ransom, Another would be," though his failure would entail real loss and require "not a second crucifixion: perhaps—who knows—not even a second Incarnation . . . some act of even more appalling love, some glory of yet deeper humility" (126). That the future will be secured at such a price makes Ransom even more daunted by the "frightful freedom that was being put into his hands. . . . It lay with him to save or to spill" (126). Once again, reassurance comes in the form of a repetition that secures the future through the recollection of singular events in the past:

> The thing still seemed impossible. But gradually something happened to him which had happened to him only twice before in his life. It had happened once while he was trying to make up his mind to do a very dangerous job in the last war. It had happened again while he was screwing his resolution to go and see a certain man in London and make to him an excessively embarrassing confession which justice demanded. In both cases the thing had seemed a sheer impossibility: he had not thought but known that, being what he was, he was psychologically incapable of doing it; and then, without any apparent movement of the will, as objective and unemotional as the reading on a dial, there had arisen before him, with perfect certitude, the knowledge "about this time tomorrow you will have done the impossible." The same thing happened now. His fear, his shame, his love, all his arguments, were not

altered in the least. The thing was neither more nor less dreadful than it had been before. The only difference was that he knew—almost as a historical proposition—that it was going to be done. . . . The future act stood there, fixed and unaltered as if he had already performed it. (126–127)

At first it seems a strange regression to find Ransom attempting to bestow the fixity of the past on the uncertainty of the future. But the very fact that Lewis regards the openness of time as a necessary condition of freedom underscores the distinctive character of this moment. At an elementary level, Ransom has simply hit on an effective means of bolstering individual resolution in the face of a dreadful and seemingly impossible situation. At another level, and in a spirit more reminiscent of Kierkegaard than Bergson, Ransom is choosing to meet the wave that is rolling his way and clearing the last obstacle to the fulfillment of his destiny.[13] In his reckoning with the Voice of Maleldil, he has reached the point where it is no longer meaningful to distinguish freedom and necessity: "You might say, if you liked, that the power of choice had been simply set aside and an inflexible destiny substituted for it. On the other hand, you might say that he had [been] delivered from the rhetoric of his passions and had emerged into unassailable freedom. Ransom could not, for the life of him, see any difference between these two statements. Predestination and freedom were apparently identical" (127). In this raising up to a higher dimension of awareness, Ransom foresees his impending action in the light of the Eternal One for whom our future deeds are as much an accomplished act as our past deeds are to us.

VII

What ensues from Ransom's spiritual crisis is an extended ordeal with the powers of darkness. In one respect, Ransom's confrontation with the Un-man is an archetypal journey to the underworld: after driving the Evil One from the surface of Perelandra, the hero descends to the interior of the planet where he endures a series of trials before finally destroying his enemy. In the symmetrical structure of *Perelandra*, the four chapters of this section (chapters 12–15) are the antithesis to the four-chapter celebration of life on the surface of the planet (chapters 3–6), and they pose a serious challenge to the hero's faith in Maleldil and His creative activity. Ransom's trial is at once physical and spiritual. After reconciling himself to a physical contest, he awakens on the first morning of the conflict to find that "he thought better of himself as a human animal" (128) and proceeds directly to battle with the Un-man.[14] But soon enough a new struggle commences as Ransom pursues his wounded enemy across the vast expanses of the sea and begins to feel a sense of isolation and estrangement from his surroundings. He is disturbed by the sea-birds whose cry "had least to do with Man" (135) and by other sounds and smells that intimidate not by their enmity but by their complete indifference to him:

> It was not hostile: if it had been, its wildness and strangeness would have been the less, for hostility is a relation and an enemy is not a total stranger. It came into his head that he knew nothing at all about this world. Some day, no doubt, it would be peopled by the descendants of the King and Queen. But all its millions of years in the unpeopled past, all its uncounted miles of laughing water in the lonely present . . . did they exist solely for that? It was strange that he to whom a wood or a morning sky on earth had sometimes been a kind of meal, should have had to come to another planet in order to realise Nature as a thing in her own right. The diffused meaning, the inscrutable character . . . which would be, in one sense, displaced by the advent of imperial man, yet, in some other sense, not displaced at all, enfolded him on every side and caught him into itself. (135–136)

Soon afterward, the experience of the "illimitable ocean," compounded by sea-creatures with nearly human faces but no link to humanity, begins to take its toll on Ransom's mind. Unlike the Edenic floating islands, the open seas of Venus feel haunted "not by an anthropomorphic Deity, rather by the wholly inscrutable to which man and his life remained eternally irrelevant" (140).

Ransom's encounter with indifferent nature gradually turns into a reckoning with scientific naturalism, or rather the dualism that arose in the scientific revolution of the seventeenth century and established a sharp division between mind and matter, human consciousness and an external world conceived in strictly quantitative and mechanistic terms. Ransom is plagued by what he had once dismissed as "The Empirical Bogey . . . the great myth of our century with its gases and galaxies, its light years and evolutions, its nightmare perspectives of simple arithmetic in which everything that can possibly hold significance for the mind becomes the mere by-product of essential disorder" (140). The erudite Ransom has been reasonably well fortified against scientific naturalism, but given that he has always assumed the centrality of man in the divine scheme of creation, the recognition that so much of the natural universe is irrelevant to humanity begins to erode the pillars of his faith. As we shall see, Ransom's problem does not simply evaporate once he emerges from the underworld. He remains troubled by the questions raised during the journey, and before the novel ends he will be compelled to rethink his conception of humanity's place in the universe.

The dying Weston tries to exploit Ransom's vulnerability with his ghastly vision of darkness and emptiness beyond the grave. Just as the hospitable surface of Perelandra rests on a vast abhorrent interior, so our earthly lives, Weston declares, are merely the outer rind of an existence that in time will sink into an abyss of eternal suffering:

"If your God exists, He's not in the globe—He's outside, like a moon. . . . He doesn't follow us in. You would express it by saying He's not in time—which you think comforting! In other words He stays put: out in the light and air, outside. But we are in time. We 'move with the times.' That is, from

His point of view, we move *away*, into what He regards as nonentity, where He never follows." (143–144)

Under ordinary circumstances, Ransom might not be disturbed by such a distortion. He knows that God in Christ follows man into the grave and redeems him with His own death. But already suspicious of the anthropomorphic character of his beliefs, and soon to be exposed to the vast indifferent core of the planet, Ransom comes to wonder whether his conception of God encompasses anything more than the superficies of the human condition and the universe we inhabit.[15] He is being lured from a legitimate concern over the centrality of "imperial man" to the nihilistic conclusion that there is only "the meaningless, the un-made, the omnipotent idiocy to which all spirits were irrelevant and before which all efforts were vain" (154). He will soon be delivered from the nightmare of nihilism, but the issue of man's place in the divine scheme of the universe will remain unresolved until the final chapter.

After the slaying of the Un-man and the slow ascent from the underworld, the exhausted Ransom is carried upward by a stream that deposits him in a blissful mountain setting. Here he begins his convalescence, which is rendered as a rebirth, "a second infancy, in which he was breast-fed by the planet Venus herself" (159). Later he is unable to recall how long he remained in this place, since the ordinary experience of passing time has been suspended, and the very sense of past and future—the problem of recollection and anticipation that first tempted him on Venus—has dissolved in the satisfaction of the present. Similarly, as he ascends the Holy Mountain, "he had no desires and did not even think about reaching the top nor why he should reach it. To be always climbing this was not, in his present mood, a process but a state, and in that state of life he was content" (165). But the anticipation begins to mount as he approaches the summit—"He dared not go up that pass: he dared not do otherwise" (165)—and enters into a valley where he senses the presence of the *eldila,* who inaugurate the final movement of the novel.

VIII

In the last two chapters (16–17), Ransom becomes at once a witness and a participant in the ceremonial transfer of guardianship from the transcorporeal *eldila* to creatures "that breathe and breed like the beasts" (169). Just as the Lady delighted in each new wave as it passes, the *eldila* who have presided over Mars and Venus feel no sadness over the passing of their order. Instead, they welcome the new King and Queen, Tor and Tinidril (as the Green Lady is now called), whose arrival signifies the restoration of humanity—or rather the *animale rationale* who now assumes the role originally meant for our own species—to its proper position as guardian over the rest of creation. After a lengthy scene that reveals his wisdom and humility, the King looks ahead to the days when his people will multiply and mature, and even the beasts "shall awake to a new life in us as we awake in Maleldil" (181). But as the King presents his triumphant vision of a flourishing world, the clouds start to darken for Ransom when it appears that after thousands of years of creative progress there is no definitive end in sight. The final transfiguration that Ransom assumes will be "the end of your world" turns out to be merely the approach to "the beginning of all things" (182). Although at that time the Earth will be redeemed, the Last Days will mark not the end of time "but the wiping out of a false start in order that the world may *then* begin" (182). Ransom is troubled by this prospect of illimitable time just as he was previously overcome by the vista of limitless space. This vertiginous extension of time and space deprives the earthly drama of its centrality and "gives me a universe, with no centre at all, but millions of worlds that lead nowhere or (what is worse) to more and more worlds for ever, and comes over me with numbers and empty spaces and repetitions and asks me to bow down before bigness" (183). Perhaps more disoriented by modern science than he had realized, Ransom assumes that the loss of a center—or rather what was once regarded as the center—implies a universe without design or purpose: "Is the enemy easily answered when He says that all is without plan or meaning? As soon as we think we see one it melts away into nothing, or into some other plan that we never dreamed of, and what was the centre becomes the rim, till we doubt if any shape or plan or pattern was ever more than a trick of our own eyes, cheated with hope or tired with too much looking. To what is all driving? What is the morning you speak of? What is it the beginning of?" (183).[16] The answer to these questions comes in the form of a Hymn of Praise that culminates in a vision of the Great Dance. This section is often compared to Spenser's *Mutabilitie Cantos*, but it involves more than a traditional reconciliation of time and eternity. After proclaiming the eternal presence of the Creator, the Hymn unfolds a vision of creative evolution that includes and transcends the failure of the Fall:

> "Never did he make two things the same; never did He utter
> one word twice. After earths, not better earths but beasts;
> after beasts, not better beasts, but spirits. After a falling, not
> a recovery but a new creation. Out of the new creation, not
> a third but the mode of change itself is changed for ever.
> Blessed is He!" (184)

The Hymn is especially striking in its vision of the relationship between the Creator and His creation. The response to Ransom's distress over the loss of a center is that each created thing is the center, or more precisely, that Maleldil is the center and "He dwells (all of Him dwells) within the seed of the smallest flower and is not cramped" (184). Each of the peoples—Malacandrans, Thulcandrans, and Perelandrans—is "at the centre" (185); but so is every other creature of the universe, and even the "Dust itself," which "utters the heart of the Holy One with its own voice. . . . each grain, if it spoke, would say, I am at the centre; for me all things were made" (185). As in the ancient hermetic formulation, God is the circle whose center is everywhere and circumference is nowhere:

> "Where Maleldil is, there is the centre. He is in every place.
> Not some of Him in one place and some in another, but in

each place the whole Maleldil, even in the smallness beyond thought. There is no way out of the centre save into the Bent Will which casts itself into the Nowhere. Blessed be He!" (185)

The *animale rationale* is "the keystone of the whole arch" (178), but it must live in the humble recognition that the rest of creation does not "await your coming to put on perfection. . . . you are not the voice that all things utter, nor is there eternal silence in the places where you cannot come" (185).

As an updated form of Christian Neoplatonism, the cosmology of the Hymn of Praise recalls a historical moment prior to the modern dissociation of nature from its divine source. In its dual emphasis on the transcendence of God and His immanence within each created thing, this vision is particularly reminiscent of the works of the influential bishop and philosopher, Nicholas of Cusa (1401–1465).[17] Of course, the Hymn does not address the complex philosophical and scientific issues surrounding the various Neoplatonic systems from Nicholas to Henry More (the seventeenth-century Cambridge Platonist on whom Lewis once planned to write his doctoral thesis); nor does it explore the reasons why the scientific revolution took an entirely different course.[18] Lewis's own contribution is to integrate this Christian Neoplatonism with a new conception of time that challenges the mechanistic assumptions that dominated modern science until the close of the nineteenth century. To this end, he develops what appears to be a version of Nicholas's remarkable *coincidentia oppositorum*—the transcendent God who is immanent in each element of the universe—into a dynamic cosmology that unites a Bergsonian anti-mechanistic vision of continuous and novel development with a Christian understanding of the singularity, sanctity, and divine indwelling within each moment of the creative process.

The final stanzas of the Hymn are the most dark and difficult. The only way to orient oneself in the vast web of interlocking centers is to "set your eyes on one movement and it will lead you through all patterns and it will seem to you the master movement" (186). We are offered assurance that "the seeming will be true," but the concluding stanza relates the disturbing tension between "seeming" and "truth" to an ineluctable element of trial and testing in this world:

> "Yet this seeming also is the end and final cause for which
> He spreads out Time so long and Heaven so deep; lest if we
> never met the dark, and the road that leads nowhither, and
> the question to which no answer is imaginable, we should
> have in our minds no likeness of the Abyss of the Father, into
> which if a creature drop down his thoughts for ever he shall
> hear no echo return to him. Blessed, blessed, blessed be He!"
> (186–187)

The finale hints at a divine purpose in the very scale and complexity of the universe—a purpose tied to the destiny of the one creature that seeks to comprehend the universal design. Once more the issue is free will and its relation to the openness of time: each creature is at the center, but only a free agent can choose either to obey Maleldil's will or to walk out of the center "into the Bent Will which casts itself into the Nowhere" (185). Earlier in the novel, Ransom explains to the Lady that the proscription on the Fixed Land puts us in a position to "do something for which His bidding is the *only* reason" (101). Later on, the King tells Ransom that we must learn to follow Maleldil with "no assurance. No fixed land. Always one must throw oneself into the wave" (181). The conclusion of the Hymn points to a similar issue at stake in our relation to the enigmas of the universe. The very condition of our finitude—our vulnerability within a world that seems to overwhelm us with its immensity and threaten us with uncertainty—situates us on a precipice that opens onto "the Abyss of the Father." Only a portion of the cosmic pattern is within our grasp. We are asked to walk forward in the awareness of our limitations with only the assurance that the "seeming will be true." If we deny these limitations and attempt to reduce the heavens to our measure, we are walking into the "otherwise" and will end up with a distorted knowledge that ultimately denies the Creator Himself. We are the glory of the creation not in our capacity to penetrate the mysteries of the Heavens but in our choice to live faithfully within the bounds of our finitude.

The Hymn of Praise passes into the Great Dance, which reveals the complex totality of the cosmic design in a vision of intersecting cords "leaping over and under one another and mutually embraced in arabesques and flower-like subtleties" (187). It is a pattern with a temporal dimension as one "master-figure" is incorporated into another while "finding in its new subordination a significance greater than that which it had abdicated" (187). But surprisingly, the Great Dance itself is not the end. At this point, Lewis commences a process that turns the Great Dance into "the mere superficies of a far vaster pattern in four dimensions, and that figure as the boundary of yet others in other worlds . . . the relevance of all to all yet more intense, as dimension was added to dimension" (188). This movement continues to accelerate and the pattern grows ever more vast and ecstatic until "at the very zenith of complexity, complexity was eaten up and faded . . . and a simplicity beyond all comprehension, ancient and young as spring, illimitable, pellucid, drew him with cords of infinite desire into its own stillness" (188). In this vision, Lewis builds on his amalgamation of Bergson and Neoplatonism by drawing upon his acquaintance with mathematical techniques for extrapolating beyond the familiar dimensions of space and time.[19] In the early twentieth century, these methods of extrapolation were acquiring a new relevance as models of a multidimensional space-time began to overtake the scientific assumptions of the previous centuries. Lewis was intrigued by this new frontier, which he believed would issue not in further disenchantment of the world but in the recognition of a multiticred universe with "Natures piled upon Natures" (*M* 252)—a creation far more complex, but also more hospitable to spiritual presence, than the "one-floor reality" (251) of nineteenth-century science.

After the vision fades, Ransom finds himself alone with the King and Queen. It is still morning, as it was when the vision appeared, but the King announces that it is "not the same morning" (*P* 188), for in the seemingly momentary epiphany an entire Perelandran year has passed. In this new moment, the King also begins to sense another phase in the development of his species: "I believe the waves of time will often change for us henceforward. We are coming to have it in our own choice whether we shall be above them and see many waves together or whether we shall reach them one by one as we used to" (188). By contrast, as he washes Ransom's bleeding heel and recalls that in the long-lived generations after Adam's Fall "the men of your race did not learn to die quickly" (189), he reminds us of the unnaturalness of the sorrow, suffering, and death that marks the passage of time on our own planet. Then as the King and Queen proceed with Ransom to the casket that will convey him back to earth, "all felt an impulse to delay" (189):

> "It is like a fruit with a very thick shell," said Tinidril. "The joy of our meeting when we meet again in the Great Dance is the sweet of it. But the rind is thick—more years thick than I can count."
>
> "You see now," said Tor, "what that Evil One would have done to us. If we had listened to him we should now be trying to get at that sweet without biting through the shell."
>
> "And so it would not be 'That sweet' at all," said Tinidril.
>
> "It is now his time to go," said the tingling voice of an eldil. (189)

In this context, the impulse to delay reminds us of the inevitable sorrows and losses of our time-bound condition and offers a hint of compassion for our desire to transcend its limits. But it also suggests that we must endure, if not embrace, the trials of finite freedom. The image of rind and core harks back to Weston's final tormented vision (see p. 81), though here the relations of surface and depth are reversed: instead of a brief flicker of life on the rind followed by eternal darkness, the often bitter passage through the rind is relieved by the recognition that this is the ordained route to an eternal joy.

IX

The representation of time in *Perelandra* suggests that it is a mistake to approach the novel as a clear-cut conflict between "Religious" and "Materialist" viewpoints and ignore the once influential *via media* of "creative" or "emergent" evolution. Admittedly, in his novel as well as his expository writings, Lewis was often dismissive of vitalism and condemned it as a seductive pseudo-religion, a disguised form of naturalism whose danger lies in the very way it promises to deliver us from mechanistic determinism. As he put it in *Mere Christianity*, the "Life-Force philosophy" is an "achievement of wishful thinking," an alluring but ultimately defective utopian vision through which fallen man might imagine his way beyond "a mere mechanical dance of atoms" and regain a sense of purpose and belonging in the scheme of the universe.[20] However, we have seen that Lewis was intrigued by certain aspects of this "In-between view," especially its insights into the nature of time and the complexities of temporal experience. In this respect he seems to have taken Bergson's creative evolution seriously enough to transfigure its spiritualized naturalism into a Christian vision that reconciles divine transcendence with continuous development in the created universe. Or stated in more dynamic terms, just as Bergson transfigured orthodox Darwinism, Lewis transfigured Bergson's creative evolution. In his own accounts of his intellectual development, Bergson attributed his rethinking of the concept of time to his early encounter with Herbert Spencer's "mechanistic" theory of evolution. Born in 1859—the year of Darwin's *Origin of Species*—Bergson developed a new philosophy of time and change from a theory of development still embedded in the spatial categories of the past. In the process, he established the autonomy of the vital realm and demonstrated that the dynamic phenomena of "life" cannot be contained within the mechanistic assumptions of nineteenth-century science. Lewis, who was born as Bergson was consolidating his reputation, came to age in an intellectual milieu overflowing with new philosophical and scientific ideas that radically challenged traditional conceptions of time and space. Lewis assimilated these momentous developments, and beginning *Perelandra* in the year of Bergson's death, he reversed the philosopher's naturalization of the supernatural and reshaped Bergson's vision of cosmic development into a Christian epic of Becoming.

III ~

That Hideous Strength

A Specter Haunting Britain: Gothic Reenchantment on Planet Earth

> Haunting belongs to the structure of every hegemony.
> —Jacques Derrida, *Specters of Marx*

> If you must see ghosts, it is better not to disbelieve in them.
> —C. S. Lewis, *That Hideous Strength*

The last of the Ransom novels is generally regarded as the black sheep of the series. Unlike the "interstellar romances" of the first two installments, *That Hideous Strength* takes place entirely on our own planet, and it sacrifices the sustained appeal of an imaginary world for what many consider an incongruous mixture of the realistic and the supernatural. Longer than the first two books combined, this outsized amalgam of medieval legend and modern mayhem also suffers from the monotonous rhythm of its plot as it shifts ceaselessly back and forth between its two opposing sites. To compound these problems, the novel ventures headlong into controversial matters of scx and gender in a way that has estranged many readers, whether or not they share Lewis's religious convictions. In particular, the portrait of the female protagonist, Jane Studdock, lends weight to the claim that the major Christian apologist of the modern century not only perpetuates the inherently patriarchal assumptions of the Judaeo-Christian tradition but also goes to considerable lengths to bolster them. Taken together, these liabilities seem to confirm Lewis's fear that his new book was "all rubbish" and "bosh" (*L* II, 571, 4/29/43; 574, 5/17/43), and more than half a century later they still provide the basis for the novel's reputation as the misshapen conclusion to the series.

In light of these difficulties, it may be profitable to reexamine the formal complexities of the novel, whose provocative subtitle, "A Modern Fairy-Tale for Grown-Ups," is indicative of its peculiarly hybrid character. Lewis scholars are aware that the shift from interplanetary travel to a terrestrial setting also involved a shift in literary affiliations. If David Lindsay's *Voyage to Arcturus* (1920) and H. G. Wells's *The First Men in the Moon* (1901) provide the formal prototypes for the earlier novels, it is the "spiritual shockers" (or "supernatural thrillers") of Lewis's friend and fellow Inkling, Charles Williams, that inform the distinctive "mixture of the realistic and the supernatural" (*L* II, 682, 12/6/45) in the final novel of the trilogy.[1] But as valid as it may be to describe *That Hideous Strength* as "a Charles Williams novel by C. S. Lewis" (Green and Hooper, *C. S. Lewis: A Biography* 205), we foreclose prematurely on Williams's influence if we ignore his roots in the modern tradition of "supernatural" or "fantastic" fiction inaugurated by the blending of "the Probable and the Marvellous" ("The Novels of Charles Williams" *OS* 21) in the Gothic romances of the eighteenth century.[2] Much has been made of Williams's study of magic and the occult as a member of A. E. Waite's Fellowship of the Rosy Cross, but the necromancers as well as the revenants, doppelgangers, and other spectral presences that populate Williams's fiction have long been the staple of Gothic tradition.[3] What Williams offered to Lewis was a compelling generic formula, prefigured by early twentieth-century authors such as R. H. Benson, Arthur Machen, and Evelyn Underhill, that employs the unsettling resources of Gothic tradition at once to stir up doubts about the naturalistic ethos of modern civilization and to reaffirm a traditional Christian conception of the supernatural (Cavaliero 1983, 1995). While the villains of Williams's *War in Heaven* (1930) and its sequels violate the boundary between natural and supernatural in an attempt to secure their own power, many of the quotidian modern protagonists of these novels undergo trials that awaken them to the dazzling splendor and "dreadful goodness" (*Descent into Hell* 16) of the divine Omnipotence who has fashioned us in His image. This beatific sublimation of Gothic terror, which is akin to the transfiguration of modern evolutionary theory in *Out of the Silent Planet* and *Perelandra,* is also a constitutive feature of *That Hideous Strength.* In one register, Lewis appropriates the dark tradition of the Gothic to depict the horrors (or what we might call "the demonic sublime") of the new totalitarian order, which threatens to transform the basic terms of existence in the modern world. Seen from this perspective, the Gothic is at once symptomatic of the modern secular condition to which it ostensibly responds and prophetic of the ghastly "posthumanity" (*AM* 75) toward which we are heading. At the same time, Lewis employs the distinctive hybridity of the Gothic—its peculiar suspension between past and present, the marvelous and the probable, supernatural and material viewpoints—to overturn the naturalistic assumptions of his modern protagonists and light the way to the apprehension of a more glorious reality that ultimately turns the tables on the Gothic itself.[4] In a manner that will become more evident as we proceed, Lewis also follows Williams in drawing on the menacing power of Gothic romance to enrich and in a sense to update the long tradition of ancient, medieval, and renaissance romance from which the Gothic itself descends.[5]

Lewis does not refer to the Gothic as such, but his own blend of the realistic and the supernatural is a virtual catalogue of Gothic conventions: the pervasive atmosphere of "terror," "dread," and "horror" (the terms occur frequently); nightmares that record actual events otherwise unknown to the dreamer; imprisonment and persecution in the "haunted castle," the domain of oppressive authority; the interest in the relations between love and power, and the attendant problems of marriage, family, and inheritance in a changing but intractably patriarchal society; the creation of a "monster"—"that hideous strength"—associated with lust for the kind of knowledge that confers mastery over life itself; and the ancient crypt that marks the ever present threat of a "return of the repressed"—the power of the past to haunt or invade the world of the living.[6] Lewis's double deployment of these motifs is played out in the relations between the two main protagonists, Jane and Mark Studdock, and the opposing locales with which each is associated. In the "realistic" atmosphere of the opening chapters, the tension between wife and husband is expressed in the sharp division between the home—the site of Jane's "solitary confinement" (*THS* 12)—and the workplace of Bracton College, where Mark curries favor to advance the career that his wife herself would like to pursue. As the plot develops, each of these sites is replaced by another less "realistic" locale that highlights its essential attributes: the domestic sphere by the Manor at St. Anne's, which harbors a small Christian community, and the College by the estate at Belbury, which houses the N.I.C.E. (National Institute of Co-ordinated Experiments) and its increasingly violent plot to take control of the nation. The change in settings also signals a shift from the everyday world of "middle things" to a sharply defined collision between Good and Evil, a decisive confrontation between a frame of mind that accepts our finite and creaturely condition, and one that seeks to transcend it. The conflict between these powers is further articulated in the internal divisions within each of them: St. Anne's becomes the scene of the struggle of "Grace against Nature," as Jane gradually overcomes her own resistances and eventually embraces the supernatural reality upon which the community is founded; while Belbury serves as the site of the struggle of "Nature against Anti-Nature" (*L* III, 498, 7/30/54), as Mark rushes into the N.I.C.E. only to find himself trapped, arrested, and subjected to compulsory "reconditioning" in an updated version of the "haunted castle." The conflict between these citadels is also gendered and generic. St. Anne is the mother of the Virgin Mary, and her Manor is closely identified with the feminine, the maternal, the natural fecundity of the earth, and by virtue of its ties to the celestial presence of Venus, with the divine love that is the source of the affections, sympathies, and charity that sustain an organic community. By contrast, the only visible women at Belbury are the perversely masculine Chief of Police (Fairy Hardcastle) and her stable of submissive hyper-feminine playmates. Moreover, the project of this essentially male conspiracy, which employs the violence and terror of the modern totalitarian state, involves the triumph over our finite organic condition—the limitations of the body, the burden of mortality, and the humiliating constraints of a reproductive process that depends on the distinctive capacities of the opposite sex.

The conflict of genres between St. Anne's and Belbury is more difficult to identify, and it points to a level of complexity that is occluded by the mortal struggle between them. Given St. Anne's association with Arthurian and other literary elements of medieval and renaissance tradition, we may initially conceive its generic relationship to Belbury as the literary equivalent of the battle between traditional and modern viewpoints—that is, as a clash between "romance" and "realism," the older literary tradition whose marvels and enchantments presuppose a supernatural source, and the tradition of modern "realism" with its commitment to the representation of "actual life" and naturalistic forms of explanation. Midway through the novel, however, the seemingly modern "scientific" orientation of the N.I.C.E. is undercut by the discovery that its leaders are steeped in the occult and are searching, in collusion with demonic forces, for the grave of Merlin the Magician in a scheme to combine the power of ancient magic with the modern magic of scientific technology. At this crucial juncture, Belbury relinquishes its increasingly tenuous affiliation with "realism" and shifts to a different generic terrain. If nothing else, the quest to master the secrets of life (reminiscent of traditional necromancers and of Victor Frankenstein and his many modern successors) indicates that Belbury no longer represents the antithesis of the romance tradition but its aberrant Gothic offspring. In line with the Augustinian notion that "bad things are good things perverted" (*PPL* 66), the initial opposition between St. Anne's and Belbury modulates progressively into a relation between a divinely sanctioned original and its grotesque derivative. Furthermore, while the "dark contrivers" of the N.I.C.E. continue to pursue their dreams of totalitarian dominion, they also begin to lose their edge and succumb to the farcical confusion between Merlin and an ordinary tramp who serves as his unwitting "double." Hence the peculiar combination of terror and travesty in the second half of the novel as St. Anne's takes the initiative and the "hideous strength" of Belbury mutates into its own serio-comic parody. As a result of this generic metamorphosis, the final victory of the Christian community over its demonic adversaries signifies not only the restoration of a traditional worldview but also the triumph of the divinely enchanted world of traditional romance over the sinister but comically deluded enchantments of its distorted Gothic double. In this respect, the final novel of the trilogy exhibits the same relationship between "archetype" and "ectype"— i.e., the "original" and its misshapen modern image—that we find in the interstellar romances that precede it.[7]

This relationship between traditional and Gothic romance is not a one-way street. While the former prevails over the latter, it also absorbs some of the distinctive features of its modern derivative. As we should expect of a novel founded on the works of Charles Williams, Lewis's use of Gothic convention is not confined to the conspiracy at Belbury but permeates the community at St. Anne's and the very "mixture of the realistic and the supernatural" (L II, 682, 12/6/45) that constitutes the fictive world of the novel itself. In this story, Merlin is at once the magician of medieval romance and a Gothic ancestor whose crypt embodies a patrimony that has been usurped, or more precisely, a spiritual heritage that has been cast aside by the powers on whose ground he is buried. Jane Studdock's Gothic credentials are evident from the outset: the sense of marital entrapment; the inherited ability to see actual events in her dreams; and above all, the shocks and surprises that from the opening scene of the novel precipitate the erosion of the axial distinctions between mind and reality, the natural and the supernatural, and even the seemingly irreducible difference between life and death, upon which her modern sensibility depends. As we shall see, her initial experience at St. Anne's, especially her attraction to its enigmatically appealing Director, amalgamates the myth of Cupid and Psyche (to which Lewis would later devote an entire novel) with the "female" Gothic paradigm that ultimately descends from it.[8] Similarly, St. Anne's itself is not simply an avatar of medieval romance but a carefully crafted composite of traditional and modern elements that simultaneously sublimates and satirizes the "miserific" enchantment of Belbury. At the same time, this admixture of traditional romance and its Gothic offspring may also be implicated in some of the more aesthetically and ethically disquieting features of the text: the air of the contrived and artificial—a prominent feature of Walpole's *The Castle of Otranto* (1764)—that surrounds the resuscitation of the Arthurian order in the midst of modern Britain; the related sense of the outré and incredulous that accompanies the literal return of Merlin, a figure who has always hovered equivocally between the historical and the legendary like the Arthurian order itself; the tonal dissonances produced by the attempt to mix "fantasy" and "farce"; and perhaps even the gruesome carnivalesque violence with which the traditional order reasserts its authority. Whether or not the author intended them, these disturbing effects seem bound up with the same process of retrofitting traditional romance by appropriating both the hybrid form and the characteristic motifs of its modern Gothic progeny.

I

In the ostensibly "realistic" atmosphere of the opening scene (see the figure on p. 98), Jane Studdock's resentment of domestic "solitary confinement" (*THS* 12) reflects the ongoing debate, especially vexed in the first few decades of the twentieth century, over the role of women, the condition of marriage, and the future of the reproductive process

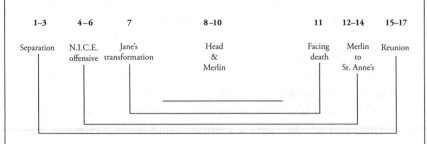

| 1–3 | 4–6 | 7 | 8–10 | 11 | 12–14 | 15–17 |

Separation | N.I.C.E. offensive | Jane's transformation | Head & Merlin | Facing death | Merlin to St. Anne's | Reunion

Figure 3.1

As in the previous two novels, we are given no formal indicators beyond the numbered chapters, though each chapter now possesses a title and markers that divide it into separate scenes. Structurally, we find once again a central core (chapters 8–10) circumscribed by a series of symmetrical frames. The inner frame (chapters 7 and 11), which plays a crucial role in all three books, surrounds the middle section and is surrounded in turn by another symmetrical set (chapters 4–6 and 12–14)—the first triad depicting the N.I.C.E. offensive, the second setting the stage for St. Anne's counter-offensive. Chapters 1–3 and 15–17, which contain numerous corresponding details, constitute the outer frame of the novel. From this vantage point, we can observe some significant variations in the seemingly monotonous oscillation of the narrative as it shuffles back and forth between the two principal protagonists and the opposing sites into which they are drawn. Consider, for example, the two chapters of the inner frame (7 and 11). St. Anne's is the setting of all four scenes in chapter 7 that portray Jane Studdock's spiritual awakening during her decisive encounter with the Director. By contrast, St. Anne's disappears entirely in chapter 11, when Jane and Mark each come to terms with the imminent prospect of death. The final scene of chapter 11 also underscores its distinctive theme: whereas every other section of the novel closes with a scene devoted to a significant step in Jane's development, this one ends with Mark's incarceration and painful self-scrutiny as he awaits his impending execution.

in modern society.[9] For certain readers, the first few paragraphs may also call to mind the situation of Emma Bovary and other restless housewives in nineteenth- and twentieth-century literary "realism." But the generic affiliations begin to change when Jane's attempt to maintain her tenuous hold on a professional career is interrupted by a glance at the newspaper, which contains the picture of a man who appeared in her dream the previous night. The "terror" (12) and inscrutability of this nightmare are menacing enough—the frightened face of the prisoner, the intimidating visitor with *pince-nez* and pointed beard who suddenly unscrews the prisoner's head, and the unaccountable switch to the head of an "ancient British, druidical" (13) corpse that revives before her eyes. But the real problem lies in the inexplicable reversal of cause and effect that makes the room around her "swim before Jane's eyes" (14). Although she nearly manages to convince herself that she must have seen a photo prior to her dream, the residue of uncertainty introduces an uncanny element that begins to shake her assumptions about the world she inhabits. In addition, the dream and its aftermath are strangely entangled with Jane's domestic distress. In the dream, her identification with the suffering prisoner reflects her own sense of internment. But the headline in the newspaper—"EXECUTION OF ALCASAN . . . SCIENTIST BLUEBEARD GOES TO GUILLOTINE" (14)—reveals a different side of the condemned man, and Jane goes on to read about the distinguished radiologist who has poisoned his wife. The reference to Bluebeard—the fairy-tale figure behind the patriarchal oppression of many Gothic novels—casts a sinister shadow on Jane's own situation. Despite the last-minute rescue of Bluebeard's final victim, the story of this serial wife-killer illustrates the results of the twin transgressions of female curiosity and conjugal disobedience. The name Alcasan, which hints at alchemy and its association with the wonders of modern radiology, also looks forward to the strange misogynistic brew of science and magic that impels the secret agenda of the N.I.C.E.[10] Finally, as Jane tries to return to her thesis on Donne's "triumphant vindication of the body" (12), the various strands of this remarkable opening scene come together in the closing couplet of *Love's Alchymie:*

> *Hope not for minde in women; at their best*
> *Sweetnesse and wit, they are but Mummy possest.* (14)

In this courtly male satire, the speaker scoffs at the illusion that love possesses a "hidden mysterie" (Donne 1933, 39) beyond the coupling of bodies, and Jane draws the appropriately bitter conclusion: "Did any man really *want* mind in women?" (*THS* 14). The conclusion of the couplet is enigmatic, but whatever Donne may have meant by these words, the reference to "Mummy" in this context implies a double "beheading," simultaneously reducing women to mere body and reminding them, as in the tale of Bluebeard, of the price of presuming otherwise.[11] As the antithesis of Belbury's male dream of a disembodied "mind" that may live forever, the "Mummy" also establishes a bond between women and death that points to the abhorrence of organic reproduction—or more importantly, the finitude entailed in the perpetual cycle of life and death—that the conspirators associate with women and their bodies.

After this introduction to the troubled wife, the scene shifts to the concurrent activities of her husband, initiating the contrapuntal pattern that recurs (with some significant interruptions) throughout the novel. The juxtaposition of the two scenes invites comparison between the private world of domestic isolation and the public realm of the workplace. Mark appears not in his home but in the street, where he meets the well-named Curry, subwarden of Bracton College. We may cringe at the ensuing exchange between the obsequious young subordinate and his condescending superior, but we should not forget that it represents a form of association, however defective, that is denied to his spouse. Moreover, while Jane struggles to preserve a shred of personal autonomy by resisting absorption into the domestic role of faculty wife, Mark harbors the illusion of independence but is secretly gratified by his new-found "insider" status and longs for acceptance into the "inner ring" (132) of the College.[12]

Unlike the perplexity surrounding Jane's dream, there is nothing to compromise the "realistic" mode of the initial portrait of Mark. But once we become acquainted with the venerable heritage of Bracton College and the ascendant "Progressive Element" to which Mark belongs, the Gothic air begins to thicken. Legend has it that Merlin the Magician is buried—or more precisely, is "buried but *not* dead, according to the story" (30)—in the Wood belonging to the College. Whether or not it actually exists, the druid's crypt signifies the enduring (non)presence of an ancient legacy that the usurping "progressive element" has disavowed and now proposes to discard altogether by selling Bragdon Wood to the N.I.C.E. The shadow of the Gothic is equally evident in Mark's first contact with the Institute. After dining with several "progressive" colleagues at the College, he is left alone with the mysterious Lord Feverstone (the villainous Dick Devine of *Out of the Silent Planet*), and feeling himself "whirled up from one plane of secrecy to another" (38), he is invited to join the N.I.C.E. and given what purports to be an insider's account of its mission. Sneering at his tepid Bracton colleagues, Feverstone outlines an agenda—"sterilization of the unfit, liquidation of backward races (we don't want any dead weights), selective breeding . . . biochemical conditioning" (40)—that goes far beyond progressive dreams of social engineering and reflects the mutation of modern eugenics from a seemingly benign program for improving the human stock into the genocidal nightmare of the Third Reich.[13] At the same time, the temptation to penetrate the immemorial mystery of life recalls the promethean hero of the male Gothic paradigm and its great exemplar, Victor Frankenstein, whose overweening ambition anticipates the project to construct the "new type of man" (40) envisioned by Feverstone and his kind. At this point, however, Mark Studdock is no more aware than the rest of the progressive element that beneath the friendly acronym of the N.I.C.E. lies a monster that will soon come back to devour it.

Like the young lovers (or siblings) of many fairy tales, Jane and Mark are soon separated and pulled in different directions. Each of the two young protagonists encounters a same-sex parental surrogate through whose agency they are transported from their respective "realistic" settings—the home and the workplace—to sites that highlight the gender/genre divisions they represent. Whereas Jane follows the recommendation of Margaret ("Mother") Dimble and forgoes a conventional psychoanalyst in favor of a woman doctor at St. Anne's, Mark races to Belbury in Feverstone's powerful car—"what fine, male energy (Mark felt sick of women at the moment)" (47). St. Anne's, as mentioned above, is closely associated with medieval romance and with the feminine, the maternal, and the fertility of the earth itself. Belbury, by contrast, is primarily a male preserve, and its aspiration to overcome the limitations of our organic condition involves the elimination of women from the process of reproduction.[14] The Gothic affiliations of Belbury may not be evident upon initial sighting; but the observation that it was "built for a millionaire who admired Versailles" (49) suggests its authoritarian as well as derivative character, and a passing reference to its "Blood Transfusion Office" (49), which builds on earlier references to the predatory white teeth of Feverstone and his colleagues, establishes the vampiric motif that links Mark's arrival at Belbury to Jonathan Harker's fate at Castle Dracula.[15] Like his counterpart in Stoker's novel, the naïve and ambitious Mark misreads the ominous signs around him, and despite the explicit warning from his senior colleague Hingest, a distinguished chemist who sees through the façade and plans to depart, the young novitiate is drawn into the net that will soon ensnare him.

Ironically, where Mark rushes in, Jane fears to tread. Upon her arrival at St. Anne's, the wary young woman is attracted to its fertile gardens and to the strong and appealing presence of the woman who greets her, Camilla Denniston (who bears the name of Virgil's warrior queen). The female doctor, Grace Ironwood, is also a commanding figure, but Jane is baffled and somewhat resentful when she hears that she cannot be cured because "'there is nothing wrong with you'" (62). Even more distressing is the discovery that she possesses an inherited gift of second sight—"the power of dreaming realities" (63)—which implicates her in the gathering storm of a major spiritual conflict. Jane is unprepared for such talk, finding it far less disconcerting to stick with Freud and interpret her dreams as an expression of personal pathology rather than an objective "vision" (63) of contemporary events.[16] The latter would undermine the most basic modern assumptions about the human mind and demand an acknowledgment of powers that an enlightened adult should dismiss as mere illusion. Furthermore, it would involve the acceptance of unwanted entanglements, and as she hastens away from St. Anne's at the end of chapter 3, Jane's self-protective wish to preserve her fragile autonomy elicits the marital discontent with which the novel began: "Some resentment against love itself, and therefore against Mark, for thus invading her life, remained. She was at least very vividly aware how much a woman gives up in getting married. . . . Though she did not formulate it, this fear of being invaded and entangled was the deepest ground of her determination not to have a child—or not for a long time yet. One had one's own life to live" (71). As the first indication that she may bear at least some responsibility for her own unhappiness, Jane's resistance to conjugal "invasion" goes hand in hand with her resistance to St. Anne's and the menacing rupture with naturalistic explanation that takes place in Miss Ironwood's office.

II

At the start of chapter 4, "The Liquidation of Anachronisms," a new phase of the action begins abruptly with "Mother" Dimble's eviction from her cottage. The narrative pendulum continues to oscillate between wife and husband, but over the next several chapters (4–6) the plot centers on the violence and terror of the N.I.C.E. as it launches its assault on the region. At the College, the "Progressive Element" discovers that its machinations have come back to haunt it. The N.I.C.E. loses no time clearing the land it has purchased, and as insolent workers and institutional police stir up unrest in the town, the dons are overwhelmed by the roar of construction, the threat of rioting crowds, and the shattering of their precious glass windows. Meanwhile, Mark is dispatched to explore a scheme for demolishing a nearby village, diverting the course of its river, and relocating its "anachronistic" population. His progressive convictions inure him to the fate of its inhabitants, as they do to the groan of vivisected animals, "which the Institute could afford to cut up like paper on the mere chance of some interesting discovery" (100). Much harder to ignore, however, is the fate of his colleague Hingest, who is intercepted and brutally beaten to death for attempting to leave the N.I.C.E.[17]

A strikingly different picture emerges when we shift from the N.I.C.E.'s *blitzkrieg* to Mark's experience of its headquarters at Belbury. Wither, the vague and evasive Deputy Director, routinely deflects the young man's efforts to pin down the terms of his employment, and the occasional assignment to "phantom committees" (79) only indicates that "the real work of the N.I.C.E. must go on somewhere else" (78). In this respect, Mark's residence at Belbury resembles the enigmatic situation in Kafka's novel *The Castle* (which Lewis had read several years before).[18] Like the land surveyor K., who is summoned to the spectral castle for a purpose he is never able to discover, Mark receives no answer to his strangely insistent demands for clarification of "my own position" (83). Moreover, when Mark attempts to assert his autonomy by threatening to resign, he discovers that the one determinate aspect of his position is that he cannot leave. As the example of Hingest makes clear, the power of the N.I.C.E. is as coercive as it is elusive, and the indeterminate menace of Kafka's multilevel modernist Gothic has stiffened into the brutal coercion of the totalitarian reign of terror.

Closely related to Mark's disorientation is the linguistic mystification that surfaces in these chapters (see Myers 1994), anticipating the explicit identification between Belbury and its biblical prototype. At this point, however, the Babel of tongues is not the consequence but the instrument of tyrannical power. The sense that language has been torn from its referential moorings is evident in the Deputy

Director's meandering circumlocutions, particularly in his "tortuous and allusive narrative" (79) of Hingest's death, which inaugurates the profusion of mendacious stories designed to confuse the populace and obscure the real intentions of the N.I.C.E. Instances of narrative distortion recur throughout this section. For instance, as Mark prepares for a brief visit home, he spends his time contriving the narrative that would "cut a good figure in the eyes of his wife" (87). The novel's reliable narrator also gets into the act with a reminder of the way in which "every narrative is false" (106). This focus on the gap between events and their representations culminates in the plot to "engineer" (126) a seemingly spontaneous riot in the town. Significantly, Mark surrenders the last remnants of his moral integrity by agreeing to "report" the riot before it occurs. His construction of two different accounts—one for the high-brow press, the other for the tabloids—not only inverts the relationship between story and event but also completes the process of transforming language into a free-floating medium that proliferates spectral counterfeits of the reality it presumably represents.

While a cloud of confusion descends on the public realm, Jane vividly "sees" the murder of Hingest in a dream. Nevertheless, she still resists the revelation that her dreams are really "News" (115), remaining self-protective and indignant that "the bright, narrow little life which she had proposed to live was being irremediably broken into" (81). Jane also continues to harbor suspicions of St. Anne's, despite her attraction to "Mother" Dimble and other members of the Company. She is disturbed to hear that a male authority (Mr. Fisher-King) presides over the seemingly feminine enclave, and her resistance soars when Camilla's husband informs her that she must obtain her own husband's "permission" (114) to join the community: "For a moment she looked on Mr. Denniston with real dislike. She saw him, and Mark, and the Fisher-King man . . . simply as Men—complacent, patriarchal figures making arrangements for women as if women were children or bartering them like cattle. ('And so the king promised that if anyone killed the dragon he would *give* him his daughter in marriage.') She was very angry" (115). Her resentment seems justified, especially at a time when her spouse has joined the opposing side, but soon she is overtaken by a new wave of events. It begins with a recurrent dream in which Alcasan's mysterious visitor—the man with the *pince-nez* and pointed beard—quietly sits by her bedside and takes notes "like a doctor" (121) in a manner reminiscent of a psychoanalytic session. Once again, Jane tries to dismiss her dreams, and at this point there is still no reason for her to surmise that the "doctor" is a real incorporeal presence who (as we later learn) has solicited the aid of supernatural powers to tap her mind. But when she sees the same man on the street in Edgestow, Jane is seized by revulsion and "her body, walking quickly past, seemed of itself to have decided that it was heading for the station and thence for St. Anne's" (134). Dreams and reality have become impossibly entangled, and as happens so often in the novel, it is not the protagonist's confused or misguided mind that finds the proper solution, but a kind of intuitive knowledge that is lodged within the body.[19]

Jane is helped along by a second occurrence, which takes place in the final scene of this section and leads directly to the remarkable chapter to follow. It begins in vintage Gothic fashion when Jane is suddenly seized by the impression that she has been "buried alive" (133). Soon she realizes that she is dreaming, and now having learned enough about herself to think of it as "a piece of news" (133), she summons the courage to follow the dream to its conclusion. Slowly groping along a dark subterranean chamber, she arrives at what seems to be a table of stone and suddenly discovers that she is touching the foot of a corpse. Still quite frightened but determined to continue, Jane feels "as if she had slipped through a cleft in the present, down into some cold, sunless pit of the remote past" (133). The dream then breaks off with an unexpected image, "a picture of someone, someone bearded but also (it was odd) divinely young, someone all golden and strong and warm coming with a mighty earth-shaking tread down into that black place" (133). Once she awakens there is no further discussion of the dream, and it remains cryptic (in both senses of the term) at this point in the novel. Nevertheless, the passage from darkness to light forecasts the conclusion of this section and the transition to the next. As her train to St. Anne's ascends above the fog that has pervaded these chapters, Jane is struck by "the *size* of this world" (135) that is opening before her, and recalling her sense of confinement in a town that felt "even out-of-doors, as if in a room," she realizes "she had come near to forgetting how big the sky is, how remote the horizon." The trajectory of the dream also anticipates the generic complexity of the following chapter, which sublimates the classic Gothic encounter with a mysterious male authority into an unforeseen spiritual transformation, and translates the reader from the stifling air of Gothic oppression to the "marvelous" realm of traditional romance.

III

When Jane arrives at St. Anne's, the contrapuntal rhythm of the narrative is temporarily suspended and, for the first time, an entire chapter remains focused on a single protagonist. Jane's decisive meeting with Mr. Fisher-King—the former Elwin Ransom, from now on the Director—brings to mind the medieval Perceval's first encounter and subsequent quest for the Holy Grail, and it secures the association between St. Anne's and the supernatural world of chivalric romance.[20] It also resembles Lewis's later account (in *Till We Have Faces*) of the initial meeting between Psyche and Cupid, the prototype not only of fairy tales such as *Beauty and the Beast* but also of the recurrent female Gothic encounter between an impressionable young woman and the ambiguously appealing master of the house.[21] When Jane first approaches the Director's room, she reminds herself, "'Be careful. Don't get let in for anything. All these long passages and low voices will make a fool of you, if you don't look out. You'll become another of this man's female adorers'" (139). But true to the myth and its subsequent iterations, the young woman's precautions prove unavailing: "Jane looked; and instantly her world was unmade" (139). The initial perception of a boyish face and bandaged foot paradoxically heightens the effect of the full beard, powerful physique, and especially the regal bearing: "she had long since forgotten the imagined Arthur of her childhood—and the imagined Solomon too. . . . for the first time in all those years she tasted the word *King* itself with all linked associations of battle, marriage, priesthood, mercy, and power" (140). Although "the ordinary social Jane" (140) manages to reassert herself, she remains "shaken . . . even shaking" (141), and once they are left alone, "all the most intolerable questions he might ask, all the most extravagant things he might make her do, flashed through her mind in a fatuous medley. For all power of resistance seemed to have been drained away from her and she was left without protection" (141). As if this vulnerability weren't enough, Jane quickly finds herself admitting to the Director that she doesn't love her husband, and when he mentions the role of "obedience" in sustaining conjugal love, she discovers that instead of provoking anger or laughter, "the word Obedience—but certainly not obedience to Mark—came over her, in that room and in that presence, like a strange oriental perfume, perilous, seductive, and ambiguous. . . ." (145). The Director's sharp response ("'Stop it!'") dispels this romantic reverie, but it will be some time before the erotic fantasy of the Gothic plot is fully transfigured into agapic love and Jane comprehends, like naive Perceval of Chrétien's romance, the true import of her encounter with the "Fisher-King."

Some hints of this transfiguration appear at the end of the meeting, when the conversation takes a lighter turn, and the Director, referring to the fairy tales of George Macdonald, summons an after-dinner squad of docile mice to illustrate his point "that obedience and rule are more like a dance than a drill—specially between man and woman where the roles are always changing" (147). Whether or not she ought to be offended by this analogy, Jane is struck chiefly by the enormous size of humans in comparison to mice when suddenly she has an Alice-like sensation that "something intolerably big, something from Brobdingnag was pressing on her," and she is "shrinking, suffocated, emptied of all power and virtue." The Director himself has contracted into "a very small object," and the entire room is dwindling to the size of "a mouse's hole . . . tilted aslant— as though the insupportable mass and splendour of this formless hugeness, in approaching, had knocked it askew." This sudden shift into the world of modern fantasy (Swift, Carroll, and MacDonald's Curdie stories) seems commensurate with the nascent state of Jane's development, as if she must first enter through the looking-glass and recover a primal receptivity to the "marvelous." At the same time, the extraordinary conclusion to her interview with the Director looks forward to the radical transformation of her horizons that occurs later in the novel, when the seemingly evanescent realm of the "spiritual" becomes as immediate and physically compelling as the "natural" world itself.

As she proceeds home on the train, Jane is "so divided against herself that one might say that there were three, if not four, Janes in the compartment" (147). The "real" Jane who prides herself on "her status as a grown-up, integrated, intelligent person" is disgusted by the little girl who has "surrendered without terms at the mere voice and look of this stranger" (148). But then "a new and unexpected visitant" emerges from "some unknown region of grace or heredity"— the "moral Jane," whose feelings for another man have awakened not only "guilt and pity" for her husband but also "a resolution to give Mark much more than she had ever given him before." And this in turn gives rise to the "fourth and supreme Jane" (149) who is "simply in the state of joy":

> The other three had no power upon her, for she was in
> the sphere of Jove, amid light and music and festal pomp,
> brimmed with life and radiant in health, jocund and clothed
> in shining garments. She thought scarcely at all of the curious
> sensations which had immediately preceded the Director's

dismissal of her and made that dismissal almost a relief. When she tried to, it immediately led her thoughts back to the Director himself. Whatever she tried to think of led back to the Director himself and, in him, to joy. (149)

There is nothing disingenuous in these feelings, since without entirely comprehending what has happened, Jane has experienced the first taste of divine Love, and her newborn delight in the world around her, as well as the appreciation of her own beauty as a source of joy to others, points toward the later stages of her spiritual awakening. But this condition of ecstasy ends immediately upon her return to Edgestow, which the N.I.C.E. has engineered into a state of chaotic violence. In a sudden descent into Gothic horror, Jane is seized by the N.I.C.E. police and finds herself face-to-face with the sinister Fairy Hardcastle. A modern avatar of the fairy-tale "ogress" (152) and her Gothic counterpart, the wicked prioress, the Chief of Police takes sadistic pleasure in using a lit cigar to extract information (for reasons as yet undisclosed) on the prisoner's whereabouts. At a certain level, Miss Hardcastle externalizes Jane's own feelings of guilt—"'You hadn't been getting up to mischief while Hubby was away, had you?'" (151)—and in delivering Jane to Belbury, she is reasserting the claims of patriarchal authority, whose coercive power seems all the more insidious when wielded by women themselves. In this instance, however, the heroine is not destined for a protracted period of persecution. Jane's interrogation is interrupted by other events, and after her captors abandon her to escape the tumult in the town, she is eventually spotted by a pair of benevolent strangers and taken to her new home at St. Anne's. There are still shocks and trials ahead, but after her brief ordeal in captivity she is spared the plight of Ann Radcliffe's Emily St. Aubert and her Gothic descendants. In a reversal of typical gender/genre roles reminiscent of Jonathan Harker's fateful trip to Transylvania, it is not Jane but her husband who ends up imprisoned in the Gothic "castle."

IV

The three central chapters (8–10) of the novel, like those in *Pere-landra,* form a coherent unit that occupies a pivotal position in the novel. Returning to the rhythmic alternation between husband and wife, the section starts with the surprising disclosure that Mark is merely the bait with which to capture Jane, and over the succeeding chapters we proceed from the enigma surrounding Belbury's Head (chapter 8), to the unveiling of Belbury's most carefully guarded se-cret (chapter 9), and then to the first indications of the turning of the tide (chapter 10). A crucial measure of these developments is Mark's transformation from collaborator to defector, a process facilitated by his subjection to a ghastly succession of horrors. By contrast, Jane experiences a series of more beneficent shocks, through which she is gradually initiated into the strange new world of St. Anne's and prepared for her part in the section that follows.

In the first of these chapters we move progressively closer to Mark's crucial encounter with the Head, which echoes Jane's encounter with the Director in the preceding section. The suspense begins to build when the ordinarily tough-minded Fairy Hardcastle flinches at the prospect of standing before the Head. The Chief of Police remains apprehensive and queasy as she approaches the door to the inner sanctum, where she is met by the corpulent physiologist, Filostrato. The scene terminates at the threshold—a device used more sparingly than we might expect in a contrapuntal narrative—and we shift to a rather leisurely account of Jane's first morning at St. Anne's. When we return to Belbury in the following scene, Mark is also enjoying the morning, but the suspense slowly rises during a long conversation with Filostrato, later joined by the "mad parson" Straik, which gradu-ally homes in on the identity of the Head. Filostrato prepares the way by moving beyond Mark's modest dreams of social progress, and even beyond Feverstone's program of racial cleansing, to a future state in which the human Mind has been freed of its dependence on the body and the earth itself has been "purified" of all organic life.[22] From the lips of an oversized physiologist this distaste for the body is somewhat ironic, but more significantly, Filostrato's aversion to the "budding and breeding" (170) of organic life is accompanied by sexual revulsion—"There will never be peace and order and discipline so long as there is sex" (170)—and a scarcely concealed misogyny—"'As for your wife . . . What have I to do with men's wives? The whole subject disgusts me'" (171). Anticipating the moment when we (i.e., men) "throw away the anachronism" (170) and "reproduce ourselves without copulation," Filostrato's vision of a sterilized universe is aimed ultimately at "the conquest of death. . . . to bring out of that cocoon of organic life which sheltered the babyhood of mind the New Man, the man who will not die, the artificial man, free from Nature. Nature is the ladder we have climbed up by, now we kick her away" (173–74). As Straik enters the room, all of these elements—the triumph over the body, organic life, and mortality itself—coalesce in the figure of the Head, who is not (as Mark assumes) the nominal Director of the N.I.C.E., the venerable Horace Jules, but the artificially preserved brain of the femicidal Alcasan—the Bluebeard guillotined for poisoning his wife and then re-beheaded in Jane's initial dream. Announcing that the reanimated Alcasan has sent for Mark, Straik recasts the significance of the Head in apocalyptic terms: "'Do you understand—*the Head?* You will look upon one who was killed and is still alive. The resurrection of Jesus in the Bible was a symbol: tonight you shall see what it symbolised. . . . we are offering you the unspeakable glory of being present at the creation of God Almighty. . . . you shall meet the first sketch of the real God. It is a man—or a being made by man—who will finally ascend the throne of the universe. And rule forever'" (174–176). The secular neophyte is dumbfounded by this speech, but urged on by alcohol and "a not wholly disagreeable thrill at the thought of sharing so stupendous a secret" (176), he acquiesces once again and is led through the interior labyrinth toward the chamber in which the dead are still alive. It is vintage male Gothic—and even more so for the way it mirrors Jane's "female" Gothic meeting with the Director while simultaneously associating the Faustian quest of the male plot with the supersession of women.

Chapter 8 ends as Mark draws near the mysterious chamber, and the next chapter begins with Jane's "dream" of his appearance before the Head. To a certain extent, the indirect account of Mark's experience mitigates its horror, since it informs us that St. Anne's is aware of his ordeal, and as the Director puts it, "'If we win we will rescue him; he cannot be far gone yet'" (180–181). In the following scene, we return to Mark himself, who awakes the next morning with a massive *head*ache and recalls the "impossible . . . nightmare" (182) of the previous night. As his thoughts turn to Jane, Mark is torn between the desperation to save his own life by handing her over to his bosses and the desire to save her from "this whole outfit of horrors" (183), which is his first glimmer of "something like disinterested love." The latter is a gesture in the right direction, but almost immediately the young man endures a series of further frights. Alarmed by Miss Hardcastle's duplicitous report that his wife has gone insane, Mark proceeds to the Deputy Director's office to announce his departure. When his knock receives no answer, he enters the room on his own, and as he approaches Wither's desk he discovers he is "looking into the face of a corpse" (185). The Deputy Director is not dead, or even asleep, but with his eyes fixed on the distant horizon it seems as if his soul were "floating far away, spreading and dissipating itself like a gas through formless and lightless worlds, waste lands and lumber rooms of the universe." When Wither finally speaks—"'I know who it is. . . . Your name is Studdock. What do you mean by coming here? You had better have stayed outside. Go away'" (185–186)—Mark is entirely unnerved and starts for home immediately. But just as he reaches the edge of the premises "something impossible was happening. There was a figure before him on the path: a tall, very tall, slightly stooping figure, sauntering and humming a little dreary tune: the Deputy Director himself" (186). Mark's response to this apparition is not simply shock but the instant evaporation of his new-born resolve. He stops, slowly turns around, and "tired, so tired that he felt the weak tears filling his eyes, he walked slowly back to Belbury."[23]

The narrative breaks off once again, but Mark's travail in the haunted castle has just begun, and when we return to him four scenes later at the start of chapter 10, he is back in Wither's office and threatened with arrest for the murder of Hingest if he fails to deliver his wife. He then attempts another escape, and once more the looming figure of Wither bars his way. This time, however, "ancestral impulses lodged in his body—that body which was in so many ways wiser than his mind" (210)—take aim at the head of this specter, which instantly vanishes, leaving the narrator to ponder the Gothic question of whether it was a hallucination or the wraith of Wither himself. In either case, Mark manages to escape, but he is jolted once more when his effort to locate Jane takes him to the office of Mr. Dimble, who astounds the young man with his intimate knowledge of the N.I.C.E. and simultaneously denies him the crucial information about his wife. Structurally, this brief encounter with a representative of the other side corresponds to Jane's brush with Miss Hardcastle, and its primary effect is to show Mark how contemptible he appears in Dimble's eyes. For a moment it seems as if the competing voices within him—comparable to the four Janes who emerged from the Director's room in chapter 7—might lead to decisive action. Mark asks for time to think things over, but before he can sort out the implications of his exchange with Dimble, he is arrested for murder by the Institutional Police and placed in a cell at Belbury. The correspondences between the two protagonists remind us that in one sense we have come full circle from the opening of the novel. In a criss-cross reminiscent of F. Anstey's *Vice Versa* (1882), one of Lewis's favorite fantasies, it is now the initially indifferent husband who feels the effects of "solitary confinement" and suffers the cascade of terrors usually reserved for the imprisoned Gothic heroine.[24]

Jane is safe in her new home, but she too is subjected to a series of surprises, albeit instructive and often comic, as her conventional expectations collide with the wondrous ways of the house. The initial shock comes soon enough: awakening to a new contentment in her first morning at St. Anne's, she opens the bathroom door and shrieks at the sight of an enormous bear that is sitting on the floor. Mr. Bultitude (named after the family in Anstey's *Vice Versa*) is as tame as the other beasts at St. Anne's, and Jane quickly warms to his presence. But soon new oddities come her way as she learns about the human inhabitants of the house. Jane is proud of her democratic principles, but as a middle-class woman she is startled to discover that her former housecleaner, Ivy Maggs, is not simply a maid but a full-fledged member of the Company. Mrs. Maggs's status is especially perplexing in light of the Director's assertion that "equality is not the deepest thing" (145), and as a new initiate Jane finds it difficult to square the social equality of the house with the less acceptable notions of spiritual hierarchy to which its occupants assent. "'It's a funny house really'" (162), says Mother Dimble, who helps her to adjust to the amiable friction between the sexes and to the disconcertingly old-fashioned views of marriage that prevail at St. Anne's. After this sequence of surprises, we might assume that a modern secular woman would be particularly astonished by the claim that the house and its Director are under the direction of supernatural powers. Her instructor, however, is the resident skeptic, Mr. MacPhee, whose methodical doubts about the Director's interstellar journeys and their divine sponsorship "almost neutralised the strangeness of what he was telling her" (189). Jane certainly shares these doubts, but MacPhee's very presence lends credibility to St. Anne's, and his skeptical approach to the supernatural actually paves the way for Jane's acceptance of this strange community and her participation in its mission. Hence the sequence of salutary shocks that greets the heroine upon her arrival at St. Anne's—the beatific counterpart of her husband's traumas at Belbury—is at once a means of challenging her modern naturalistic views and another stage in the process of her redemptive transformation.

Jane's most terrifying "dream," which registers the horror of her husband's encounter with the Head, introduces the crucial chapter that stands at the center of this section and of the novel as a whole. Most of the scenes in chapter 9 take place at St. Anne's, but following the pattern of Jane's dream, they are directed mainly to the machinations of the N.I.C.E. and indicate that the Company is aware of its secret designs. The Director understands the implications of the bodiless Head:

> "It means that if this technique is really successful, the Belbury people have for all practical purposes discovered a way of making themselves immortal. . . . It is the beginning of what is really a new species—the Chosen Heads who never die. They will call it the next step in evolution. And henceforward, all the creatures that you and I call human are mere candidates for admission to the new species or else its slaves— perhaps its food." (194)

As significant as "the emergence of the Bodiless Men" (194) may be, the innermost secret of the N.I.C.E. lies buried beneath the Wood it has purchased from the College. The Institute is searching for the body of Merlin, who "had not died. His life had been hidden, sidetracked, moved out of our one-dimensional time, for fifteen centuries. But under certain conditions it would return to his body" (199). The N.I.C.E. is not concerned solely with "modern or materialistic forms of power" (198), and if it succeeds in reviving and enlisting the Druid to its cause, the conspirators will use the secrets of ancient magic to compound the might of modern technology. The result would be "a junction . . . between two kinds of power which between them would determine the fate of our planet" (200).[25] There have been some previous hints of occult practices at Belbury—Wither's states of dissociation, the tapping of Jane's mind—but the Director's revelation is the decisive step in transforming our conception of the opposing forces. We can no longer think in terms of a clear-cut opposition between spiritual and secular, religious and naturalistic worldviews. As the Director goes on to explain, these nineteenth-century antitheses, which provided some safety by limiting scientific aspirations to the material realm, have eroded to the point that "babble about the *élan vital* and flirtations with panpsychism were bidding fair to restore the *Anima Mundi* of the magicians. Dreams of the far future destiny of man were dragging up from its shallow and unquiet grave the old dream of Man as God" (200).[26] For the same reasons, even if we were still inclined to do so, we can no longer conceive the relationship between St. Anne's and Belbury in terms of the generic opposition between medieval romance and modern realism. Taken together with the telltale attempt to commandeer an ancient inheritance, the desire of its "dark contrivers" to fuse magical and scientific knowledge in effect resituates the N.I.C.E. on a different ground, and from this point on Belbury represents not the antithesis of St. Anne's but rather its demonic gothic double. Moreover, the disclosure of the mystery of the Wood, which takes us back to the opening of the novel, also propels us forward into the second half. As the pieces of the puzzle fall into place, the Director suspends the Company's "passion of patience" (191)—a phrase lifted from Charles Williams—and at the end of this section, with Merlin's character and allegiances very much in doubt, he sends out an armed party—Dimble, Denniston, and the "seer" Jane, who still knows "nothing of Maleldil" but pledges "obedience" (226) to the Director—to search for the crypt of the wizard.

V

By chapter 11, it appears as if Jane and Mark have reversed positions since the outset of the novel: whereas the one who suffered "solitary confinement" now sets forth on a perilous adventure, the one who abandoned her to domestic isolation now ponders his fate in a cell. At this point, however, the differences between wife and husband should be considered in light of their common plight: each of them knows that they are in mortal danger, and for the first time in their lives each of them comes face-to-face with the terrifying prospect of death. In this respect, the eleventh chapter stands as a singular unit in the novel as well as the dark counterpart to Jane's spiritual awakening when she meets the Director in the equally singular chapter 7. Taken together, these two chapters, like the corresponding chapters in *Perelandra*, establish the first of a series of frames around the central section of the novel (chapters 8–10) and begin to reveal its structural symmetries.[27] Chapters 7 and 11 are also related in the opposing ways that they interrupt the prevailing pattern of contrapuntal narration: St. Anne's is the setting of all four scenes in chapter 7, while it disappears entirely during the reckoning with death in chapter 11. Furthermore, insofar as the latter chapter constitutes a discrete section of the novel, its conclusion underscores its distinctive theme: whereas every other section closes with a scene devoted to a significant step in Jane's spiritual development, this one ends with Mark's incarceration and painful self-scrutiny as he awaits his imminent end.

The search for Merlin sets the stage for Jane's confrontation with death. As the three members of the company descend deeper into the woods on a dark rainy night, their fears are intensified by the lack of visibility in this "phantasmal world" (229). At this point, we may or may not recall the similar role played by Mina Harker in the hunt for Dracula, but as the female guide of a male expedition in pursuit of "something dead and yet not dead" (229), Jane experiences the same sense of dread that accompanies the courageous avengers in the second half of Stoker's novel. Dimble shares this dread of a more-than-human figure out of the shadowy past. As a scholar who has long pondered the obscurities of the "The Dark Ages," he is appalled at the thought that "now they were going to step right into that Darkness. . . . and now all that age, horribly dislocated, wrenched out of its place in the time series and forced to come back and go through all its motions yet again with doubled monstrosity, was flowing towards them and would, in a few minutes, receive them into itself" (229–230). For Jane, the confrontation with this monstrosity "meant death" (230), but now she tries to see death in the "new light" (231) of her life at St. Anne's, and for the first time she begins to consider "the reality behind what she had been taught at school as 'religion'": "Because, really, it now appeared that almost anything might be true. The world had already turned out to be so very unlike what she had expected. The old ring-fence had been smashed completely. One might be in for anything. Maleldil might be, quite simply and crudely, God. There might be a life after death: A Heaven: A Hell" (231). The shattering of the "ring-fence" foreshadows events to come, but this "blaze" in her mind soon passes, and the scene ends inconclusively in the same phantasmal state of confusion and anxious apprehension with which it began.

Sitting in his prison cell, Mark also takes up "the question of immortality" (241), but his thoughts are directed primarily to the fate of his body: "On any view, this body—this limp, shaking, desperately vivid thing, so intimately his own—was going to be returned into a *dead* body. If there were such things as souls, this cared nothing about them. The choking, smothering sensation gave the body's view of the matter with an intensity which excluded all else" (241). Mark may not be ascending the spiritual ladder toward Maleldil, but we should not dismiss this concentration on the body—his *own* body—as the hopeless desperation of a materialist, especially in a text where spiritual transgression takes the form of a revolt against embodiment. For a man who has "lived only in his brain" (244), the crisis of the body leads to the searing recognition that he has sacrificed the promptings of his "blood and heart." As he sheds the "public self" (244) he has tried so hard to cultivate, Mark now sees himself for what he has been—"the odious little outsider who wanted to be an insider" (243). He also sees that his self-betrayal has entailed the surreptitious betrayal of others, including the family and friends of his youth, and more recently his own wife, whom he would reduce to an appendage of his own career: "If all had succeeded, if he had become the sort of man he hoped to be, she was to have been the great hostess—the secret hostess in the sense that only the very esoteric few would know who that striking-looking woman was and why it mattered so enormously to secure her good will"

(244). At this moment, Mark is looking at his life not with "moral considerations" (243) but simply "with a kind of disgust at its dreariness." The existential encounter with death has shocked him into self-awareness, and his reversion to the concrete reality of the living body, before which all of his intellectual pretensions evaporate into thin air, has provided a level of self-objectification sufficient to reveal to himself the creature that he is.

It is no accident that in this death-haunted chapter the figure of Frost—*pince-nez,* pointed beard, and icy good looks—emerges into full view for the first time. From his initial appearance in Jane's dreams, the enigmatic Professor has been lurking in the background as an ominous silent presence until this moment, when we discover that Wither considers him an equal as well as the secret sharer of his concealed agenda. These demonic co-conspirators make an incongruous pair—Wither in the detachment from his own body, Frost in his reduction of all thought and feeling to bodily functions—and together they represent the final stage of the modern dissociation between mental and physical processes. At the same time, each of these men dramatizes the ominous erosion of this dissociation in the early twentieth century: Wither employs his disembodied spirit as a brutal instrument of practical control, while the materialistic Frost, as we now discover, has established contact with occult "authorities" (236)—the demonic powers incongruously labeled "macrobes" (253)—who have given him access to Jane's dreams. But there is more to the relationship between these two old men. As their conversation proceeds, Wither and Frost draw so close together that "their faces almost touched, as if they had been lovers about to kiss" (240). Startled by the sound of a book (*Who's Who*) that crashes unaccountably to the floor, they lurch forward "locked in an embrace from which each seemed to be struggling to escape," and the scene breaks off in the midst of this grotesque entanglement with the swelling of "a cackling noise that seemed in the end rather an animal than a senile parody of laughter." However we respond to this scene, it may be considered the dark complement to the sudden disturbance that terminated the interview between Jane and the Director in chapter 7, and in its grim humor the passage looks forward to the comic reduction of this demonic duo in the section to follow. But for now the ghoulish relationship between Wither and Frost contributes to the prevailing atmosphere of horror and death, and when the latter reappears in Mark's cell at the end of the following scene—the last in this disturbing chapter—he has reassumed the intimidating predatory sang-froid from which, as Mark now sees, "any child would have shrunk away . . . and any dog would have backed into the corner with raised hackles and bared teeth" (245).

VI

The figure of Merlin looms over the penultimate section of the novel (chapters 12–14). Both sides are searching for the ancient wizard, and once he joins the Company at St. Anne's while his parodic double (a simple tramp misidentified as the mage) confounds the conspirators at Belbury, the final outcome is no longer in doubt. In the symmetrical structure of the novel, this set of chapters corresponds to the section in which the N.I.C.E. begins its assault on the surrounding community (chapters 4–6). In contrast to the thick fog that descends on the earlier section, the night sky begins to clear in the opening scene of its structural counterpart. Instead of a sanctuary for the persecuted, St. Anne's is now the springboard for a decisive counter-offensive, while Belbury begins to succumb to the confusion it was once so adept at sowing. Thematically, St. Anne's now emerges as the original of which Belbury is the monstrous distortion. As Wither floats further into disembodied spiritualism and the materialistic Frost subjects Mark Studdock to Pavlovian "reconditioning," St. Anne's exemplifies the incarnate union of mind and body in the natural order that human beings inhabit—first in its affirmation of the affects we share with other animals, indicating that our animal nature is more than mere matter, and then in the arrival (on horseback) of the physically imposing figure of Merlin, whose magic represents not the brute power to manipulate matter but an ancient union between the spiritual and the natural lost to the modern world. Somewhat more surprisingly, the developments at St. Anne's signify not only the reenchantment of the physical world but also (so to speak) the reembodiment of the spiritual world. In another series of startling developments, Jane is astonished to discover that the "spiritual" cannot be dissociated from "sex and sense" (312), and in the midst of her struggle with the recognition that the supernatural may be as tangibly "real" as the natural world itself, she comes to the realization that she is no longer thinking about the spectral realm of "Religion," but standing in the presence of God.

Once we learn that Wither and Frost constitute the "inner ring" of the organization, Belbury becomes a site for examining the convolutions of the antinomy between mind and matter in the modern world. We are already acquainted with the tendencies of the Deputy Director, who has been drifting toward a spiritual condition divorced entirely from the natural order:

> He had learned to withdraw most of his consciousness from the task of living. . . . Colours, tastes, smells, and tactual sensations no doubt bombarded his physical senses in the normal manner: they did not now reach his ego. . . . That detachment of the spirit, not only from the senses, but even from the reason, which has been the goal of some mystics, was now his. . . . The face had no expression; the real man was far away suffering, enjoying, or inflicting whatever such souls do suffer, enjoy or inflict when the cord that binds them to the natural order is stretched out to its utmost but not yet snapped. (247–248)

Frost presents a somewhat more complicated case, which issues from the two-step process that Lewis outlines in *The Abolition of Man* (1943). As a result of the initial division between subjective and objective realms, we can regard the natural world as mere matter and proceed to the task of subjecting it to our will. But once we have reduced external reality in this manner, there is nothing to prevent us from turning the process of objectification back on ourselves: "It is in Man's power to treat himself as a mere 'natural object' and his own judgements of value as raw material for scientific manipulation to alter at will" (*AM* 72). This version of the "dialectic of enlightenment" clarifies the peculiar position that Frost assumes in this section.[28] As opposed to Wither, the Professor treats Man as mere material, but his aim is not simply to assert that mental life is reducible to physiological functions but to root out the thoughts, volitions, and feelings—the haze of "subjective reactions" (*THS* 256)—that stand in the way of "the total objectivity of mind" required for the technocratic transformation of Man, who will eventually shed his "large body" and become "all head."[29]

In an unexpected turn of events, Mark discovers that he is not only the Professor's prisoner but also his chosen disciple—an ironic fulfillment of his dream of joining the "inner ring"—and as a prospective member of the technocratic elite, he will be purged of all "affectional feelings" (255) that resist the ruthless Objectivity necessary for leadership in the new dispensation.[30] At certain moments, Mark finds himself possessed by the dark temptation of this "movement opposite to Nature" (266), but in the midst of his trials in the Objectivity Room—where surrealist paintings are among the devices used to disorient and assault the senses—the very deprivations of this "asceticism of anti-Nature" (296) produce within him "some kind of vision of the sweet and the straight . . . something he vaguely called the 'Normal' . . . solid, massive, with a shape of its own, almost like something you could touch, or eat, or fall in love with" (296–297). Mark's attempt to sustain this vision is propped up by the arrival of the tramp who is mistaken for Merlin. With his disarming simplicity and hearty appetites, this figure provides the uncertain young man with a welcome companion and an unlikely ally in his efforts to resist the strange lure of "total objectivity." At the same time, the instinctive "animal cunning" (310) with which the tramp misleads the conspirators into providing him with creature comforts enables Mark to take heart from the folly of his captors, whose solicitude for the unwitting "pseudo-Merlin" (330) completes the transformation of Belbury into a parodic double of its enemy.

Frost may be losing the battle for Mark's soul, but the discussion of animal sentience at St. Anne's confirms that the Professor is right about one thing—there is an intrinsic connection between our "subjective reactions" and our embodied condition: "'What friends those two are!' said Ivy Maggs. She was referring to Pinch the cat and Mr. Bultitude the Bear" (257). In the ensuing exchange, at once serious and comic, the skeptical MacPhee puts forward a more benign version of Frost's physiological materialism, asserting that "friendship" between animals is merely an anthropomorphic projection on a more elemental "desire for warmth . . . a sense of security . . . and likely enough some obscure transferred sexual impulses" (258). The Director mediates between the two positions, but in a manner that shifts the basis of the argument:

> "I think MacPhee is introducing into animal life a distinction that doesn't exist there, and then trying to determine on which side of that distinction the feelings of Pinch and Bultitude fall. You've got to become human before the physical cravings are distinguishable from affections—just as you have to become spiritual before affections are distinguishable from charity. What is going on in the cat and the bear isn't one or other of these two things: it is a single undifferentiated thing in which you can find the germ of what we call friendship and of what we call physical need. But it isn't either at that level. It is one of Barfield's 'ancient unities.'" (258)[31]

The Director's intriguing formulation invites extensive commentary, but in this context his principal aim is to reaffirm the unity of rational and animal nature in the constitution of our own kind. While rationality confers a special privilege, the union of the physical and the affective in animal life indicates that our bodies are not reducible to mere matter, and as the seat of our natural sentiments they are the foundation of the higher virtues—the "'ordinate affections' or 'just sentiments'" (*AM* 16)—which have found expression in the Tao (or "natural law") that has traditionally provided the moral compass for civilized peoples throughout the world. In an epoch founded on the radical separation between the mental and the physical, the Director is addressing himself to the far-reaching consequences of privileging the former to the point of denying any inherent value to the possession of the latter.[32]

Merlin's arrival extends this reenchantment of the body to the entire natural world. The reanimated mage, who appears on a huge horse "all in a lather of sweat and foam," has the body of a "giant" (*THS* 260) and a face with a "strangely animal appearance: not sensual nor fierce but full of the patient, unarguing sagacity of a beast" (284).[33] As Dimble informs us, Merlin's animal nature, and his instant rapport with the beasts at St. Anne's, comes from a time when "the Earth itself was more like an animal. . . . and mental processes were much more like physical actions" (281). The druid is "the last vestige of an old order in which matter and spirit were, from our modern point of view, confused" (282):

> "For him every operation on Nature is a kind of personal
> contact, like coaxing a child or stroking one's horse. After
> him came the modern man to whom Nature is something
> dead—a machine to be worked, and taken to bits if it won't
> work the way he pleases. Finally, come the Belbury people,
> who take over that view from the modern man unaltered and
> simply want to increase their power by tacking onto it the aid
> of spirits—extra-natural, anti-natural spirits. Of course they
> hoped to have it both ways. They thought the old *magia* of
> Merlin which worked in with the spiritual qualities of Nature,
> loving and reverencing them and knowing them from within,
> could be combined with the new *goeteia*—the brutal surgery
> from without. No. In a sense Merlin represents what we've got
> to get back to in some different way." (282–283)

Dimble envisions a "regenerate science" (*AM* 79) that reveres "the spiritual qualities of Nature." At the same time, there is no going back to "the old *magia*." As Merlin learns from the Director, "the soul has gone out of the wood and water" (*THS* 285). The old magic, insofar as it served as an instrument for power over Nature, was never "*very* lawful, even in your day," and it "withered" (282)—the reference to the N.I.C.E. Deputy Director is telling—the minds of even its most benevolent practitioners.[34] In any case, Merlin's skills would be of little avail against "the Hideous Strength" (286): the new magicians have not only trampled on the terrestrial creation but also crossed the cosmic frontier "into the Heavens" (287), and as a consequence of their transgression, they have "pulled down Deep Heaven on their heads" (291). To his surprise and horror, Merlin discovers that instead of wielding his ancient power over Nature, he has been chosen (by virtue of the receptive capacity of his "withered" mind) to serve as the self-sacrificial conduit through which "the celestial powers: created powers, not in this Earth, but in the Heavens" (286) will descend on the earth and break the might of the enemy. The plot may seem somewhat strained at this point, but thematically there is more at stake than the attempt to transform Merlin into a Christ-like figure of sacrificial redemption. Lewis is shifting from the critique of the modern dissociation between mind and matter to the related and equally problematic split between the natural and the supernatural realms. The burden of the first part of this section is to identify the elements of "mind" that are lodged in the body, which is irreducible to mere matter, and the "spiritual qualities" of Nature that the modern epoch has chosen to ignore. By contrast, the aim of the last part is to reinvest the "spiritual" realm with the sort of qualities that we ordinarily associate with the "natural"—not for the purpose of reducing the "spiritual" to the terms of the "natural" but in order to awaken us to the awesome power and palpable presence that modern thought has eliminated from the former and restricted to the latter.

Over the course of this section the narrator continues to move back and forth between the opposing camps. The balance slowly tips, however, in the direction of St. Anne's, and the concluding chapter dwells mainly on the decisive stage of Jane's transformation. As she prepares a bridal chamber for Ivy Maggs, her working-class double whose husband has been released from prison, Jane's literary memories of the "archaic" world of "bridal beds and marriage bowers" (298) modulate almost imperceptibly into an astonishing vision: a giant flame-robed Mother Dimble, accompanied by a handful of "chubby, gnome-like little men, quite insufferably familiar, frivolous, and irrepressible" (301), who enter the house—"they were all coming at her" (302)—and set fire to the room. Jane is alarmed by the spectacle, but just as the terror becomes unbearable, she sees "that what was curling up from everything the torch had touched was not flame after all, but vegetation" (302), and the sequence comes to an abrupt end with the arrival of the real Mother Dimble. A modern interpreter would make quick work of this dream-vision, but in a lengthy discussion with the Director, Jane discovers that far more is involved than "Freudian repressions" (312) of her own internal conflicts. According to the Director, the Huge Woman in the dream may be the "earthly wraith" (313) of Perelandra (Venus), the counterpart of the celestial intelligence who will soon descend upon St. Anne's. Perhaps more importantly, the dream itself signifies that the "world beyond Nature" may be as sexually charged and frightfully demanding as the natural world itself:

> Some knowledge of a world beyond Nature she had already gained from living in this house, and more from fear of death that night in the dingle. But she had been conceiving this world as "spiritual" in the negative sense—as some neutral, or democratic, vacuum where differences disappeared, where sex and sense were not transcended but simply taken away. Now the suspicion dawned upon her that there might be differences and contrasts all the way up, richer, sharper, even fiercer, at every rung of the ascent. How if this invasion of her own being in marriage from which she had

recoiled, often in the very teeth of instinct, were not, as she had supposed, merely a relic of animal life or patriarchal barbarism, but rather the lowest, the first, and the easiest form of some shocking contact with reality which would have to be repeated—but in ever larger and more disturbing modes—on the highest levels of all? (312)

In other words, as Jane learns from the Director, whose masculinity now seems "steeper, more emphatic, than that of common men" (312), there is no escape from the sexual: "If it were a virginal rejection of the male, He would allow it. . . . for it exists only on the biological level. But the masculine none of us can escape. What is above and beyond all things is so masculine that we are all feminine in relation to it" (312–313). Many readers are troubled by this controversial formulation, which seems to challenge male dominion at one level—"we are all feminine in relation to it"—only to reconstitute it at a higher level.[35] But at this stage of her spiritual journey Jane is offended less by the patriarchal implications of this cosmic hierarchy than by its "bright, darting, and overpowering" (313) reality. As objectionable as his explanation may sound, the Director has shattered Jane's "modern" assumption that hers was "the vivid, perilous world brought against their grey formalised one; hers the quick, vital movements and theirs the stained glass attitudes" (313). Just as her previous dreams were records of real events, Jane's latest dream-vision converts the supersensible world from the evanescent and ethereal into something more potent, tactile, and implacably real than the "real" world itself.[36]

The climactic moment of Jane's pilgrimage takes place in solitude at the end of this section:

His [the Director's] comparison between Mark's love and God's (since apparently there was a God) struck her nascent spirituality as indecent and irreverent. "Religion" ought to mean a realm in which her haunting female fear of being treated as a thing, an object of barter and desire and possession, would be set permanently at rest and what she called her "true self" would soar upwards and expand in some freer and purer world. For she still thought that "Religion" was a kind of exhalation or a cloud of incense, something steaming up from specially gifted souls towards a receptive Heaven. Then, quite sharply, it occurred to her that the Director never talked about Religion; nor did the Dimbles nor Camilla. They talked about God. They had no picture in their minds of some mist steaming upward: rather of strong, skilful hands thrust down to make, and mend, perhaps even to destroy. Supposing one were a *thing* after all—a thing designed and invented by Someone Else and valued for qualities quite different from what one had decided to regard as one's true self? (314–315)

It is easy to bristle at this passage, even if we acknowledge that the main emphasis is on the obedience that all human beings (men and women alike) owe to their Creator. For many readers the difficulties of this formulation may be insuperable, but as we can see from Belbury's misogynistic dreams of divinity, the admission that I am "a *thing* after all"—which is not the same as mere matter—may be even more difficult for the half of our species that has long assumed prerogatives of agency than it is for the half to whom it has been traditionally denied.[37] In Jane's case, the move from possessing a concept of Religion to accepting the reality of God is one with the realization that we are objects as well as subjects "and valued for qualities quite different from what one had decided to regard as one's true self" (315). As she quietly ponders this dramatic shift in orientation, Jane's pride momentarily rises up in resentment, but then, "at one particular corner of the gooseberry patch, the change came. . . . a boundary had been crossed" (315):

She had come into a world, or into a Person, or into the presence of a Person. Something expectant, patient, inexorable, met her with no veil or protection between. In the closeness of that contact she perceived at once that the Director's words [the comparison between Mark's love and God's] had been entirely misleading. This demand which now pressed upon her was not, even by analogy, like any other demand. It was the origin of all right demands and contained them. . . . In this height and depth and breadth the little idea of herself which she had hitherto called *me* dropped down and vanished, unfluttering, into bottomless distance, like a bird in a space without air. The name *me* was the name of a being whose existence she had never suspected, a being that did not yet fully exist but which was demanded. It was a person (not the person she had thought), yet also a thing, a made thing, made to please Another and in Him to please all others, a thing being made at this very moment, without its choice, in a shape it had never dreamed of. (315–316)

In response to this revelation, Jane is tempted first to resist and then to reconvert this encounter into a self-flattering "religious experience" (316). She also instructs herself to "try to get it again. It will please the Director" (316). But now there is no turning back, and in the final words of the section, we are reassured that "her defences had been captured and these counter-attacks were unsuccessful."

VII

The triumph of St. Anne's dominates the final section of the novel (chap-ters 15–17). Here Lewis weaves together his various sources, ancient and modern, into an archetypal victory of good over evil, the spirit of divine beneficence over the distortions of mind that have plunged the world into enmity and violence on an unprecedented scale. In light of Lewis's Augustinian theology, the ascendancy of St. Anne's is also a restoration of the original over its perverse imitation, a reinstitution of the "high" romance mode that overwhelms its dark Gothic double. Structurally, the last three chapters correspond to the first three, first and foremost in the ruin of the once irresistible juggernaut of the N.I.C.E. and the reunion of Jane and Mark. A variety of other details echo the events of the opening section: the climactic banquet at Belbury, recalling the College dinner during which Mark is lured into the Institute; Feverstone's attempt to escape from the carnage in his car, echoing the scene in which he first takes Mark to Belbury; and on a comic note, the reappearance of the benighted sub-warden Curry, still oblivious to the demonic powers he has helped to unleash and savoring his "Providential" (372) opportunity to establish a new College on the ruins of the old. As in some of the previous sections, Lewis temporarily suspends the pattern of switching back and forth between the two opposing camps. After the opening scene—an awe-inspiring pageant in which the Celestial Intelligences descend upon St. Anne's—the setting shifts to Belbury for ten successive scenes, culminating in the blood-soaked spectacle of its demise. Afterward, as if to underscore the restoration of normality, the contrapuntal narrative returns in the final chapter, which alternates between scenes involving Mark and other survivors of the divine retribution, and scenes portraying various members of the Company at St. Anne's, who soberly assess the victory of Logres—the spiritual kingdom that forever "haunts" their nation—and prepare the bridal chamber for the long-awaited remarriage of husband and wife.

In "The Descent of the Gods" (chapter 15), the Celestial Intelligences manifest their spectacular power and transfigure the community at St. Anne's. At the end of the previous section, Jane's recognition of the inexorable "reality" of the supernatural culminated in an intimate encounter with the divine Person. In the opening of this section, the reality of the supernatural appears as the overwhelming might that no merely mortal strength can withstand. Lewis places a premium on the direct physical impact of this cosmic epiphany. The whole house seems to be "tilting and plunging like a ship" (317). Anyone approaching the Director's room would sense "an almost physical resistance," and he "would have known

sensuously, until his outraged senses forsook him, that the visitants
in that room were in it, not because they were at rest but because
they glanced and wheeled through the packed reality of Heaven
(which men call empty space), to keep their beams upon this spot
of the moving Earth's hide" (317–318). To highlight the sense of a
vast "packed" and multitiered universe, Lewis divides the Company
into two parts—the majority downstairs in the kitchen, Ransom
and Merlin upstairs in the Blue Room—and one by one the arrival of the five planetary Intelligences is registered by its wondrous
effects on the two contingents. The Celestial descent begins with
Viritrilbia (Mercury), who downstairs inspires a prodigal display of
verbal wit and upstairs appears as "the lord of Meaning himself"
(319); Perelandra (Venus), who brings warmth and affection to those
below, and the spirit of Charity, "fiery, sharp, bright and ruthless"
(320) to Ransom and Merlin in the room above; and Malacandra
(Mars), who stirs the martial spirit of MacPhee and Camilla, and
dispels the anxiety of the others in the kitchen, while upstairs he
creates an atmosphere in which the two leaders, relieved of all fears,
"felt themselves taking their places in the ordered rhythm of the
universe, side by side with punctual seasons and patterned atoms
and the obeying Seraphim" (322). Then there is a pause in the pro-
cession, as Ransom warns Merlin to prepare for the last two spirits,
who possess genders with no relation to man or woman—there
is more to this cosmos than masculine and feminine—and bear
the "mightier energies . . . of giant worlds which have never from
the beginning been subdued to the sweet humiliations of organic
life" (322). First the cold leaden spirit of ancient Lurga (Saturn) descends upon St. Anne's, "a mountain of centuries sloping up from
the highest antiquity we can conceive, up and up like a mountain
whose summit never comes into sight, not to eternity where the
thought can rest, but into more and still more time, into freezing
wastes and silence of unnamable numbers" (323). But no sooner
has this incomprehensible and unendurable power overcome the
house than it is trumped by an even greater power—the majestic

joy embodied in Glund-Oyarsa (Jupiter), who transports the downstairs into a riotous dance, while the upstairs is turned into "a blaze of lights" (323) that transforms everything within it:

> Kingship and power and festal pomp and courtesy shot from
> him as sparks fly from an anvil. The pealing of bells, the blowing of trumpets, the spreading out of banners, are means used
> on earth to make a faint symbol of his quality. . . . For this
> was great Glund-Oyarsa, King of Kings, through whom the
> joy of creation principally blows across these fields of Arbol,
> known to men in old time as Jove and under that name,
> by fatal but not inexplicable misprision, confused with his
> Maker—so little did they dream by how many degrees the
> stair even of created being rises above him. (323–324)

In the midst of this sensory onslaught, the narrator, whose universe has already transcended the horizons of human understanding, attempts to extrapolate beyond the King of Kings himself to the Maker whose majesty we can hardly begin to fathom. But there are limits to the reach of the analogical imagination, and the scene terminates judiciously with a simple description: "Merlin received the power into him. . . . Later in the day MacPhee drove him off and dropped him in the neighborhood of Belbury" (324).[38]

After this ceremonial infusion of celestial power, it may seem incongruous to find the divinely appointed agent infiltrating enemy headquarters dressed up in extravagant priestly garb and pretending to translate the ancient tongue of the tramp for whom he has been mistaken. But the face-to-face encounter between Merlin and his unsuspecting double underscores the relationship of the original to its parodic copy that has come to define the terms of engagement between St. Anne's and Belbury. It also enables Lewis to line up the Classical and Biblical archetypes that will bestow legitimacy and multilevel significance on the violence to come. Merlin's disguise recalls the ruse of Odysseus, who masquerades as a beggar to prepare for the slaying of the suitors, while the confusion of tongues points to the retributive justice of Babel, which commences when Frost lapses into temporary aphasia and Wither unaccountably "forgets" the forthcoming banquet for the puppet director of the N.I.C.E. But before the banquet begins, Mark Studdock enters the final phase of the transformation that will exempt him from the fate of his colleagues. It takes place in the Objective Room, where Frost makes a last attempt to recondition his prisoner by ordering him to trample on a "ghastly and realistic" (331) crucifix. The religionless Mark tries to cover his reluctance by referring to it as a "pure superstition" (332), but Frost still possesses enough of his faculties to know that the symbol represents "a dominant system in the subconscious of many individuals whose conscious thought appears to be wholly liberated" (332). Moved by the helplessness of the figure on the cross, the young man takes a step beyond his recent affirmation of "the Straight or Normal or Wholesome" (332) and finds himself looking at the suffering Christ "as a bit of history. . . . a picture of what happened when the Straight met the Crooked, a picture of what the Crooked did to the Straight—what it would do to him if he remained straight. It was, in a more emphatic sense than he had yet understood, a *cross*" (333). This is the closest Mark comes to an awareness of the Divine, but in its own way it is as momentous as the more formal conversion of his wife, and it brings about his first and only act of open defiance—"It's all bloody nonsense, and I'm damned if I do any such thing" (334)—a refusal which is all the more courageous in light of the knowledge that his disobedience will lead to his death.

The penultimate chapter of the novel is devoted entirely to the climactic banquet at Belbury. As the oration of the titular Director (a thinly veiled stand-in for a doddering H. G. Wells) devolves from occasional malapropism into sheer nonsense, the curse of Babel descends upon the entire gathering. Confusion turns into chaos when Miss Hardcastle takes out her revolver and kills the Director in a general shooting spree. But this is merely the prelude to the main action, which begins with the sighting of a beast—a tiger—who quietly disappears beneath the tables and reemerges suddenly to make quick work of the Chief of Police. Then other beasts appear, and soon an entire stampede of creatures, released by Merlin's magic, bursts through the door of the banquet hall ("made in imitation of Versailles" 346) and charges into the crowd. Some have been troubled by the grisly and arguably gratuitous violence of the ensuing slaughter, as if the use of emancipated beasts enabled the author to indulge in a sadistic bloodbath without implicating any members of the Company of St. Anne's. Others have been content to regard this one-sided spectacle as an act of just retribution, as if Nature itself is rising up to avenge the violation of its most fundamental laws. Whether or not we approve of the process, each of the major operatives perishes in a manner commensurate with his own aberrations, following the well-established precedent of Dante's *contrapasso*.[39] Wither and Frost, like Faust, are given the last-minute opportunity to repent. The former, unable to act on the knowledge that he may yet be saved, compels Filostrato and Straik at knifepoint to undress and worship the Head, and after guillotining the physiologist and slashing the throat of the mad preacher, the man who has spent his life perfecting the dissociation of spirit from the animal side of his nature comes face to face with a huge bear (Mr. Bultitude), with "its mouth open, its eyes flaming, its fore-paws spread out as if for an embrace" (353). Frost, who reduced human nature to a physiological machine, now watches helplessly as his own body enters the chamber of corpses and prepares the fire that will consume them all. Finally aware "that he had been wrong from the beginning, that souls and personal responsibility existed" (356), he rejects a final offer of redemption, and thrusting himself "back into his illusion. . . . eternity overtook him as sunrise in old tales overtakes [trolls] and turns them into unchangeable stone" (356).[40] Finally, the crafty Feverstone manages to escape by car, but a strange presence in the back seat (later identified as Merlin) assumes control over his actions, and as we learn in the next chapter, he is eventually swallowed up in the same earthquake that destroys the College he had helped to corrupt. As excessive as it might appear, this decisive display of celestial power seems designed not only to crush the beast at Belbury but also to reinvest supernatural agency with the wonder and terror of the *mysterium tremendum*, which the new principalities and powers have sought to seize from the heavens and turn into a perpetual state of totalitarian terror.

In the final chapter we return to the normal pattern of narration, the eight scenes alternating regularly between St. Anne's and sketches of various survivors of the N.I.C.E. debacle—Mark Studdock, released by Merlin, at the start of the journey back to his wife; Feverstone, who is buried alive by the earthquake that destroys the town and its university; the insensible and self-satisfied Curry, now planning to capitalize on the havoc to which he contributed; and again the penitent Mark, who approaches his destination in the double state of desire for his wife and recognition of his own unworthiness. At St. Anne's itself, the women prepare for the ceremony of (re)marriage as the celestial power of Venus "comes more near the Earth than she was wont to—to make Earth sane" (376).[41] In one final after-dinner conversation, the Company reflects on the extraordinary events they are witnessing. Nowhere is the peculiar mixture of Medieval and Gothic romance more in evidence. We learn that the Director is about to join Arthur and others "who have never died" (366) in a sacred realm of the undead: "There are many places in the universe— I mean, this same physical universe in which our planet moves— where an organism can last practically forever" (366). The ever skeptical MacPhee objects that all this is "clean contrary to the observed laws of Nature" (366), but he is reminded that the modern concept of Nature has artificially restricted our sense of the possible: "The laws of the universe are never broken," but they far exceed "the little regularities we have observed on one planet for a few hundred years." In an open homage to Charles Williams, we also hear about the operations of "the haunting. . . . how something we may call Britain is always haunted by something we may call Logres. . . . the whole work of healing Tellus [Earth] depends on nursing that little spark, on incarnating that ghost, which is still alive in every real people, and different in each" (367–369). As for the fate of the N.I.C.E., we return to the preeminent myth of the early Gothic, Mary Shelley's "hideous progeny," the prototype of the "artificial Man" envisioned at Belbury and the fountainhead of modern science fiction. When the compassionate Mother Dimble questions the wholesale annihilation of the University, she is reminded that for all their naiveté and silliness, the intellectuals have brought this doom upon themselves. Like Victor Frankenstein, they created the monstrous progeny that in the end came back to destroy them: "was there a single doctrine practiced at Belbury which hadn't been preached by some lecturer at Edgestow? Oh, of course, they never thought any one would *act* on their theories! No one was more astonished than they when what they'd been talking of for years suddenly took on reality. But it was their own child coming back to them: grown up and unrecognisable, but their own" (369–370).[42]

As the Company deliberates, Venus is descending upon St. Anne's, and soon their reflections give way to the first stirrings of love in the raucous but "decent" (374) mating of the beasts who have been liberated from Belbury. Then the healing spirit of eros descends on Ivy Maggs, who awaits the return of her husband, and finally on Jane Studdock, who takes her leave of the Director—the Pendragon whose earthly mission is now accomplished—and proceeds to the Lodge where her husband is waiting. Given the network of allusions that has been gathering force over the last few chapters, the finale is steeped in romance tradition, recalling the reunion of Odysseus and Penelope and the various kin and lovers of Spenserian and Shakespearean romance who have been separated by malevolence, chance, or their own folly.[43] The conclusion also bears the mark of the prototypical female Gothic, Mrs. Radcliffe's *Mysteries of Udolpho,* and its major variant, Brontë's *Jane Eyre*—in the victory of the relatively passive and long-suffering heroine, the reunion with her wayward and chastened lover, the final affirmation of the companionate marriage, and perhaps above all, in the triumph of feminine values manifested in the Celestial Venus, who restores a measure of peace, sanity, and the spirit of divine Love to a tormented and self-destructive planet.

VIII

For all its differences in setting and generic allegiance, the final novel of the Trilogy exhibits a transpositional strategy that is strikingly similar to that of its predecessors. As we have seen, Lewis's imaginary worlds on Mars and Venus derive their most salient characteristics from the same "developmental" tendencies they are designed to attack. Similarly, the very mix of the realistic and supernatural that constitutes the fictive world of *That Hideous Strength* is constructed according to the Gothic blueprint provided by the N.I.C.E.'s fusion of ancient magic and modern science. Adopting Augustine's "privative" notion of evil as nothing other than the distortion of the Good, Lewis turns the apparent antithesis between Christianity and the post-Darwinian currents of modern thought into a relationship between a transcendent original and its parodic imitation. At the same time, we can observe a significant change in the character of the satirical target over the course of the three novels. In *Out of the Silent Planet*, Lewis is aiming at an evolutionary naturalism grounded in materialist assumptions and issuing in a vision of ceaseless conflict between or within the species. In *Perelandra*, the demonic tempter espouses a doctrine of "creative" or "emergent" evolution that arises from a critique of mechanistic science and offers a "middle way" between "spiritual" and "material" points of view. And just as the target of the second novel shifts from the material to the organic realm, the "developmental" dreams of the final novel project us beyond the organic world itself into the spiritual realm of the "new man who never dies." Although the desire to transcend our finite condition underlies all three novels, the progression from interplanetary colonization to "creative" development to the techno-magical transformation of man into God follows a distinctive trajectory from the material to the spiritual plane.

Given Lewis's strategy of constructing sublimated versions of the very "falsehoods" he condemns, it is not surprising to find that as the target alters from one book to the next, there is commensurate change in its "beatific" transfiguration. The difference between the opening and the close of the Trilogy is especially instructive in this regard. In *Out of the Silent Planet,* Lewis responds to the evolutionary naturalism of H. G. Wells by constructing an imaginary world in which universal reason transcends the differences between the species and provides the basis for their mutual acknowledgment and shared participation in a divinely ordered cosmos. By contrast, in *That Hideous Strength,* where the enemy aspires to transcend the natural order itself, the transfiguration of the myth of "development" runs in the opposite direction. The emphasis is no longer on the rational harmony that transcends our animal nature but on the affirmation of our organic, embodied, and finite condition. Or more precisely, the focus is on the incarnate union between the spiritual and the natural whose distorted trace may be found in Belbury's attempt to transform the human into the divine by mixing ancient magic and modern technology, the occultism of Wither and the scientism of Frost. Once again, Lewis takes the Platonic step of conceiving a divinely sanctioned "original," or first "principle," which in turn reduces its modern derivative—ironically the very stuff out of which it was conceived—into a perverted copy. But in this case, the traditional Augustinian view, which affirms the essential goodness of the creation while insisting on its finite and dependent status, overcomes the parodic distortion of its perennial gnostic counterpart, which seeks in knowledge, either scientific or occultic or the fusion between them, a means of transcending our creaturely condition. At the same time, the climactic manifestation of celestial power, as excessive as it seems, is designed to reinvest supernatural agency with the wonder, as well as the terror, which has been expropriated from the heavens by the New Leviathan and dissociated from the mysterious union of goodness and grace that are reconciled in divine Love.

Conclusion ∾

Further Transpositions: Ransom,
Violence, and the Sacred

> I think the most significant way of stating the real
> freedom of man is to say that if there are other rational
> species than man, existing in some other part of the
> actual universe, then it is not necessary to suppose that
> they also have fallen.
> —*The Problem of Pain*

> "My name also is Ransom."
> —*Perelandra,* chapter 11

In each volume of the Trilogy there comes a moment when the protagonist shifts from a relatively passive state to one that requires personal decision, commitment to violent action or painful self-scrutiny, and a confrontation with death. It is no coincidence that this moment occurs at the same point—immediately after the pivotal central section—in each of the three novels: first, the hunting expedition that terminates Ransom's visit to the *hrossa* (*OSP* chapter 13); next, the silent and shocking self-debate that calls him to mortal combat with the demonic Un-man (*P* chapter 11); and finally, the double reckoning with death as Jane Studdock joins the search for the as-yet mysterious Merlin, while her incarcerated husband, now the victim of force and fraud, silently examines the ugly waste of his own past existence ("Battle Begun" *THS* chapter 11).[1] It is also noteworthy that in each instance the crisis is closely tied to the specific phase of the developmental paradigm—material, organic, or spiritual—with which the novel is concerned. Each situation turns on the tension between a particular version of the evolutionary model and its original "principle," and in every case the protagonist's actions demonstrate that the deficiencies of the former lie precisely in its distortions of the latter. In this respect, the personal crises of these chapters represent the decisive moments at which the ethical implications of the developmental paradigm are simultaneously tested and transfigured. At yet another level, these three chapters also represent three axial moments in the cosmic drama issuing from the presence of free agency in the created universe. At the risk of modulating into allegory, we may refer to these moments as Adamic (or tragic), Christic (or salvific), and Ecclesiastic (or agapic) respectively. Taken together, they map the narrative progression arising from the complex relationship between divine and human will, a narrative that situates the ordeal of strife, suffering, and death within the larger story of the creation of a "rational animal," endowed with the capacity for discriminating right from wrong, and the sacrificial redemption of its afflicted freedom. Often excused or excoriated for their legitimation of violence, these interrelated passages exhibit not only the structural symmetries of the Trilogy as it evolved from one volume to the next, but also the relationship between the manner in which we conceive the universe and the fateful decisions that each of us—without exception—is called upon to make.

The hunting scene in *Out of the Silent Planet* dramatizes the gap between the terrestrial conception of the "struggle for existence" and its transfiguration onto a higher plane. The *hrossa* long to pursue and slay the *hnakra*—"our enemy" and "our beloved" (76)—but in this unfallen world of peaceful coexistence between different rational species, the ritualized violence between rational and irrational creatures is an inherent and mutually uplifting element of the natural order. The hunt also takes place at a timely moment in the narrative, offering Ransom the opportunity to restore his compromised sense of courage and exercise the martial virtues required for the impending struggle on earth. It is therefore perplexing that just as the search for the sea monster is approaching its climax, an *eldil* appears to ban his participation in the fight. One clue to this enigma is that Ransom's Martian companions readily obey the divine decree, even though it means that they must row the earthling ashore and thereby give up their long-awaited "share in the hunt" (80). As honorable as it seems, Ransom's heat-of-the-moment refusal to forsake the adventure—"it was in obedience to something like conscience that he exclaimed: 'No, no. There is time for that after the hunt. We must kill the *hnakra* first'" (81)—is at another level an act of disobedience that echoes the archetypal transgression of our ancestral forebears. In following his own heroic promptings at this crucial juncture, Ransom at once ignores a divine prohibition and demonstrates the difference between the rationally governed Martians and the damaged relationship between reason and passion, "spirit" and "blood," that makes our own species so susceptible to the furies let loose by the shedding of blood. The fruits of this triumph of "blood" over "spirit" are evident in the tragic outcome of Ransom's resolve, which brings victory over the *hnakra* but death to his *hrossan* friend. Although it appears as if Weston and Devine shoot the seal-shaped alien under the mistaken assumption that he is a beast, Ransom admits that the ruthless terrestrials "would kill even a *hnau,* knowing it to be *hnau,* if they thought its death would serve them" (83). The Martians engage successfully in an originary form of violence, but in our hands this "principle" easily disintegrates into the violent, fear-ridden state represented in modern thought by the Hobbesian "war of all against all" or its modern equivalent, the Darwinian "struggle for existence." It is therefore no wonder that modern thought, to the extent that it reduces man from a spiritual to a purely biological entity, elevates the state of inexorable competition, conflict, and self-serving aggression from a tragic lapse of our ordained destiny into the primary principle of the natural order. In other words, while the anti-pacifist Lewis may be grooming the unsure Ransom for future warfare, the otherwise mystifying ban on his participation in the hunt, along with the lamentable consequences of his defiance, introduces an element of hesitation, an ambivalence that acknowledges the insufficiencies of any reconciliation between the ends for which we were created and the apparent inevitability of resorting to violence in a violent world.[2]

The Adamic character of the hunt is reversed in the Christological drama that takes place in the corresponding section of *Perelandra*. Whereas in the first novel Ransom impetuously disregards the divine interdict, in the sequel he struggles to evade the unthinkable divine summons to a raw fistfight with the Devil. Lewis's hero is prepared for a "*spiritual* struggle" (122), but the call to unarmed physical combat, which ignites images of "the deadly cold of those hands . . . the long metallic nails . . . ripping off narrow strips of flesh," seems as degrading as it is terrifying and repellent. If at one level this chapter is designed to justify, if not sanctify, the recourse to arms against Nazi aggression, the emphasis lies not in any fantasy of battlefield glory but in the terrible recognition of how much depends on the self-sacrificial acts of ordinary men: "And at that moment, far away on Earth, as he now could not help remembering, men were at war, and white-faced subalterns and freckled corporals who had but lately begun to shave, stood in horrible gaps or crawled forward in deadly darkness, awaking, like him, to the preposterous truth that all really depended on their actions" (121).[3] In this way the divine injunction also addresses the "creative evolution" that the novel simultaneously "raises up" and reduces to a parodic distortion. Unlike the brutal "struggle for existence" targeted in *Out of the Silent Planet*, the buoyant "Life-Force philosophy," which offers "all the thrills of religion and none of the cost" (*MC* 26–27), overlooks the snares as well as the tribulations of free agency in a world perpetually threatened by fear, enmity, and the specter of death. In the initial section of *Perelandra*'s inner frame (chapter 7), Weston had spoken of his own spiritual "surrender" (81) to the impetus of the Life-Force, but in response to Ransom's ethical interrogation, the self-deceived reprobate casually cast aside "mere moralism" (82) and exhibited no hesitation in his readiness to employ any means—deceit, murder, treason—to serve his illusory cause. In the complementary section that completes the inner frame (chapter 11), Ransom's internal resistance is not a fool-proof guarantee of the validity of the divine summons, but the very process of protracted self-debate serves as a means of testing the "Voice" even as he accepts its summons to a seemingly absurd and impossible act of self-sacrificial obedience.

The new Eden on Venus will be spared the fate of our own first world, but the pre-demption of this blissful and ever-evolving paradise is contingent upon the same self-surrender to which Ransom's divine exemplar—"My name also is Ransom" (126)—remained faithful unto death. In this respect Ransom's crisis evinces the astonishing humility of the archetypal act of divine self-sacrifice, while the gradual surrender of his own "voluble self" (120) to the silent voice of divine authority re-enacts the drama of the Cross in "the self's surrender to God. . . . the pure will to obey, in the absence, or in the teeth, of inclination" (*PP* 98).[4] Whereas the hunting scene reveals the tragic potential of our freedom, Ransom's ultimate assent to the horrifying, violent, and prospectively fatal encounter with the Unman demonstrates "that the supreme cancelling of Adam's fall, the movement 'full speed astern' by which we retrace our long journey from Paradise . . . must be when the creature, with no desire to aid it, stripped naked to the bare willing of obedience, embraces what is contrary to its nature, and does that for which only one motive is possible" (100). Once again the focal point of free agency is the problem of violence as it manifests itself in the tension between divine and human will, but in this instance "the bare willing of obedience" shows us the process by which "a rational creature consciously enacts its creaturely *rôle,* reverses the act by which we fell, treads Adam's dance backwards, and returns" (100).

The corresponding chapter in *That Hideous Strength* reprises both the hunting expedition and the redemptive trial of self-sacrifice. Jane's search for Merlin echoes Ransom's pursuit of the *hnakra,* while Mark's solitary self-examination recalls the silent self-debate on Venus.

The wounded but now princely Ransom (Fisher-King/Director/ Pendragon) is conspicuously absent from this death-haunted section, as is his ecclesiastical establishment at St. Anne's. But the communal "principle of *Vicariousness*" (*M* 191) encompasses both wife and husband as they separately confront the prospect of death. Jane admits that "I know nothing of Maleldil" (*THS* 226), but her pledge of "obedience" to the Director is deemed "enough for the present," and with his benediction she ventures into the darkness with two other members of her adoptive community. Like Ransom before her, she joins the "hunt" (224) for a dangerous and possibly deadly "monstrosity" (230) at the same time that enemy forces are hunting her. But in this instance there is no conflict between reason and passion, divine and human will. Jane never succeeds in finding Merlin, but her "all-absorbing tension of excitement and obedience" (226), culminating in the realization that "Maleldil might be, quite simply and crudely, God" (231), seems at once to replay and reverse the impulsive act of "disobedience" on the Martian hunt. Mark, for his part, has little in common with Ransom, but the ordeal that takes place in his cell involves a similar demand for self-detachment, the shedding of a false and external sense of self, and the recognition of how much rests on the choices we make—in this case the awareness "that it was he himself—nothing else in the whole universe—that had chosen the dust and broken bottles, the heap of old tin cans, the dry and choking places" (244). Mark assumes that "his story is at an end" (243), and just as Ransom proceeded from his sacrificial "trial" to combat with the Adversary, Mark's painful self-scrutiny is the prelude to his spiritual struggle with Frost, who soon appears to torture him not with brute force, as Miss Hardcastle recommends, or with threats, as Wither proposes, but (like the Christ in the wilderness) with the seductive power of his own desires—the lifelong lust for the self-aggrandizement conferred by insider status. Mark, like his wife, "knows nothing of Maleldil," but the renunciation of his former self seems "enough for the present," and it prepares the way for his climactic refusal to trample the image of Christ on the Cross, a symbolic identification with the innocent victim of violence that almost certainly entails his own violent death. As we might expect from the parallel scenes in the earlier novels, the dual transformation of wife and husband is also tied to the third and final phase of the developmental model that their persecutors represent. Wither and Frost are wedded, however incongruously, to the same Babelian dream—the transcendence of our embodied, finite, and mortal condition. Just as Jane's turn from a vague "religion" to a concrete and insistent "God" manifests the transfiguration of Wither's disembodied spiritualism, Mark's death-row conversion reveals that there is more to the body than appears in Frost's materialism. It is hardly an accident that Mark's regeneration is set in motion by the awareness of his own trembling body, and that his awakening comes about, like Jane's concurrent experience in the woods, as he contemplates the approach of death—"a result . . . which the Deputy Director and Professor Frost had possibly not foreseen" (243). In creatures for whom spirit cannot be dissociated from the body, "bodily Death, the monster, becomes blessed spiritual Death to self, if the spirit so wills—or rather if it allows the Spirit of the willingly dying God so to will in it" (*M* 210).

The striking confluence of these three identically situated chapters indicates that we must attend not only to the internal configuration of each individual novel but also to the correlations and embedded sub-narratives established by their shared design. This particular set of chapters, which focuses on the "frightful freedom" (*P* 126) of an inherently fallible species, explores the relationship between the choices that we make and the way we conceive ourselves, our relations to others, and the rest of the natural universe. As we have seen, in each case the exercise of free agency is closely associated with a particular phase of the developmental paradigm and exposes its ethical deficiencies. The Adamic transgression of *Out of the Silent Planet* speaks to an evolutionary theory that denies the priority of rationality over animality, "spirit" over "blood," and thereby fuels the insecurity, suspicion, and strife that reduces human relations to a violent "struggle for existence." The Christic self-surrender of *Perelandra* addresses an optimistic counter-theory that presumes to correct the conceptual shortcomings of its predecessor but ignores the persistence of evil, and hence the arduous course of right action, in an ever-changing and precarious world. Similarly, the transformation of Jane and Mark Studdock in *That Hideous Strength* cannot be dissociated from the blindness of the N.I.C.E., which disavows the incarnate union of the spiritual and the organic, either by the elevation of one side of our composite nature at the expense of the other, or more presciently, by the merger of spiritualism and materialism into a techno-magical project that promises a future unconstrained by the burdens of our mortal condition.

At the same time, the very strategy that uncovers the flaws of these evolutionary schemas is also responsible for their affirmative transfiguration into an originary principle. Whether or not we relish the violence of the hunt, this sublimated form of the "struggle for existence" highlights the primacy of rational governance in a world whose several rational species have overcome the fears and furies that divide our own species into perpetually warring factions. It affirms "the *good* element in the martial spirit, the discipline and freedom from anxiety" (*L* II, 702, 2/15/46) through which we march in step with "the ordered rhythm of the universe, side by side with punctual seasons and patterned atoms and the obeying Seraphim" (*THS* 322). On Venus, the affirmative vision of creative evolution is not so much negated as perfected in the mobile new Eden, transfigured both by the reinstitution of divine transcendence and by the voluntary submission and self-giving required to preserve the beneficent dynamism of the natural order. Once again, the situation in *That Hideous Strength* is more complex, but while the presumption of the N.I.C.E. is crushed by the just violence of divine retribution, its aspiration to overcome the limitations of our present state is paradoxically fulfilled—not by the disavowal of the sympathies or the sufferings of our embodied condition, but as the redemption of Jane and Mark Studdock makes clear, by the self-giving love expressed in the communal remembrance and individual reenactment of the "accepted Death" (*PP* 102) through which Death itself is overcome. If "bad things are good things perverted," as Lewis faithfully maintained, then the ultimate act of transfiguration is the regeneration and "raising up" of an anguished creation into new life, or as he put it elsewhere (*L* III, 520, 1/11/54), "the process of turning finite creatures (with free wills) into—well, into Gods."

Appendix A: "The Dark Tower" ~

Much confusion surrounds the posthumous appearance of this unfinished tale. According to Lewis's literary executor, Walter Hooper, the untitled sixty-two-page manuscript was salvaged from a fire to which Warren Lewis had consigned his brother's papers soon after his death. Since its publication in *The Dark Tower and Other Stories* (1977), scholars have debated not only the merits of the story but also its date(s) of composition, and in the case of one outspoken critic, the authenticity of the manuscript itself. On the basis of internal and external evidence, Hooper speculates that it was composed in 1938–39 and designed as a sequel to *Out of the Silent Planet* (*DT* 8, 92). John Rateliff, citing references in J. R. R. Tolkien's letters and *Notion Club Papers*, offers a measured argument for redating the manuscript to 1944–45; but he agrees that if the novel had been completed it would have followed *Out of the Silent Planet* in the final sequence. Jared Lobdell (2004) splits the difference by suggesting that Lewis composed the opening chapters in 1938–1939, and then resumed work in 1944–1945 and perhaps again around 1956 before putting it aside entirely. In *The C. S. Lewis Hoax* (1988), Kathryn Lindskoog doubts whether Lewis ever wrote the manuscript. Her impassioned argument, which openly casts suspicion on Hooper himself, is based on several factors: the absence of any explicit reference to this work by Lewis or his acquaintances during his lifetime; the inferiority of the writing and the departures in style and content from the rest of the Ransom series; and in her view most tellingly, some striking resemblances to passages in Madeleine L'Engle's *A Wrinkle in Time* (1962), implying that the story must have been composed by someone other than the ailing Lewis, who died in the following year. Lindskoog's case was compelling enough to have kept the controversy alive, but most scholars who have seen the manuscript regard it as genuine, and after the recent testimony of Lewis's student, Alistair Fowler (2003), the burden of proof is increasingly on those who question its authenticity. Critical reception of "The Dark Tower" has been mixed: many of its first readers, eagerly awaiting the release of a lost novel by C. S. Lewis, were sadly disappointed. Others have found it an interesting experiment that sheds light on Lewis's more successful ventures into other-dimensional travel. Some have speculated on the outcome of the story—we have enough to justify some fruitful extrapolation (see especially Lobdell 2000)—but few doubt the wisdom of the author's decision to scuttle it.

In its fragmentary form, "The Dark Tower" may be divided roughly into two sections. The first four chapters, which take place at Cambridge, allow us to peer through a newly devised "chronoscope" into a "dark tower" (hence Hooper's title) of a mysterious "Othertime," and they culminate in an equally mystifying "exchange" between the inventor's assistant (Scudamour, out of Spenser's *Faerie Queene*) and his Othertime double. In chapter 5, the scene shifts to Scudamour's adventures in the "alien" world, where we remain until the manuscript breaks off abruptly in the midst of chapter 7. As in *Out of the Silent Planet*, Lewis's point of departure is the trail-blazing fiction of H. G. Wells. Echoing the opening scene of Wells's *The Time Machine*, the story begins with a discussion of time travel that includes the inventor Orfieu, Scudamour, and three guests from the Space Trilogy—Ransom, MacPhee (not yet the official skeptic), and the narrator identified as Lewis. Orfieu dismisses the Wellsian premise of a "time flying-machine" (*DT* 19): it is illogical to assume that the human body can transport itself to a past or future state in which its own matter would be distributed elsewhere. He then shifts to the faculty of recollection and reveals that as a result of his isolation of "the Z substance" (23)—a reference to recent excitement over the neurotransmitter "substance P"—he has designed a "chronoscope" that enhances "time-perception" just as the telescope extends the natural apparatus of sight. But the fact that Orfieu's contraption has a material basis in human physiology is less significant than his attempt to reorient time travel from physical to mental processes—memory, cognition, and imagination—while eschewing any affiliation with the "mystical" (20).

Orfieu's discussion of memory is informed by two early twentieth-century books that had caused quite a stir in intellectual circles. The first, entitled *An Adventure* (1911) by C. A. E. Moberly and E. F. Jourdain, is the documentary account of an excursion to Versailles by a pair of respected Oxford educators, who were walking through the gardens behind the palace when they suddenly beheld "a whole scene from a part of the past long before their birth" (21). The second,

J. W. Dunne's *An Experiment with Time* (1927), demonstrates our capacity to "remember" not only past but also future events. Dunne uses his own dreams as the main source of evidence, but assuming the stance of a strictly objective investigator, he lays out an experimental procedure for testing his claims, and as a military officer, engineer, and innovative aeronautical designer, he possessed a level of credibility that tended to put the skeptics on the defensive. Dunne's attempt to couch his hypothesis in a theory that employs the fourth, fifth, and higher dimensions—so that successive moments in a lower dimension appear as simultaneous to an observer in a higher dimension—seemed only to heighten his authority, at least among those who were ready to believe. This remarkably influential book, which provided an ostensibly scientific explanation of occult phenomena, encouraged various kinds of literary experimentation with narratives that transcended the common-sense image of time. It influenced many writers of the period, including E. R. Eddison, James Hilton, J. B. Priestley, and J. R. R. Tolkien (see Flieger [1997] and the review of Dunne by J. L. Borges [1940]). For Lewis, who was also experimenting with nonlinear notions of time, Dunne's book offered a means of replacing Wells's purely mechanical "time flying-machine" with a device more closely related to the operations of the mind and a conception of time travel that strikes a better balance between physical and psychological processes. Or as the reflective Ransom observes, it is "the fact of having minds" that function in a certain way which "puts us into time" (*DT* 23).

In the next few chapters (2–4), we are introduced to Othertime and follow Orfieu and his colleagues as they try to comprehend the whereabouts (or *when*abouts) of this strange new world. The chronoscope lights on an eerie chamber decorated throughout with images composed of swarms of identical sub-images, such as the floral pattern made up of individual flowers "repeated till the mind reeled" (30). The import of these designs is evident in the "idol" consisting of innumerable human bodies and culminating in "a single large head . . . the communal head of all those figures" (31). Sitting in this chamber of the "dark tower" is a corpse-like "Stingingman" who transforms what appear to be ordinary human beings into goose-stepping automatons, reminiscent of the silent drones that populate the totalitarian dystopia of Joseph O'Neill's *Land under England* (1935). Our five observers are appropriately repulsed by this scene; the one exception is the new arrival Knellie, an aging aesthete whose attraction to Othertime speaks to the paradoxical kinship, explored by Thomas Mann and other writers of the time, between the "complete moral freedom" (52) of a detached and decadent aestheticism and the contemptuous violation of time-honored ethical standards in modern totalitarian regimes. In this sense the alien world seems to represent what our own world is in danger of becoming.

As Orfieu and his colleagues behold the spectacle of human degradation, they remain perplexed over the relationship between Othertime and our own time. The narrator wonders whether it is past or future, while Ransom seems convinced that the chronoscope is peering into Hell. But when Scudamour sees his own "double" replacing the Stingingman, the group begins to suspect that they have opened a door to "something going on alongside the ordinary world and all mixed up with it" (48). It now becomes clear that we are not witnessing a form of linear time travel in the manner of Wells's *The Time Machine;* nor are we peering into the transcendent spiritual or higher dimensional world that appears in Wells's earlier novel, *The Wonderful Visit* (1895). Instead, we are making contact with what appears to be a parallel or alternative universe that bears an as-yet undetermined connection to our own. Wells himself had broached this idea in *The Wonderful Visit,* where the descent of an Angel from the Fourth Dimension prompts his terrestrial host to speculate that "there may be any number of three-dimensional universes packed side by side, and all dimly dreaming of one another. There may be world upon world, universe upon universe" (26). It took several decades, but stories of this sort began to appear in the 1930s, when British authors such as Stapledon were considering the proliferation of simultaneous universes, and various American pulp writers—Murray Leinster, David R. Daniels, C. L. Moore, W. Sell, and Jack Williamson among others—were expanding beyond the linear conception of time travel to tales that involve alternate time-tracks and parallel worlds (see Nahin 1993, *Time Machines,* for a comprehensive survey).

Wells's seminal short story, "The Crystal Egg" (1897), anticipates yet another aspect of "The Dark Tower." Early in the story, Orfieu and his associates begin to suspect that crossworld surveillance is running in both directions, and gradually it becomes evident that the Othertimers are not only examining us but constructing replicas of artifacts in our world, including the "dark tower" itself, which is identified as a copy of the new Cambridge library. The interaction between the two worlds takes a giant step forward when Scudamour, seeing his Othertime "double" prepare to sting the likeness of his own fiancée, Camilla Bembridge, somehow manages to leap through the chronoscope while his sinister counterpart ends up on the loose in our own world. As contrived as this "exchange" may seem, the existence of Othertime doubles indicates that these parallel worlds are intimately if inexplicably tied to each other. Moreover, the introduction of a love motif explicitly echoing the confusions of identity in Spenser's epic—Hooper tells us that Camilla's surname was originally Ammeret, recalling Scudamour's lover in *The Faerie Queene*—adds emotional weight to what might otherwise be a merely mechanical exchange between worlds.

In the second section of the fragment (chapters 5–7), we fast forward to Scudamour's return and the account of his Othertime exploits. As a result of his intervention, Scudamour rescues the Othertime Camilla from his own Stingingman, whom he replaces as Lord of the Dark Tower. In his new role, Scudamour retains his terrestrial mind and character but feels the same impulses, including the urge to sting, as his Othertime "double." He also receives updates on the movements of an enemy force, the "White Riders," whom he regards as the potential salvation of this dreary and oppressive world. But the principal disclosures of this section take place in the Tower library, where Scudamour becomes acquainted with a world that has "specialized in the knowledge of time" (84) to the same degree that ours has been based on the "knowledge of space." There are hints of Bergson in this distinction, but Lewis cuts some new ground (more akin to Dunne than to Bergson) as his Othertimers begin to speculate on the possibility of multi-dimensional time. Just as our geometers progress from one spatial dimension to the next by constructing a new axis perpendicular to the existing one, so the Othertime chronometers have extrapolated from a one-dimensional time *line* to a two-dimensional *square* in which time may flow not only "backwards-forwards" along a horizontal axis but also "andwards and eckwards" along a vertical axis (86). Proceeding from Lewis's pet idea that images in myths and dreams may be glimpses of "realities which exist in a time closely adjacent" to one's own (88), Othertime researchers have begun to construct artifacts designed to replicate and thereby "attract" their other-dimensional counterparts. Reminiscent of Weston and his kind, they have also "sacrificed" children and prisoners in an attempt to produce "exchanges" between their world and ours. We are led to wonder if the Camilla whom Scudamour rescues in Othertime has been the victim of such an exchange, since she is far more appealing and humane than her disagreeable double in our own world. But the narrative breaks off before our suspicions can be confirmed.

The manuscript terminates in mid-sentence, but assuming that the disclosures in the library are reasonably accurate, we have sufficient information to construct a cogent explanation of the commerce between Othertime and our time. We may never know Lewis's plans for completing the story, but the plot has proceeded far enough to raise questions that we expect to have answered by the end. What happens to Scudamour between his lessons in the library and his return to our world? Will he join the White Riders and redeem this shabby totalitarian domain, which seems at once a "downwards" transposition of our own world and an ominous sign of what it might become? Will Orfieu or Ransom (as their names imply) enter into Othertime and participate in Scudamour's rescue or other events in the alien world? What sort of trouble will Scudamour's double stir up before he is returned to his own time, and how will the author resolve the issue of the two seemingly misplaced Camillas? In addition to questions of plot, we are still left wondering about the character of this multiverse and the relations between its different time-tracks. Are these two (or more) worlds entirely separate until they develop technologies of contact? If so, how do we explain the connection between the myths and dreams of one universe and the realities of another, or the uncanny presence of our own doubles, which suggests a bond between worlds more intimate than the apparatus of replica-construction and the body-swapping of lookalikes seem to indicate? Do these alternative worlds issue from a single transcendent source, or as Charles Williams's Lord Arglay speculates in *Many Dimensions,* do they arise from our own actions, so that "whenever a man made a choice, a real choice—whenever he definitely did one of two things he also did at the same moment the other and brought an entire new universe into being that he might do so" (53)? The reason our questions are never answered may lie in the conceptual uncertainties of the project itself. It may have been launched as an exercise in time travel, but like the five protagonists who leap from one hypothesis to the next, Lewis ends up experimenting with various ways of imagining the relations between alternative or parallel universes. As an exploration of temporal processes, *Perelandra* has far more to recommend it, and as a study of parallel worlds the result is often unsatisfying or confusing, especially in the conflation of temporal and spatial orientations and in the use of crudely mechanical means to represent a considerably more complex relationship between the disparate worlds. If Lewis has not yet arrived at the elegant cosmic design of *The Chronicles of Narnia,* this discarded fragment reveals some of the other possibilities he might have pursued, and it throws into relief the distinctive benefits of the road he later chose to take.

Appendix B: Table for Converting Page References to Chapter Numbers ～

Quotations from the Space Trilogy are from the Scribner trade paperbound editions published in the United States (2003). The page references are to those editions. The table below will enable readers using other editions to find the reference by chapter number.

Out of the Silent Planet

pp. 9–16: ch.1
pp. 17–22: ch.2
pp. 23–26: ch.3
pp. 27–31: ch.4
pp. 32–37: ch.5
pp. 38–41: ch.6
pp. 42–47: ch.7
pp. 48–51: ch.8
pp. 52–59: ch.9
pp. 60–65: ch.10
pp. 66–72: ch.11
pp. 73–77: ch.12
pp. 78–84: ch.13
pp. 85–90: ch.14
pp. 91–96: ch.15
pp. 97–103: ch.16
pp. 104–115: ch.17

pp. 116–123: ch.18
pp. 124–131: ch.19
pp. 132–140: ch.20
pp. 141–149: ch.21
pp. 150–152: ch.22
pp. 153–158: Postscript

Perelandra

pp. 9–18: ch.1
pp. 19–28: ch.2
pp. 29–39: ch.3
pp. 40–50: ch.4
pp. 51–61: ch.5
pp. 62–73: ch.6
pp. 74–84: ch.7
pp. 85–92: ch.8
pp. 93–106: ch.9
pp. 107–118: ch.10

Notes ∼

1. Of the many edifying studies of Lewis's fiction, Myers (1994) stands out for its emphasis on his debt to the intellectual, cultural, and literary developments of the early twentieth century. While her insightful readings of the Ransom novels differ from my own, they demonstrate the rewards of situating Lewis in the context of his own times. See also Stableford's (1985) sweeping survey of the distinctive and somewhat neglected British tradition of modern "scientific romance."

2. See Douglas (2007) on the prevalence and significance of this "ring composition" in world literature.

3. According to Lewis, David Lindsay is "the real father of my planet books" (*L* II, 630, 10/29/44). Although deploring his predecessor's "almost Satanic" spirituality and "laughably crude" style, Lewis writes that "from Lindsay I first learned what other planets in fiction are really good for: for *spiritual* adventures. Only they can satisfy the craving which sends our imaginations off the earth. Or putting it another way, in him I first saw the terrific results produced by the union of two kinds of fiction hitherto kept apart: the Novalis, Macdonald, James Stephens sort and the H. G. Wells, Jules Verne sort" (*L* II, 753, 1/4/47). Lewis turned to other sources for the actual plots of his two "interstellar romances": *Out of the Silent Planet* is a rewriting of Wells's *The First Men in the Moon* (1901), and *Perelandra* is a reconstruction of Milton's *Paradise Lost* and, in its pivotal temptation scenes, his *Paradise Regained*. The earthbound *That Hideous Strength* is deeply indebted to the fiction of Charles Williams.

4. It is worth quoting the entire passage: "What the Christian story does is not to instate on the Divine level a cruelty and wastefulness which have already disgusted us on the Natural, but to show us in God's act, working neither cruelly nor wastefully, the same principle which is in Nature also, though down there it works sometimes in one way and sometimes in the other. It illuminates the Natural scene by suggesting that a principle which at first looked meaningless may yet be derived from a principle which is good and fair, may indeed be a depraved and blurred copy of it—the pathological form which it would take in a *spoiled* Nature" (*M* 189–190).

5. In his other writings, Lewis often employs the notion of "up-grading" or extrapolating from a lower level to a higher one. The *locus classicus* may be found in his essay "Transposition" (*WG* 91–115), which assumes a three-level hierarchical ladder and focuses on (1) the modern tendency to reduce middle-level "human" (cp. Bergson's "vital") phenomena to lower-level "material" causation, and (2) the correspondences that enable us to glimpse beyond the "human" to the "divine" level. The origins of this idea lie in Plato and the longstanding neo-Platonic tradition with which Lewis was intimately acquainted, but the hierarchical division into three planes of being—the material (or "mechanistic"), the organic (or "vital"), and the spiritual (or "theological")—is a prominent feature of early twentieth-century Catholic responses to Bergson, who distinguishes sharply between the material and organic planes but virtually equates the organic with the spiritual (see p. 55). Students of Anglo-American modernism may be more familiar with the exposition of this critique in T. E. Hulme's posthumous *Speculations* (1924), which influenced T. S. Eliot and other like-minded intellectuals in the twenties and thirties. Lewis's three-tier hierarchy also draws on another modern source—the idea of four-dimensional space. In "Transposition" and elsewhere, he turns to Edwin Abbott's immensely influential *Flatland: A Romance of Many Dimensions* (1884) as a model for extrapolating beyond the (three-dimensional) world we inhabit to a higher dimension—"God's dimension" (*MC* 162)—of which the elements on the lower plane of our own existence may provide a certain degree of comprehension. On the sometimes startling results of the movement "upwards" and "downwards" (also conceived as "inwards" [Gk. "andwards"] and "outwards" [Gk. "eckwards"]), see Lewis's account of this transpositional process as it operates in the passage from our time-bound experience to our comprehension of the eternal

(*MC* 170, *M* 231); in the imputed "sublimation" of some of the all-too-human sentiments expressed in the Psalms (*RP* 112–116); in the transfiguration of our Old Nature into the New (*M,* chapter 16); and, picking up on a cardinal point in the theological works of Charles Williams, in the Athanasian formulation of the Incarnation as proceeding "'not by the conversion of the godhead into flesh, but by taking of (the) manhood into God'" (*RP* 116). It should be mentioned that Lewis is well aware that there are certain things which lie entirely beyond our grasp, and that certain matters which seem intractable at our level, such as the relationship between free will and predestination, may simply evaporate at a higher level in a manner that we can scarcely begin to fathom. Nevertheless, while he is sensitive to the apophatic discourse (or "negative theology" as it is now often called) that has weighed so heavily in the Christian mystical tradition, Lewis leans in the direction of the positive affirmation of Divine presence. In this respect, selected images and analogies may provide us with a glimpse of the transcendent as long as we remain cognizant of their snares and the limitations of their reach. See *Perelandra* (pp. 126–127, 186–187), *The Great Divorce* (chapters 13–14), and Downing (2005) on Lewis and the mystical tradition; and De Vries (1999) on the fascination with "negative theology" in the recent turn to the religious in Continental philosophy, especially in the works of Jacques Derrida.

6. The difference between the transfiguration of the material realm on Mars and the organic realm on Venus is evident in the physical description of the two planets as well as the celestial intelligences (Oyarsas) who preside over them. When the Oyarsas of Mars and Venus appear side by side at the end of *Perelandra,* they exhibit the traditional planetary distinction based on gender (masculine and feminine) and governing virtue (martial discipline and love), but they also bear the difference between the inorganic and the vital realms embodied by their respective planets: "The Oyarsa of Mars shone with cold and morning colours, a little metallic—pure, hard, and bracing. The Oyarsa of Venus glowed with a warm splendour, full of the suggestion of teeming vegetable life" (*P* 171). See Ward (2008) for a comprehensive discussion of the traditional "Seven Heavens" in *The Chronicles of Narnia* and Lewis's other works. My own "Why Wells Is from Mars, Bergson from Venus" (2008) lays out the case for a more modern reading of Lewis's Celestial Intelligences in the Space Trilogy.

7. According to Lewis, "the germ of *Perelandra* was simply the picture of the floating islands themselves, with no location, no story . . ." (*L* III, 162,

1/31/52). There is no reason to doubt that this image was the "germ" of the novel, but the picture of "floating islands" is insufficient to account for the extensive exploration of time and of the complexities of temporal experience that Lewis erected upon it. So are Milton's suggestive remarks about paradise as a progressive state in which "bodies may at last turn all to spirit, / Improved by tract of time, and winged ascend / Ethereal, as we, or may at choice / Here or in heavenly paradises dwell" (*Paradise Lost* V.497–500). See Hannay (1977) on the elaborate parallels between *Perelandra* and *Paradise Lost,* and Huttar (in Martin 2000) for a well-informed discussion of Milton's presence in Lewis's works, including some observations on *Perelandra* (177–179). Lewis is heavily indebted to Milton, but it is arguable that for Lewis's readers, the very focus on his great predecessor has directed attention away from the modern elements in his invented paradise.

8. Lewis's affection for the "discarded image" of traditional cosmology is apparent throughout his works, nowhere more so than in the epilogue to the volume of that title, where he declares "that the old Model delights me as I believe it delighted our ancestors. Few constructions of the imagination seem to me to have combined splendour, sobriety, and coherence in the same degree." It is important to remember that Lewis follows this well-known statement with the remark that for all its appeal, this Medieval Model "had a serious defect; it was not true" (*DI* 216). It should also be noted that in this late work Lewis is less concerned with the "truth" of the old Model, or that of the developmental model that replaced it, than he is with the manner and degree to which these relatively stable but impermanent paradigms shape the particular forms of knowledge and the process of inquiry in each successive epoch. As Peter Schakel points out (*Imagination and the Arts* 18), Lewis wrote these words around the same time that Thomas Kuhn was publishing his milestone work, *The Structure of Scientific Revolutions* (1962), which focused on the longstanding "paradigms" that govern scientific thought and on the conditions of their construction, perpetuation, and eventual transformation.

CHAPTER I

1. On the metaphysical and religious issues surrounding the surprisingly long history of the debate over the "plurality of worlds," see Crowe (1986),

Dick (1982, 1996), and Guthke (1983). Nicolson (1948) and Hillegas (1969) examine Lewis's particular debt to the interplanetary probes of the seventeenth and eighteenth centuries, which developed the ancient tradition of cosmic voyaging into extended accounts of extraterrestrial intelligence on the moon and other bodies in our own solar system. H. G. Wells begins *The War of the Worlds* with an epigraph from Kepler, whose *Somnium, Sive Astronomia Lunaris, Joannis Kepleri* (1634; see Lear, 1965) represents this new line of speculation, which also includes some highly influential books by John Wilkins (1638), Henry More (1647), and, near the end of the seventeenth century, Fontenelle (1686), Huygens (1698), and many others. An intriguing early work by Kant, *Universal Natural History and Theory of the Heavens* (1755), attests to the survival of this tradition many decades later. See Markley (2005) on the complex history of scientific controversies and literary representations of Mars in the last hundred years.

2. In his late post-Sputnik essays on extraterrestrial intelligence, Lewis explains that the shared "rationality" with which he is concerned is "not merely the faculty to abstract and calculate, but the apprehension of values, the power to mean by 'good' something more than 'good for me' or even 'good for my species.' If instead of asking, 'Have they rational souls?' you prefer to ask, 'Are they spiritual animals?' I think we shall both mean pretty much the same. . . . It is spiritual, not biological, kinship that counts" ("Religion and Rocketry" *WLN* 85, 91; see also "The Seeing Eye" *CR* 167–176 and "Unreal Estates" *OS* 143–153). In these later writings, Lewis bases his vision of a prospective encounter with rational aliens on the disheartening history of relations within our own species: "They [our ambassadors to new worlds] will do as their kind has always done. What that will be if they meet things weaker than themselves, the black man and the red man can tell. . . . Against them we shall, if we can, commit all the crimes we have already committed against creatures certainly human but differing from us in features and pigmentation" ("Religion and Rocketry" *WLN* 89–90). Moreover, here on earth our perpetual intraspecies strife cannot be separated from our relations to other species, since we readily justify our crimes against other human beings by subordinating them to the status of beasts. With respect to these other species, Lewis retains the traditional criteria of rationality and speech to distinguish human and nonhuman animals, but he holds out the possibility that other animal species may possess a "rational

soul," and, if so, we would have "no more right to enslave them than to enslave our fellow-men" ("The Seeing Eye" *CR* 174). In general, Lewis's anthropocentrism is tempered by his respect for the sanctity and perhaps the final redemption of every living thing, his recognition of the limits and responsibilities associated with divinely appointed stewardship, and his realization that, if "spiritual animals" are distinguished by their capacity to acknowledge something beyond "natural ends" ("Religion and Rocketry" *WLN* 85), they are also the only animals with a demonstrated history of pursuing ends that violate and corrupt the natural order. In the conclusion of this chapter (section VII), we will return to Lewis's later reflections on interplanetary travel, which place more emphasis on the relations between extraterrestrial, human, and animal intelligences than his more commonly cited letters of the thirties and forties.

3. Lewis predates the passionate preoccupation with "the Other" in contemporary discourse, but his own use of the term proceeds from the same post-Hegelian tradition that lies behind its widespread currency in recent philosophy, literature, and social science. Ever alert to our tendency to reduce, embellish, or otherwise distort objects of perception to suit our own purposes, Lewis uses "other" and "otherness" as substantives primarily (1) to call attention to the distinctive and singular reality of another person (e.g., "H. [Lewis's deceased wife] rushes upon my mind in her full reality, her otherness" [*GO* 55]); (2) to describe a domain or imaginary "world" that stands apart from and is irreducible to the familiar horizons of our own world; or (3) in the manner of Rudolf Otto's modern reassertion of the Divine as "wholly Other" (*The Idea of the Holy* 25), to refer to the separateness, transcendence, and unfathomable mystery of God.

4. On Lewis's relationship to Wells, see Filmer (1987), Lake (1992), Myers (1994), and Peters (1998). Myers provides a detailed account of the extensive structural similarities between *Out of the Silent Planet* and *The First Men on the Moon.* Wells's later novel, *Men Like Gods* (1923), which transports an unruly cohort of modern Englishmen into a future utopian world, also bears comparison to *Out of the Silent Planet,* particularly in Wells's account of the conflict between the haughty imperialism of the English and the civilized life of our rational descendants, who curb the aggression of the intruders and ultimately dispatch them back to their own savage century.

5. See Brantlinger (1988) and Wilt (1981) on the anxiety over the long-term consequences of imperial dominion as it appears in the fiction of Wells,
H. Rider Haggard, Bram Stoker, and other popular turn-of-the-century writers.

6. Lewis does not deny the "struggle for existence" in the natural world, nor
those other aspects of nature that seem to contradict the Christian doctrine
of the essential goodness of the creation. Instead, he argues on empirical
grounds that the modern view is one-sided, and on other grounds that the
natural order, which from our perspective often seems indifferent or cruel,
may still reflect a higher principle of "which is good and fair" (*M* 190).

7. In these opening chapters, Lewis employs the ancient themes of hospitality
to strangers and sacrificial violence to undermine Western pretensions to
superiority over "primitive" peoples. In the deceitful semblance of hospitality
toward Ransom, Lewis ties modern violence to archaic practices that speak
to our age-old suspicions and hostility toward the outsider. With respect to
sacrifice, Lewis relates modern rationalizations for discarding other living
beings in the name of progress to the primordial need for rituals of violence
to deflect what appears to be the ever-present threat from powers beyond our
control. (Weston will later acknowledge that his principal aim, which may
require the sacrifice of any "lower forms of life" [136] that impede its realization, is to gain control of the basic conditions of existence—to "make man
live all the time" [138] by overcoming death itself.)

8. By the 1930s, the high tide of "gun and gospel" imperialism had long since
passed. But if imperial ideology was on the defensive, the vast British Empire
was still intact, and many of the older assumptions and attitudes survived
well into the mid-twentieth century. A distinguished array of interwar authors, including E. M. Forster, George Orwell, Evelyn Waugh, and Graham
Greene, precedes Lewis in attacking the heritage and enduring realities of
Empire. Recalling his early experience of English public schools, Lewis
maintains that "I hated whatever I knew or imagined of the British Empire"
(*SJ* 173). Although he came from a prosperous line of Ulster Anglicans and
spent much of his life in Oxford, Lewis continued to regard himself as Irish
rather than English and shared the age-old Celtic resentment of the Saxon
oppressor.

9. In a number of essays, Lewis treats Darwinian theory as a symptom rather
than the cause of the developmental paradigm: "The clearest and finest
poetical expressions of the Myth come before the *Origin of Species* was

published (1859) and long before it had established itself as scientific ortho-doxy" ("Funeral of a Great Myth" *CR* 83). At the same time, he claims that, irrespective of its affiliations to earlier expressions of the Myth, the theory of biological evolution should be taken seriously and tested as a "genuine scientific hypothesis" (83). His most extensive account of this position appears in "Is Theology Poetry?" (*WG* 116–140). But if he respects evolutionary biology as a "scientific hypothesis," Lewis is a harsh critic of the evolutionary assumptions of nineteenth-century anthropology. See Stocking (1987) on the formation of evolutionary anthropology (which also precedes the appearance of Darwin's work) and its ties to imperial ideology in the second half of the nineteenth century. See also his follow-up study (1995) on the breakdown of the evolutionary paradigm and the transformation of British anthropology in the twenties and thirties. To a certain extent, the situation of the three species on Malacandra mirrors the new anthropological paradigm (which has itself come under fire in recent years) with its respect for the integrity and coherence of each of the distinctive cultures that constitute the human "family."

10. As established by Darwin's cousin Francis Galton (1822–1911), the new science of eugenics held out the promise of systematic improvement of the species through conscious management of the reproductive process. The history of the eugenics movement has been well documented in recent years (see Barkan [1992] and Kevles [1985] for comprehensive studies; Jones [1980] for the British movement; Black [2003], Carlson [2001], Currell [2006], and Stern [2005] for the rapidly expanding literature devoted to the United States). In the United States, twenty-four states passed legislation permitting involuntary sterilization of the mentally retarded. By the time the practice became discredited in the 1940s, tens of thousands of Americans had been sterilized. It is significant that the debate over eugenics at first cut across the usual ideological divisions, with advocates and adversaries on either side of the political spectrum. The movement was perpetually tainted by charges of class snobbery and racism, but prior to the 1930s, when eugenics became ever more closely associated with Nazi excesses (see Burleigh [2000], Proctor [1988], and Weikert [2004]), progressives such as Haldane (see his *Dædalus* [1924]) often promoted their own ambitious programs for biological improvement of the species. Among the earliest and most outspoken opponents of eugenics were Catholics such as G. K. Chesterton, whose *Eugenics and*

Other Evils (1922) is often considered the first sustained critique of the movement. In the diary he kept during the twenties, Lewis refers to the popular topic of eugenics on several occasions, and his entry for June 13, 1926, indicates that he was reading Chesterton's book (*AMR* 214; see also 149, 153, 163, 401, 412). Lewis does not abandon the problem of eugenics after the opening incident of *Out of the Silent Planet*. As a major component of twentieth-century "Westonism," it remains a significant undercurrent of the first two novels and returns as a primary issue in *That Hideous Strength*. Needless to say, in the age of genetic engineering eugenics is a major issue once again. See Habermas (2003) for one recent sounding that employs arguments reminiscent of Lewis's reflections in the *The Abolition of Man*. For some of the more prominent critiques of racism during the thirties, see Voegelin (1933), Huxley and Haddon (1936), and Barzun (1938).

11. Hynes (1976) traces the conflict between uneasy protagonists and powerful aggressors in the major poets of the thirties, including W. H. Auden, C. Day Lewis, Louis MacNeice, and a large supporting cast. Many of their longer poems and plays involve symbolic journeys beyond the familiar frontiers of an enervated society, and their typical protagonist is preoccupied with his own fears and the discipline required to master them. An especially interesting case is Auden's play *The Ascent of F6* (1937; in Auden, *Complete Works,* 1988), whose hero—an introspective scholar named Ransom!—is drawn into the dangerous world of imperial rivalry when he is asked to lead an expedition up an unscaled peak on the border between two colonies controlled by rival powers. Hynes identifies a similar pattern in the proliferation of travel books that exhibit the characteristic thirties' concern with courage and heroic action in unfamiliar, threatening, or openly violent conditions. See Cunningham (1988) for a more recent and comprehensive overview that touches on many of these issues, Schweizer (2001) on travel writing in the thirties, and Hughes (1966) on the similar concern with heroism in French writers of this period.

12. See "The Conditions for a Just War" (*GD* 325–327), originally a letter in response to E. L. Mascall's "The Christian and the Next War" (1939). Lewis's most fully developed statement on pacifism, "Why I Am Not a Pacifist" (*WG* 64–90), is a posthumously published address apparently delivered to an Oxford pacifist society in 1940.

13. One of the detrimental effects of this vision of the "heavens" is that it tends to project the reader (especially one familiar with the author's reputation)

too far ahead of Ransom. To the extent that we regard Ransom's subsequent misprisions on Malacandra merely as residual effects of his initial Wellsian illusions, we lose sight of the striking accuracy of his perceptions and the cogency of his often erroneous conjectures, conditioned as they are by his own terrestrial experience. By ignoring the step-by-step process of Ransom's reorientation, we also miss the insights generated along the way by the tension between his slowly altering perspective and the realities of the new world he is gradually coming to understand. Time and again, it is through Ransom's judicious *misconceptions* about the relations among the three rational species that Lewis explores the problematic divisions within our own species and our relations to the rest of the animal kingdom. Consider, for instance, the moment when the mammalian *hrossa* first inform Ransom of the existence of other rational species, including the frog-like *pfifltriggi*. At one level, Ransom's silent conjecture that "apparently, three distinct species had *reached* rationality" (70; my italics) reflects the limitations of the evolutionary perspective he has transported to Mars. At another level, this inference prompts us to reconsider the origins and development of the species on our own planet, whether from the religious vantage point of a creation that has been ruptured by human transgression or from a naturalistic perspective that permits us to imagine an evolutionary process that might have turned out otherwise.

14. In *Animals and Why They Matter* (1984), philosopher Mary Midgley offers some intriguing thoughts on the tension between exclusivity and openness in human societies. Despite the tendency to establish our identity by exclusion of others, human communities are selectively permeable. Many societies are receptive to some degree of heterogeneity, and members of different groups can intermingle or live peacefully in close proximity, however limited and precarious these arrangements have proven to be. From an anthropological perspective, it is also notable that our societies are selectively open to other species. We not only seek the company of certain beasts but also identify with their situation and develop relationships of mutual affection. Midgley has read Lewis's novel and commends him for reconciling these opposing tendencies through his portrayal of rational species that live separately among their own kind but respect the equality, and occasionally enjoy the company, of other rational species. From a more radical contemporary perspective that extols the migratory and hybrid, Lewis's vision may seem rather

retrograde, but Midgley, who is no friend of sectarianism, recognizes and urges acceptance of the widespread desire to live among one's own.

15. Ransom's pseudo-explanation that "he had come out of the sky" (*OSP* 68) also echoes the encounters between white adventurers and native tribesmen in Haggard's *King Solomon's Mines* (1885) and other imperial adventure fiction of the late nineteenth and early twentieth centuries.

16. The anti-imperial subtext of Gulliver's last voyage comes to the fore when he contemplates the futility of any European attempt to colonize the seemingly vulnerable Houyhnhnms, hoping instead that the latter "were in a Capacity of Disposition to send a sufficient Number of their Inhabitants for civilizing *Europe;* by teaching us the first Principles of Honour, Justice, Truth, Temperance, publick Spirit, Fortitude, Chastity, Friendship, Benevolence, and Fidelity." Lewis, like Swift, uses the encounter with other rational species for the double purpose of satirizing the condition of our own species and attacking Western presumptions to the right of dominion over "idolatrous and barbarous People" (Swift, *Gulliver's Travels* 278). See Hawes (2004) on this aspect of Swiftean satire and Hodgkins (2002) on the contributions of Swift and Lewis to a longstanding Protestant tradition of anti-imperial protest.

17. The hunting scene also begins to reveal the distinctive symmetry of the book's twenty-two chapters—the same structure of a nucleus surrounded by a series of successive frames that Lewis would employ in *Perelandra* and *That Hideous Strength.* See the figures on pages 28, 66, and 98.

18. See Thiébaux (1974) and Berry (2001) on the significance of the hunt, and the countercurrent of ethical reservations regarding the hunt, in medieval and Renaissance literature.

19. Scholars have noted the correspondences between the three Martian species and the professions of the three earthlings on their planet. The contemplative *sorns,* poetic *hrossa,* and artisanal *pfifltriggi,* which represent in turn the intellectual, aesthetic, and practical spheres, have their respective counterparts in the physicist Weston, the philologist Ransom, and the businessman Devine. In this distribution of functions, the aesthetic realm appears to occupy the middle ground between the intellectual and the practical. Ransom is an intellectual, but language is his specialty and he is still most comfortable with the sociable and poetic *hrossa.* For their parts, Weston and Devine are situated at opposite ends of the spectrum, one representing the perversion of the intellect and the other the misuse of practical enterprise. Given

these correspondences between earthlings and Martians, we should not forget that unlike the former, who are a single rational species distinguishable by function, the latter are actually three different species—corresponding roughly to humans, other mammals, and amphibians, respectively—who are united by the shared faculty of reason. To a considerable extent, it is the tension between the functional similarities and the biological differences of the two planetary conditions that generates the complexity of the novel.

20. Jacques Derrida (2008) also plays on Descartes' formulation in "L'Animal que donc je suis (à suivre)" ["The Animal That Therefore I Am (More to Follow)"], one of several probing reflections on the problematic boundary between humans and other animals. See also his "And Say the Animal Responded," and Wolfe (*Animal Rites*, 2003; *Zoontologies*, 2003) and Lawlor (2007) on Derrida and animality.

21. Lewis would return to the problem of modern gnosticism—and the double estrangement between mind and body, man and beast—in *That Hideous Strength*, and his lifelong fascination with talking beasts would come to full fruition in *The Chronicles of Narnia* (1950–1956). Lewis's most refined discussion of animal suffering appears in the last chapter of *The Problem of Pain* (1940). See Laurent (1993) and Myers (1998) on his discussions of animals and their plight in the modern world. From a contemporary "post-human" perspective, Lewis's criterion for distinguishing human from nonhuman animals—"the charm of speech and reason" (*OSP* 59)—perpetuates the traditional anthropocentric claim to superiority over the other species. For recent developments in animal discourse, see the collections by Wolfe (*Zoontologies*, 2003) and Atterton and Calarco (2004), and for literary study along these lines, see Wolfe (*Animal Rites*, 2003), who follows Derrida and other contemporary theorists in challenging both traditional views and the residual anthropocentrism of the recent "animal rights" movement.

22. "'It is in her right,' said Weston, 'the right, or, if you will, the might of Life herself, that I am prepared without flinching to plant the flag of man on the soil of Malacandra: to march on, step by step, superseding, where necessary, the lower forms of life that we find'" (136). Ransom translates as follows: "'He says . . . that because of this it would *not* be a bent action—or else, he says, it *would* be a possible action—for him to kill you all and bring us here. He says he would feel no pity. He is saying

again that perhaps they would be able to keep moving from one world to another and wherever they came they would kill everyone'" (136). Ransom usually manages to find a "rational" equivalent to Weston's declarations, but occasionally after several attempts he concedes, "'I cannot say what he says'" (135).

23. The principal documents are two essays, "Religion and Rocketry" (*WLN* 83–92) and "The Seeing Eye" (*CR* 167–176), and the 1962 roundtable discussion with Brian Aldiss and Kingsley Amis published posthumously as "Unreal Estates" (*OS* 143–153).

24. As he puts it in "Unreal Estates," "Most of the earlier stories start from the opposite assumption that we, the human race, are in the right, and everything else is ogres. I may have done a little towards altering that, but the new point of view has come very much in. We've lost our confidence, so to speak" (*OS* 147). The new postwar "point of view" was launched in dramatic fashion with the appearance of Ray Bradbury's *The Martian Chronicles* (1950), which depicts the devastating if unintended effects of terrestrial (and specifically American) exploration of Mars. That the intruders are portrayed not as monstrous or hostile but as naïve and oblivious to the self-protective instincts of the Martians is merely the other side of the same temptation to assume that "we, the human race, are in the right" (*OTOW* 161).

25. See the remarkable discussion of the African "Pongos" in note "J" of the *Second Discourse* (203–13). In his probe of the accounts of ostensibly dispassionate observers, Rousseau uncovers the naïve ethnocentrism of early modern anthropologists by demonstrating that the very gestures and practices which Europeans regard as the actions of a nonhuman species might be readily explained as the behavior of normal human agents. "For the three or four hundred years since the inhabitants of Europe have inundated the other parts of the world, and continually published new collections of voyages and reports, I am convinced that we know no other men except the Europeans. . . . One does not open a book of voyages without finding descriptions of characters and customs. But one is completely amazed to see that these people who have described so many things have said only what everyone already knew, that they have known how to perceive, at the other end of the world, only what it was up to them to notice without leaving their street; and that those true features that distinguish nations and strike eyes made to see have almost always escaped theirs" (210–11).

CHAPTER 2

1. As mentioned in the introduction, the term "creative evolution" is associated specifically with the French philosopher Henri Bergson, whose *Creative Evolution* (1907) became one of the most influential books of the early twentieth century. The British fascination with a dynamic conception of nature is evident not only in the "emergent" evolutionists such as Alexander (1920) and Morgan (1923) but also in Alfred North Whitehead's later works—*Science and the Modern World* (1925) and *Process and Reality* (1929)—and in the more philosophical writings of well-known physicists such as Arthur Eddington, who included a chapter on "Becoming" in his influential book, *The Nature of the Physical World* (1928). Lewis may have been critical of "emergent" evolution, but he admired Samuel Alexander (*Space, Time and Deity,* 1920) and made frequent use of his distinction between "contemplation" and "enjoyment" in our apprehension of objects (see pp. 176–177 n. 9). And if he was no friend to the process theology inspired by Whitehead's *Science and the Modern World* and *Process and Reality,* Lewis nevertheless regarded him as "our greatest natural philosopher" (*M* 168) and endorsed his Bergson-indebted critique of the mechanistic assumptions of modern science. Peter Bowler's formidable study, *Reconciling Science and Religion* (2001), situates "emergent" evolution and related developments in the context of the broader struggle between religious and scientific viewpoints in early twentieth-century Britain. See Griffin (2001) on recent process theology, and Clayton (2004) and Cooper (2006) for different accounts (pro and con) of the contemporary turn to "panentheism," which (as distinct from "pantheism") affirms both the transcendence and the immanence of the divine.

2. The quotation is from William Blake's *The Marriage of Heaven and Hell:* "The reason Milton wrote in fetters when he wrote of Angels & God, and at liberty when of Devils & Hell, is because he was a true Poet and of the Devils party without knowing it" (1982, 35). In *A Defence of Poetry,* Percy Bysshe Shelley offered another representative remark of the Romantic view of Milton: "Nothing can exceed the energy and magnificence of the character of Satan as expressed in Paradise Lost. It is a mistake to suppose that he could ever have been intended for the popular personification of evil. . . . Milton's Devil as a moral being is as far superior to his God as one who perseveres in

some purpose which he has conceived to be excellent in spite of adversity and torture, is to one who in the cold security of undoubted triumph inflicts the most horrible revenge upon his enemy, not from any mistaken notion of inducing him to repent of a perseverance in enmity, but with the alleged design of exasperating him to deserve new torments" (2002, 498).

3. There are many expository and critical studies of Bergson, a fair portion of them from the period of his enormous fame in the first few decades of the century. (See Grogin [1988], Bowler [2001]), and Quirk [1990] on Bergson's reception and the religious issues at stake in his work in France, Britain, and the United States, respectively.) Since the eclipse of his reputation in the middle third of the century, Bergson has been rehabilitated primarily through the efforts of Gilles Deleuze, and as a precursor of the ongoing shift "from the physical world to the biological universe" (Dick, *Plurality of Worlds* 10), he is again receiving attention as an original and significant voice in modern philosophy (see Ansell-Pearson [2002], Grosz [2004], Guerlac [2006], Lawlor [2006], and Mullarkey [1999]). On Bergson and the double character of late nineteenth- and early twentieth-century vitalism, see my essay in Burwick and Douglass (1992). Other essays in the volume explore various facets of the vitalist controversy from the eighteenth century to the present.

4. The main autobiographical account appears in *Surprised by Joy* (198, 204, 211). In June 1920, Lewis mentions that he is reading Bergson in a letter to Arthur Greeves (*L* I, 494; 6/19/20). His diary entry for September 17, 1923, states that he is "re-reading" *Creative Evolution*. The diary also records his reading of *Mind-Energy* (*L'Énergie spirituelle,* a collection of essays published in 1919) in January 1924 and *Matter and Memory* in February 1925 (*AMR* 269, 285, 349). Other references to Bergson appear throughout his later works.

5. In a discussion of modern "scientific cosmology," Lewis states that "the Bergsonian critique of orthodox Darwinism is not easy to answer" ("Is Theology Poetry?" *WG* 136). Of the various formulations of creative evolution, "the wittiest expositions of it come in the works of Bernard Shaw, but the most profound ones in those of Bergson" (*MC* 26).

6. In *A Preface to 'Paradise Lost,'* Lewis compares the Greek sense of time as "mere flux" to the Virgilian view of time as a developing and irreversible process: "But Virgil uses something more subtle than mere *length* of time.

Our life has bends as well as extension: moments at which we realize that we have just turned some great corner, and that everything, for better or worse, will always henceforth be different" (36). Milton is more akin to Virgil than Homer in recording "a real, irreversible, unrepeatable process in the history of the universe" (133). A few passages in *Paradise Lost* suggest that Milton regarded the Edenic state as progressive rather than static. One of them appears in the epigraph to this chapter, which records a moment prior to the Fall when Raphael tells Adam that "Your bodies may at last turn all to spirit, / Improved by tract of time, and winged ascend / Ethereal, as we, or may at choice / Here or in heavenly paradises dwell" (V.497–500). (See also *Paradise Lost* VII.154–161 and Lewis's *PPL* 68.)

7. In this and other sections of the text, readers may be struck by the similarities between Lewis and existentialist philosophers such as Heidegger, Jaspers, Marcel, and especially Sartre (whose *Being and Nothingness* also appeared in 1943). Although Lewis seems to have struggled with the little Sartre that he read, the similarities are not entirely accidental. For one thing, Bergson's reformulation of the concept of time and its relationship to human freedom anticipated and influenced many of the philosophers associated with existentialism, particularly in France. Until quite recently, most accounts of this movement followed the lead of Sartre and his contemporaries in excluding Bergson from the canonical list of seminal figures, which typically includes Kierkegaard, Nietzsche, Husserl, and Heidegger among others. See Guerlac (1997) on this problematic dismissal of Bergson by French philosophers of the succeeding generation.

8. In this chapter, Weston uses the expression "emergent evolution." Later on, Ransom refers to Weston's doctrine as "creative evolution" (*P* 104). Here and elsewhere, Lewis tends to use "emergent evolution," "creative evolution," and "Life-Force philosophy" interchangeably. The term *nisus* (80), which Weston uses to describe the tendency of creation toward higher levels of development, appears in Samuel Alexander's *Space, Time and Deity* (1920).

9. The difference between experiencing life and "stepping out of life into the Alongside" is closely related to Samuel Alexander's distinction between "contemplation" and "enjoyment" (*Space, Time and Deity* 12–13), which Lewis regarded as "an indispensable tool of thought" (*SJ* 218). Whereas in "contemplation" we are attending directly to the object of thought, in "enjoyment" we attend to our mental apprehension of the object rather

than attending to the object itself. According to Lewis, these are "distinct and incompatible" activities of mind: "The surest means of disarming an anger or a lust was to turn your attention from the girl or the insult and start examining the passion itself. The surest way of spoiling a pleasure was to start examining your satisfaction" (218). Moreover, in the process of disrupting direct attention to the object, the shift from "contemplation" to introspective "enjoyment" also distorts the object so that what we "enjoy" is the "mere sediment or track or by-product" of what we "contemplate" (219). For another variation on Alexander's distinction, see Lewis's "Meditation in a Toolshed" (*GID* 212–215).

10. The regression from the vital to the mechanistic is a significant motif in Bergson's works. In *Time and Free Will* (1889), he maintains that in our more superficial states we are less like "vital" beings who are free and constantly developing and more like "mechanical" entities that are determined and predictable. His well-known account of laughter ("Laughter" [Le Rire], 1901) is based on the same principle: laughter is produced when we see human beings lapse into behavior we associate with the repetitive character of a machine (or at least the machine as conceived prior to the cybernetic revolution). There is little to laugh about in Ransom's encounter with the Un-man, but the latter's chillingly "external" and repetitive behavior displays the telltale signs of the descent from the vital to the mechanistic.

11. Chapter 11 also begins to reveal the structural symmetry of the novel's seventeen chapters (see the figure on page 66).

12. When Ransom first raises the possibility of physical combat (*P*, chapter 2), he refers to the exigencies of "our little war here on earth" and tells the astounded narrator (identified as Lewis), "'Now your idea that ordinary people will never have to meet the Dark Eldila in any form except a psychological or moral form—as temptations or the like—is simply an idea that held good for a certain phase of the cosmic war'" (22). Lewis is emphasizing the perpetual novelty of Maleldil's actions, but he also had other reasons for this recourse to physical violence. Like many of his compatriots, Lewis looked back on his nation's reluctance to use force against Nazi Germany as the fatal error of the 1930s. As we saw in the previous chapter, he was opposed to the pacifist movement, which was especially strong among religious groups, and despite his horror at the prospect of another global conflict, he publicly defended the traditional doctrine of the "just war."

Needless to say, the donnish manner of Ransom's speech in chapter 2 is quite different from the voice of personal anguish when the prospect of direct physical combat with the Evil One turns from abstract possibility to imminent reality.

13. It is significant that when Lewis's characters are facing difficult or ostensibly impossible decisions, or struggling to uphold prior resolutions, the language often shifts from the prevailing emphasis on novelty and spontaneity to constancy and repetition. In this respect, Lewis is reminiscent of Kierkegaard in *Fear and Trembling* and *Repetition*, though Lewis differs in assigning a more central role to rationality in the process of making and sustaining one's decisions. On the latter point, recall the narrator's "impulse to retreat" from his mission to Ransom's cottage and his reliance on "the rational part of my mind" (*P* 13) to maintain his resolution to proceed. On Lewis's other affinities to existentialist philosophy, see note 8.

14. Ironically, the Un-man assumes that this conflict will be a repetition of terrestrial events epitomized by Christ's agony on the Cross: "'And you think, little one,'" it says to Ransom, "'that you can fight with me? You think He will help you, perhaps? . . . They all think He's going to help them—till they come to their senses screaming recantations too late in the middle of the fire, mouldering in concentration camps, writhing under saws, jibbering in madhouses, or nailed on to crosses. Could He help Himself?. . . . *Eloi, Eloi, lama sabachthani*'" (130).

15. Weston presses his point with the claim that contemporary physics is beginning to uncover a universe that subverts the very notion of rationality itself: "'Haven't you seen the real meaning of all this modern stuff about the dangers of extrapolation and bent space and the indeterminacy of the atom. . . . the knowledge that reality is neither rational nor consistent nor anything else. In a sense you might say it isn't there'" (144). Ransom disputes some of these remarks, but to the extent that modern physics has taught him "that the account a man gives of the universe, or of any other building, depends very much on where he is standing" (144), the new science seems only to fuel the suspicion that his God cannot survive the decentering of man. Lewis himself was usually quite favorably disposed to contemporary developments in physics and mathematics, which called into question the "one-floor reality" (*M* 251) of scientific naturalism prior to the revolution of the early twentieth century (see note 19).

16. Note that Ransom's dismay over the decentering of humankind, the earth, and Christ's incarnation are not alleviated but rather aggravated by the knowledge that God has created life on planets other than our own. On the metaphysical and religious issues raised by the long debate over the "plurality of worlds," see Crowe (1986), Dick (1982, 1996), and Guthke (1983).

17. See Nicholas Cusanus, *De Docta Ignorantia* [*Of Learned Ignorance*] (1440). Departing from the hierarchically ordered cosmology of his predecessors, Nicholas not only foreshadows Copernicus by dislodging the earth from its stationary and central (if lowly) position but also maintains that the transcendent God, who alone may be conceived as the center, is also equally close to all points in the universe and inhabits them fully and without mediation. In his own context, Nicholas was responding in part to the division between the realms of nature and grace that had arisen in late medieval scholasticism. But insofar as he anticipates the metaphysical questions attendant upon the Copernican system and the scientific revolution of the seventeenth century, Nicholas offers a resolution to the problems that torment Ransom in the aftermath of his journey to the Underworld. Nicholas constructs a cosmic vision that at once repairs the late scholastic rift between God and the natural world and avoids the modern dissociation between subjective and objective realms that eventually developed out of it. On the philosophical and historical significance of Nicholas, see Cassirer (1926), Dupré (1993), and Koyré (1957). At the beginning of *English Literature in the Sixteenth Century* (1954), Lewis refers to Cusanus as "an early believer (for his own, metaphysical, reasons) in earth's movement" and then goes on to discuss the advent of scientific methodology and triumph of dualism: "By reducing Nature to her mathematical elements it substituted a mechanical for a genial or animistic conception of the universe. The world was emptied, first of her indwelling spirits, then of her occult sympathies and antipathies, finally of her colours, smells, and tastes. . . . The result was dualism rather than materialism. The mind, on whose ideal constructions the whole method depended, stood over against its object in ever sharper dissimilarity. Man with his new powers became rich like Midas but all that he touched had gone dead and cold" (3–4). See also Lewis's poems from the same period, "Cradle-Song Based on a Theme from Nicolas of Cusa" (1954; later named "Science-Fiction Cradlesong") and "On Another Theme from

Nicolas of Cusa" (1955; renamed as "On a Theme from Nicolas of Cusa"). Given the scarcity of references to Nicholas earlier in his career, it is difficult to determine whether or to what extent Lewis drew on him directly for the cosmology of the Hymn.

18. Lewis was intimately acquainted with Neoplatonic and other alternatives to the purely quantitative and mechanistic science that emerged in the seventeenth century. He was especially interested in the metaphysical debates between Descartes and Henry More (1614–1687), and though he thought Descartes was by far the greater philosopher, his portrayal of the *eldila* may owe something to More's argument (directed against Descartes' dissociation between spirit and matter) that spiritual beings such as the angels possess extension and therefore occupy space just like material bodies. The single footnote in *Perelandra* (18–19) is a playful discussion of this issue and also suggests that something akin to More's vision of a multitiered universe may be resurfacing in the "multi-dimensional space" projected by modern geometry (see note 19). In *The Abolition of Man* (1943), Lewis offers a more extensive analysis of the scientific revolution and concludes with an intriguing call for "a new Natural Philosophy" (78) that recovers what was lost in the process of reifying the natural universe. See Dickerson and O'Hara (2008) on Lewis's approach to the "re-enchantment of creation."

19. See Neuhouser (1996) on Lewis's appropriation of higher-dimensional geometry. Lewis like many of his contemporaries was introduced to these matters, and his thinking was certainly influenced, by Edwin Abbott's *Flatland: A Romance of Many Dimensions* (1884).

20. "One reason why many people find Creative Evolution so attractive is that it gives one much of the emotional comfort of believing in God and none of the less pleasant consequences. . . . All the thrills of religion and none of the cost. Is the Life-Force the greatest achievement of wishful thinking the world has yet seen?" (*MC* 27). In a related formulation, "The more modern form of nature religion would be the religion started, in a sense, by Bergson. . . . The nature religions simply affirm my natural desires" ("The Grand Miracle" *GD* 86).

CHAPTER 3

1. Lewis first came across Williams's work in 1936, when he read *The Place of the Lion* (1931) and wrote to the author, an editor at Oxford Univer-

sity Press in London, that it was "one of the major literary events of my life—comparable to my first discovery of George Macdonald, G. K. Chesterton, or Wm. Morris" (*L* II, 183, 3/11/36). By that point, Williams had published five of his seven novels: *War in Heaven* (1930), *Many Dimensions* (1931), *The Place of the Lion* (1931), *The Greater Trumps* (1932), and *Shadows of Ecstasy* (1933, though written prior to the others). Lewis read *Descent into Hell* (1937) soon after it appeared, and along with *The Place of the Lion*, it remained his favorite. When the Press moved its London office to Oxford after the outbreak of the war, Williams became a full-fledged member of the Inklings. His final novel, *All Hallows' Eve*, appeared in 1945, the year of his death. Lewis was also indebted to Williams's theological and critical works and to his Arthurian poems, *Taliessin through Logres* (1938) and *The Region of the Summer Stars* (1944), which play a role in *That Hideous Strength*. Hart attributes several elements of *That Hideous Strength* to Williams's influence: ". . . the realistic contemporary setting, the carefully drawn emotional and spiritual conflicts of an intellectual young husband and wife, the physical immanence of supernatural forces, the domesticated bear and the severed head, the prophetic dreams" (*Through the Open Door* 127). See Cavaliero (1983, 1995) and Spencer (1986, 1987) for studies of Williams's own debt to early twentieth-century "supernatural" (Cavaliero) or "fantastic" (Spencer) fiction.

2. The terminology is notoriously slippery, but for the purposes of this essay I borrow Glen Cavaliero's designation, "supernatural fiction," to refer to the two-century modern tradition that includes but extends well beyond authors whom we would ordinarily associate with the Gothic. Cavaliero's typological distinction between (1) the "preternatural," (2) the "paranormal," and (3) the "hermetic" (or supernatural proper) is valuable in identifying the specific features of the early twentieth-century subgroup represented by R. H. Benson, Evelyn Underhill, Arthur Machen, and Charles Williams, who in reaffirming a traditional Christian conception of the supernatural belong in the last of the three categories. I will also adopt Kathleen Spencer's use (1986, 1987) of Andrzej Zgorzelski's formal designation, "fantastic fiction" (as distinct from "fantasy"), to refer to works that "consist in the breaching of the internal laws which are initially assumed in the text to govern the fictional world," and therefore "build their fictional world as a *textual confrontation of two models of reality*" ("Is Science Fiction a Genre of Fantastic

Literature?" 298). For the most part, however, I will rely on the familiar if ill-defined notion of the Gothic, partly because I wish to highlight the manner in which Williams and Lewis sublimate or transfigure the specific tropes of the Gothic into their own kind of "supernatural" or "fantastic" fiction. On Lewis's formulation of a "third kind of book" wedged between "the classical novel" and "pure fantasy" ("The Novels of Charles Williams" *OS* 21), see footnote 4.

3. On the longstanding ties between Rosicrucianism and Gothic fiction, see Roberts's (1990) study of the quest for immortality in the "Rosicrucian novel," including William Godwin's *St. Leon* (1799); Percy Shelley's juvenile *St. Irvyne; or, The Rosicrucian* (1811); Mary Shelley's *Frankenstein* (1818); Robert Maturin's *Melmoth the Wanderer* (1820); and Edward Bulwer-Lytton's *Zanoni* (1842) and *A Strange Story* (1862). Cavaliero (1983, 1995) and Spencer (1986) are among those who explore the Gothic roots of Williams's fiction, while Lobdell (1996, 2003) focuses on the influence of that Gothic offshoot, the detective story, and has collected the many detective fiction reviews that Williams wrote between 1930 and 1935, the period in which he published five of his seven novels.

4. We should note the kinship between Gothic "terror" and the primal experience of supernatural "awe" and "dread" in Rudolf Otto's seminal work, *The Idea of the Holy* (1917), which Lewis discusses in his first apologetical work, *The Problem of Pain* (1940), and later listed as one of the ten books that most influenced his development (["Booklists. . ."] 1962). Otto's Gothic-sounding account of the Divine *mysterium tremendum* descends primarily from Kant's treatment of the sublime in *The Critique of Judgment*, and in this respect as well as others, *The Idea of the Holy* is not only tied historically to the intellectual milieu surrounding the birth of the Gothic but also bears a notable resemblance to the same transfiguration of the Gothic that appears in the fiction of Williams and Lewis.

5. The *locus classicus* of the Gothic "blend" of the probable and the marvelous is the preface to the second edition of Horace Walpole's *The Castle of Otranto* (1764; 2nd ed. 1765), by all accounts the inaugural work of what became a popular craze by the 1790s. According to Walpole, the novel was "an attempt to blend the two kinds of romance, the ancient and the modern. In the former all was imagination and improbability: in the latter. . . . a strict adherence to common life" (*The Castle of Otranto* 9). Lewis's principal

discussion of this generic compound appears in his 1949 radio broadcast, "The Novels of Charles Williams." His account of a "third kind of book" situated between "the classical novel" and "pure fantasy" encompasses not only Gothic tales such as *Dr. Jekyll and Mr. Hyde,* which "intrudes its strange horror upon surroundings studiously prosaic," but also a variety of other works, comic as well as tragic, all of which suppose "that this everyday world were, at some point, invaded by the marvellous" ("The Novels of Charles Williams" *OS* 22). In a formal sense, the "fairy tale" does not reside in this space between the naturalistic and the marvelous, but Lewis's fascination with the "realistic" manner in which these stories often begin (see the preface to *That Hideous Strength*), along with his recognition of the "*real* peasant suffering and crime" that underlies their often "sinister or harrowingly pathetic" (*L* II, 595; 12/20/43) plots, indicates why he might subtitle his own work "A Modern Fairy-Tale for Grown-Ups." It is important to emphasize this tension between the realistic and the supernatural since Lewis's fiction is often disparaged as escapist "high" fantasy that expresses "a longing to transcend or escape the human" (Jackson, *Fantasy* 156). Jackson, the author of a seminal effort to redefine modern "fantasy," may be correct in identifying Lewis with a type of fiction that fulfills "a desire for a 'better,' more complete, unified reality" (2). But the problematic character of *That Hideous Strength,* which features the often painful (and painstakingly rendered) transformation of its modern protagonists, should be exempted from the charge of avoiding "the difficulties of confrontation, that tension between the imaginary and the symbolic which is the crucial, problematic area dramatized in more radical fantasies" (*Fantasy* 156).

6. These conventions are also a prominent feature in Shakespeare's Ur-Gothic masterpiece, *Hamlet,* and it is interesting to note that in his well-known essay, "Hamlet: The Prince or the Poem?" (*SLE* 88–105), Lewis contends that the main interest of the play lies not in the enigma of the protagonist's character, as most modern critics maintain, but in the fact that he is haunted by a ghost. On the threshold of modernity, Shakespeare is exploring a "certain spiritual region" (101)—the liminal condition of "man—haunted man—man with his mind on the frontier of two worlds, man unable either quite to reject or quite to admit the supernatural" (102). On the Gothic germination of *That Hideous Strength,* see Lewis's early diary record of the dream and consequent "shocker play" (never written)

that anticipates a central strand of the novel: "a scientist discovering how to keep consciousness and some motor nerves alive in a corpse, at the same time arresting decay, so that you really had an immortal dead man. I dreamed that the horrible thing was sent to us—in a coffin of course—to take care of. . . . [O]n second thoughts I am not sure that the idea of the play did not originate in another dream I had some years ago—unless the whole thing comes from Edgar Allen Poe" (*AMR* 266–267, 9/12/23). Early scholarly studies of the Gothic, none of which seem to have come within Lewis's purview, include Birkhead (1921), Railo (1927), Tompkins (1932), and Summers (1938). Despite the significant contributions of Varma (1957), Fiedler (1960), Todorov (1970), and others, the Gothic retained its second-class status until the last two decades of the century when the pioneering studies of Punter (1980) and Jackson (1981), along with feminist interest in the "female" Gothic (see note 8), launched a vast wave of scholarly activity that has established the Gothic as an enduring modern tradition standing side by side, and significantly influencing, the canonical tradition of modern "realism." Among those I have found most fruitful for examining Lewis's engagement with the Gothic are the full-length studies by Botting (1996; a breathtaking overview), Castle (1995; on the eighteenth century), Cavaliero (1995; on "supernatural fiction"), Day (1985; Gothic as a parody of the romance mode), Frye (1957, 1976; on the romance mode itself), Jackson (1981; on reconceiving modern "fantasy"), Todorov (1970; on the structure of the "fantastic tale"), Varnado (1987; on the kinship to the religious *mysterium tremendum*), Williams (1995; on "male" vs. "female" Gothic plots), and the collections by Hogle (2002) and Punter (2000). On H. G. Wells's affiliations with the Gothic, see Dryden (2003) and Hurley (1996); for more general considerations of the influence of the Gothic on the development of modern science fiction, see Luckhurst (2005) and Richter (1996). To my knowledge, Mervyn Nicholson's brief but illuminating study, "Bram Stoker and C.S. Lewis: Dracula as a Source for *That Hideous Strength*," is the only existing consideration of Lewis and the Gothic that goes beyond a passing reference (1993; see note 15). See Nelson (2000) on Lewis's reading of other "weird fantasy," focusing primarily on late nineteenth- and early twentieth-century authors such as Rudyard Kipling, H. Rider Haggard, Algernon Blackwood, William Hope Hodgson, and Walter de la Mare.

7. According to some contemporary scholars, the relationship between traditional Romance and latter-day Gothic is one of displacement (Castle, 1995) or even parodic distortion (Day, 1985), transforming supernatural enchantment into an ambiguous spectral realm and relocating the *mysterium tremendum* of the supernatural in the turbulent and seemingly fathomless depths of the human psyche. The new complexity of the psyche finds its definitive conceptual articulation in Freud's "Gothic" model of the mind, with which Lewis engages in a running debate throughout the course of the novel. On the comic and parodic character of the N.I.C.E., Lewis claims that "I wanted farce as well as fantasy" ("A Reply to Professor Haldane" *OS* 72), and in identifying the Trilogy as Romance (as opposed to Epic), he refers to "the method of Apuleius, Lucian and Rabelais, but diverted from a comic to a serious purpose" (letter to William L. Kinter, 1/14/51, cited in Green and Hooper, *C. S. Lewis: A Biography* 211). See also note 25 ("The trouble about writing satire . . ."); Lewis's brief discussion of modern "fantastic" satire from Swift to Orwell, whose "true ancestors are Rabelais, Cervantes, the *Apocolocyntosis,* Lucian, and the *Frogs and Mice*" (*ELSC* 468); Schakel (1989) on Lewis's "satiric imagination"; Neuleib (1981) on the grotesque and Patterson (1981) on the "carnivalesque" in *That Hideous Strength;* and more generally, Bakhtin (1981), Frye (1957), Relihan (1993), and Weinbrot (2005) on ancient and modern Menippean satire.

8. See Anne Williams (1995) on the distinction between "female" and "male" plots, which reflects the modern division between the home and the workplace. In Williams's account, the origins of the "female" plot lie in the myth of Cupid and Psyche and its fairy-tale offspring, "Beauty and the Beast" (*Art of Darkness* 146f; 256). The prototype of the "female" Gothic is the virtuous heroine of Ann Radcliffe's *The Mysteries of Udolpho* (1794), Emily St. Aubert, who is imprisoned in the castle of the evil Count Montoni but eventually makes her escape and reunites with her long-lost lover. Charlotte Brontë's *Jane Eyre* (1847) establishes a much-imitated variant (e.g., Daphne DuMaurier's *Rebecca*) featuring a poor young woman who is employed in the house of a wealthy and ambiguously attractive man, and after enduring a series of threats, terrors, and adversities, ends up marrying the master of the house. Massé (1992) identifies another significant variant, the "Marital Gothic" (e.g., Charlotte Perkins Gilman's "The Yellow Wallpaper"), which turns the wife into a virtual or actual prisoner in her own home (Massé,

In the Name of Love 20–39). See also the full-length studies by Ellis (1989), Hoeveler (1998), and DeLamotte (1990). The darker "male" plot typically involves the isolated over-reacher who violates civil or even natural law to satisfy his lust for pleasure or power, often by pursuing secret knowledge that confers immortality or mastery over others. Lewis echoes both "female" and "male" plots, exploring the gender issues raised by each and offering some surprising reversals before his heroine recovers her wayward husband and the strikingly feminine St. Anne's triumphs over the ruthless and misogynistic male domain at Belbury.

9. On the vast literature devoted to the changing roles of women in early twentieth-century Britain, see Jane Lewis (1984) and Pugh (1992); and on the interwar period, Beddoe (1989), Light (1991), and the essay by Wallace (1999) on the changing "marriage plot" in women's fiction, including the detective fiction of Dorothy Sayers; and Squier (1994) on the heated debates over the future of reproductive processes. On a more personal note, Lewis dedicated his novel to his old hometown friend, Jane McNeill. In private correspondence to other friends, he expresses reservations or outright distaste for her, but in his diary he records a conversation in which "she talked about her longing to get away from Strandtown and the impossibility of doing so, as she could neither leave nor transplant her mother. Her idea of going to Oxford or Cambridge had been knocked on the head years ago by her father's death" (*AMR* 174, 1/9/23). Whether or not Jane Studdock owes her name to Miss McNeill, Lewis seems to have been sympathetic to his friend's foiled aspirations. According to a later account, she apparently hated the novel (Hooper, *C. S. Lewis: A Companion and Guide* 706).

10. See Morrisson (2007) on the extensive and surprisingly reciprocal relationship between the "alchemical revival" and the discovery of radioactivity in the late nineteenth and early twentieth centuries. This interaction between occult alchemy and atomic science continued into the twenties and thirties. In more general terms, the historical conjuncture between "spiritual" and "material" realms figures prominently in Lewis's conception of the N.I.C.E.; indeed, it is this coalescence between the "occult" and the "scientific" in the twentieth century that precipitates the massive cosmic conflict at the center of the novel.

11. On the gender politics of female decapitation, see Eilberg-Schwartz and Doniger (1995), whose collection, *Off with Her Head!,* considers how "removing the female head [and other less obvious forms of beheading] relieves woman

of both identity and voice and reduces her to a mere sexual and reproductive body" (1).

12. Lewis's lecture "The Inner Ring" (*WG* 141–157) examines the pathology of this common craving. His account is reminiscent of the male Gothic desire to "penetrate" that which is secret or forbidden and links the secular and "progressive" Mark to "the lust for the esoteric, the longing to be inside. . . . the delicious sense of secret intimacy" (151) associated with the pursuit of occult knowledge and the carefully guarded secrets of the top brass at Belbury.

13. Recall that Lewis raises the problem of eugenics at the very outset of the Trilogy, when Ransom discovers that Devine and Weston are preparing to "sacrifice" the "idiot boy" Harry, "the sort of boy," as Weston puts it, "who in a civilized community would be automatically handed over to state laboratory for experimental purposes" (*OSP* 21). See chapter 1, note 10, on the development of the eugenics movement and the controversies surrounding it, including J. B. S. Haldane's influential manifesto, *Dædalus* (1924), and G. K. Chesterton's seminal critique, *Eugenics and Other Evils* (1922).

14. The shift in settings also signals a break with the everyday world of "middle things" to the dramatic showdown between opposing principles. As Lewis states it in "The Decline of Religion" (*GD* 218–223), "When the Round Table is broken every man must follow either Galahad or Mordred: middle things are gone" (220). See Myers (1993, 1994) and Patterson (1981, 1986) for more extensive analysis of the principal locales in the novel. Marina Warner's intriguing account of the cult of St. Anne in seventeenth-century France (the specialty of Lewis's older brother) suggests some of the reasons that Lewis may have chosen the name: "Anne's story echoes biblical tales of barrenness reversed by God as a special sign of his favour to the parents and a singular benediction on their late, longed-for offspring. . . . Anne was seen above all as a patroness of childless women and grandmothers, but she was also an educator, who in numerous cult images teaches her daughter to read" (*From the Beast to the Blonde* 82–83).

15. For a Gothic-minded reader, the "imitation of Versailles" calls to mind not only the imitation Gothic of Horace Walpole's Strawberry Hill—an inaugural moment of the Gothic revival—but also the authoritarian edifice at the center of *The Castle of Otranto* and many of its successors. As the subsequent N.I.C.E.-incited riots indicate, Lewis is suspicious of modern

revolutionary movements, but the climactic destruction of the banquet hall at Belbury (chapter 16), openly reminiscent of the French Revolution, represents a revolt of Nature itself against a ruthless, oppressive, and ultimately demonic regime. Mervyn Nicholson (see note 6) discusses the many connections between *Dracula* and *That Hideous Strength*, including the kinship between the two principal couples and the undercurrent of protest against the more destructive aspects of the traditional gender ideology that both novels otherwise seem to reaffirm.

16. The substitution of Miss Ironwood for a psychoanalyst is another instance of Lewis's ongoing quarrel with Freudian theory (as it was generally understood at the time), and his preference for Jung over Freud. See note 24 on Lewis's condemnation of the "occult" and his simultaneous acknowledgment of some of the phenomena associated with it.

17. Lewis was opposed to extremism at either end of the ideological spectrum, but given the course of developments leading up to the war, the tactics of the N.I.C.E. are more directly reminiscent of Hitler's consolidation of power and the behavior of similar regimes in the thirties. Lewis may also be alluding to local conditions in Britain. Scholars tend to focus on the growing apprehensions over a planned economy after the war, but the N.I.C.E. assault on the surrounding region also reflects the British government's expropriation of land for military training and production. In *The Village That Died for England* (1995), Patrick Wright offers a detailed account of the fate of one town in Dorset, and in their discussion of the genesis of *That Hideous Strength,* Green and Hooper (1974) refer to the controversy over the founding of the atomic research center at Harwell, fifteen miles from Oxford. Among his literary sources, Lewis may have drawn on several anti-fascist novels, including Joseph O'Neill's *Land under England* (1935), which he read when it first appeared (see Osborn, 2001), and possibly Rex Warner's *The Aerodrome* (1941), a remarkable portrait of the corruption and virtual conquest of a small English town by the quasi-fascist commander of the nearby military base. Lewis refers to both of these novels, along with Huxley's *Brave New World* (1932), in his 1950 preface to a new edition of his early poem, *Dymer* (1926), which anticipates some of the fears of totalitarianism that would come to the fore in the following decade. See Filmer (1987), Reilly (1997), and Schakel (1987) on the connections between *That Hideous Strength* and Orwell's *Nineteen*

Eighty-Four (1949); Horsley (1995) on the fictional representation of political power from Conrad to Orwell; and Jameson (2005) and Kumar (1987) for broad-based studies of modern utopian and dystopian literature.

18. A few references to *The Castle* and *The Trial* appear in Lewis's letters of the period (*L* II, 199, 6/28/36; *L* II, 439, 8/18/40). Lewis usually refers to Kafka only in passing, but in his preface to *George MacDonald: An Anthology* (1947) he lists Kafka together with Novalis and MacDonald as the creator of a rare type of modern "mythopoeic art": "It goes beyond the expression of things we have already felt. It arouses in us sensations we have never had before . . . gets under our skin, hits us at a level deeper than our thoughts or even our passions, troubles oldest certainties till all questions are reopened, and in general shocks us more fully awake than we are for most of our lives" (xxviii). See Bridgwater (2003) on Kafka's own affiliations with Gothic and fairy-tale traditions.

19. In *The Four Loves* (1960), Lewis distinguishes three views of the body: (1) the ascetic view that regards it as a "sack of dung" or the "tomb" of the soul; (2) the "neo-pagan" glorification of the body; and (3) the view "St. Francis expressed by calling his body 'Brother Ass'. . . . a useful, sturdy, lazy, obstinate, patient, lovable and infuriating beast" (100–101). Lewis seems most disposed to the Franciscan position, some of the implications of which are apparent (a) in our tendency to make jokes about the body—"we have here an animal which finds its own animality either objectionable or funny"— and (b) in our "uncanny" feelings about the dead, specifically with respect to corpses (bodies without spirit) and ghosts (spirits without bodies) (*M* 206–207). Nevertheless, Lewis's statements about the body often vary with the context in which it is being considered. In response to modern materialistic views of the human organism, Lewis insists on the union of spirit and flesh, rational and animal nature, associated with the concept of "personhood." By contrast, in response to the gnostic denigration of the body, which has been rekindled by the modern Cartesian dissociation between spirit and matter, Lewis emphasizes the significance of our animal nature, the joys of sensory experience, and our kinship with the rest of the created order. See *The Problem of Pain* (20f.) on Lewis's similar emphasis upon the necessity of "matter"—an argument he developed in his earlier unpublished debates (probably 1927–1928) with Owen Barfield (now available in *L* III, 1596–1646); Lewis's letter to another anthroposophist (*L* II, 513–14, 3/25/42)

on the danger of forgetting our "creatureliness"; and his lecture "*De Futili-tate*" (*CR* 57–71) on his attempt "at reversing the popular belief that reality is totally alien to our minds" (71). Also see Derrick (1981) and Patrick (1998) on the early "gnostic" tendencies in Lewis himself; Fairfield (1998) and Howard (1987, 1998) on the decidedly "anti-gnostic" theme of *That Hideous Strength;* Grimstad (2002), Jonas (1958), O'Regan (2001), and Voegelin (1933) on gnostic elements in modern thought; and King (2003) for a recent overview of gnosticism as a historical phenomenon and as a source of much recent philosophical and religious speculation. Both of Lewis's dialectical stances play a significant role in *That Hideous Strength*. But given the N.I.C.E.'s dream of transcending the limits of the body, the "anti-gnostic" theme is especially prominent, as is a striking emphasis on what we now call "body-knowledge" (after Merleau-Ponty, whose *Phenomenology of Perception* also appeared in 1945). For Jane and Mark, "the body's view of the matter" (*THS* 241) is often the most reliable guide to action and understanding of their situation. Like the figure of Merlin lying in his crypt, the body becomes the site of discarded sentiments and virtues that remain an inalienable part of our nature and continue to "haunt" an age in which they have never been properly cultivated.

20. Much has been written on the medieval aspects of the novel. See Lutton (1986) and Rawson (1983) for a comparison with the Grail motif in Eliot's *The Waste Land,* and Barber (2004) for a magisterial survey of the Grail legend and its modern revival in modern literature. On the revival of Arthurian literature in the nineteenth and twentieth centuries, see Mancoff (1998), Starr (1954), Taylor and Brewer (1983), and Thompson (1985).

21. Patterson (1979) discusses the resemblances between Jane's meeting with the Director and Psyche's encounter with Cupid in Lewis's *Till We Have Faces* (1956). See Anne Williams (*Art of Darkness,* Appendix C, 256) on the resounding structural similarities between Psyche and Cupid, Beauty and the Beast, and a variety of female Gothic plots, from *The Mysteries of Udolpho* and *Jane Eyre* to DuMaurier's *Rebecca* (1938) and Victoria Holt's *Mistress of Mellyn* (1960), the latter a landmark in the popular revival of the female Gothic during the sixties and seventies.

22. Filostrato's fantasy is not that far removed from the speculative dreams of certain intellectuals in the twenties and thirties, especially the contributors to the remarkable To-day & To-Morrow series, "a line of futurological pam-

phlets explicitly designed to explore issues currently under contestation, and thus to 'provide the reader with a survey of numerous aspects of most modern thought'" (Squier, *Babies in Bottles* 18). See, for instance, J. D. Bernal's *The World, the Flesh, and the Devil* (1929), which envisions the evolution of humanity into bodiless species. Lewis claimed that he was "spurred to write" by such speculations in J. B. S. Haldane's *Possible Worlds* (1927) and the novels of Olaf Stapledon, *Last and First Men* (1930) and *Star-Maker* (1937), which in the process of projecting the course of evolutionary development over billions of years, provide an ingenious array of forms, incarnate and discarnate, that our future descendants may assume (*L* II, 236, 12/28/38; 594, 12/7/43).

23. Lewis expresses his antipathy toward the occult in his early poem, *Dymer* (1926). His most extensive and revealing discussion appears in *Surprised by Joy* (59–60, 174–178). Nevertheless, while he seems to eschew occult practices, Lewis does not deny "preternatural" or "paranormal" phenomena, at least in this novel. Jane's "second sight" is no mere illusion; nor is the threatening specter of Wither that roams the grounds at Belbury; nor Frost's telepathic access to Jane's mind. And these are only the prelude to the miraculous manifestation of the "supernatural" in the return of Merlin and the descent of the planetary intelligences in the latter part of the text. See Oppenheim (1985) and Owen (2004) on the occult revival of the late nineteenth and early twentieth centuries; Hazelgrove (2000) and Kollar (2000) for evidence that spiritualism did not fade away in the twenties but was still alive and well at the dawn of the Second World War; section VI (*THS*, covering chapters 12–14) on the relationship between Wither's "spiritualism" and Frost's "materialism"; and note 26 on the twentieth-century coalescence of the occult and scientific that eventually pulls down "Deep Heaven on their heads" (291).

24. In *Vice Versa, or, A Lesson to Fathers* (Anstey 1882), the magic of an oriental talisman leads to an exchange in which Paul Bultitude, a pompous businessman, occupies the body of his son Dick and is compelled to suffer all the miseries of a boarding school, while Dick gets to enjoy the comfortable existence of an urban gentleman. In his autobiography, *Surprised by Joy* (1956), Lewis describes this novel as "the only truthful school story in existence" (41), and he bestowed the name Bultitude upon the domesticated bear who resides at St. Anne's.

25. A few months after the end of the war, Lewis wrote to I. O. Evans that he was previously unaware of the Nazi flirtation with magic and the occult: "I had'nt [*sic*] myself thought that any of the people in contemporary rackets were *really* dabbling in Magic. I had supposed that to be a romantic addition of my own. But there you are. The trouble about writing satire is that the real world always anticipates you, and what were meant for exaggerations turn out to be nothing of the sort" (*L* II, 672, 9/26/45).

26. It is difficult to exaggerate the significance of this breakdown of the old scientific "materialism" and the crossing of the "frontier" from the scientific to the spiritual. (See Morrisson [2007] on the historical coalescence of occult and scientific knowledge in the early twentieth century.) The collapse of the spiritual/material dualism motivates the secret plot to wed ancient magic and modern science and incites the climactic retaliation of Deep Heaven at the end of the novel. It is at this point that Belbury also sheds its association with modern "realism" and takes on the trappings of Gothic romance, turning into the parodic counterpart of St. Anne's, its sinister enchantment a warped imitation of the authentic enchantment of its enemy.

27. Recall that in *Perelandra*, the central temptation scene (chapters 8–10) is preceded by a chapter (7) that introduces the satanic tempter and is followed by a chapter (11) in which Ransom comes to terms with the horrifying recognition that he must engage in direct physical combat with his adversary.

28. The final essay of *The Abolition of Man* is a valuable guide to *That Hideous Strength,* but we should remember that its description of the human mind doubling back on humanity itself and reducing it to a mere object, as radical as it seems, is founded on a modern subject/object dialectic that disregards Belbury's profoundly disconcerting effort to invest the new totalitarian order with the sublimity and transcendent power once associated with the heavens. Lewis's dissections of the end-game of modern thought bears a striking resemblance to that of Max Horkheimer and Theodor Adorno's *Dialectic of Enlightenment* (1947), written at the same moment and from a very different point on the ideological spectrum. The kinship is based not on any immediate influence but on the longstanding similarity between conservative and radical critiques of the Enlightenment. As intellectuals from all camps struggled to comprehend the current crisis of European society, some came to regard the rise of totalitarian terror not as a defection from the Enlighten-

ment but as the ultimate development of its distinctive type of rationality. In this respect, both Lewis and Horkheimer/Adorno should be situated along a spectrum that includes Mann (*Doktor Faustus*, 1947), Orwell (*Nineteen Eighty-Four*, 1949), Camus (*The Rebel*, 1951), and a variety of philosophers, social scientists, and historians who sought to explain the moral collapse of modern civilization and to restore, revise, or replace the rationalist heritage of the Enlightenment.

29. The Technocracy movement, inspired by Thorstein Veblen and founded by an enterprising engineer, Howard Scott, flourished in the United States during the twenties and thirties. In the latter decade, Scott and some of its other spokesmen became increasingly authoritarian in their views, and Professor Frost's techno-elitism, including his penchant for Pavlovian reconditioning, comes directly from their writings. See Akin (1977) on the history of the movement, which found popular expression (somewhat belatedly) in James Burnham's classic, *The Managerial Revolution* (1941). Luckhurst (2005) discusses the influence of technocratic ideals on Hugo Gernsback, John W. Campbell, and other pioneers of American science fiction during its formative years. Frost also refers explicitly to the evolutionary ethics of C. H. Waddington, the biologist whose *Science and Ethics* (1942) served as a springboard for Lewis's defense of immutable ethical principles (the Natural Law or the *Tao*) in *The Abolition of Man* and contemporaneous essays such as "The Poison of Subjectivism" (1943). See Farber (1994) for the historical development of evolutionary ethics and a critique of the kind of moral reasoning it has encouraged.

30. Similar in its psychological manipulation to Frost's attempt to root out "affectional feelings" is Fairy Hardcastle's dream of replacing the old notion of "retributive" punishment with a more "humane, remedial treatment" that "need have no fixed limit; it could go on till it had effected a cure, and those who were carrying it out would decide when *that* was. And if cure were humane and desirable, how much more prevention?" (*THS* 67–68). See Lewis's essay, "The Humanitarian Theory of Punishment" (*GID* 287–294) for his proto-Fouauldian views on the subject and his subsequent "reply" (*GID* 295–300) to his critics.

31. In his first book, *Poetic Diction: A Study in Meaning* (1928), Owen Barfield takes exception to Max Müller's argument that concepts such as the Latin "spiritus" originate in concrete "roots" ("spirit" as "breath" or "wind") and

only subsequently assume more abstract or metaphorical significance ("spirit" as "the principle of life within man or animal"). Barfield maintains that an original unity precedes the very division into "literal" and "metaphorical" meanings. We must "imagine a time" when terms such as 'spiritus' or πνεῦμα, or older words from which these had descended, meant "neither *breath*, nor *wind*, nor *spirit*, nor yet all three of these things, but when they simply had *their own old peculiar meaning*, which has since, in the course of the evolution of consciousness, crystallized into the three meanings specified . . ." (81).

32. All three chapters of *The Abolition of Man* address this dissociation—in the domains of the psyche, social relations, and the sciences respectively. In the first, Lewis discusses the modern bifurcation between emotions and objects, especially as it distorts our understanding of language (see Myers 1994) and devalues "just sentiments" to mere "subjective reactions." In the second, he turns to the severance between values and facts that obscures the enduring moral imperatives that have been shared by all the major religious and philosophical traditions. In the final essay, he addresses the sharp dichotomy between the spiritual and natural, the knowing subject and the objects of knowledge, which has first divested nature of its inherent qualities and then turned Man himself into nothing more than a "natural" object.

33. In September 1945, Lewis wrote to I. O. Evans that his knowledge of Merlin was based primarily on medieval sources: Geoffrey of Monmouth, Layamon, and Malory (*L* II, 672–673, 9/26/45). See Downing (1998) on Lewis's use of Merlin in the novel. On the historical, literary, and spiritual interest that this figure continues to inspire, see Gollnick (1990), Goodrich and Thompson (2003), Markale (1981), Stewart (1986), Tolstoy (1985), and more generally, Starr (1954), Mancoff (1998), Taylor and Brewer (1983), and Thompson (1985) on the modern revival of Arthurian literature.

34. Lewis acknowledges the distinction between *magia* and *goetia* ("white" and "black" magic), but his suspicions of magical practices of any sort are apparent in his various discussions of the subject. See *The Abolition of Man* (76–78) and *English Literature in the Sixteenth Century* (5–14). However, "magic" and "the magical" assume a more positive significance when detached from human practice and associated with the premodern notion of an enchanted universe: "Now the value, for me, of the magical element in Christianity is this. It is a permanent witness that the heavenly realm . . . is a realm of objective facts—hard, determinate facts, not to be constructed

a priori, and not to be dissolved into maxims, ideals, values, and the like" (*LM* 104). See Walker (1958) on the revival of "magia" in Ficino and other Renaissance Platonists with whom Lewis was acquainted, and Kort (2001, especially chapter 2) on the subject of "reenchantment."

35. Among Lewis's admirers, no aspect of *That Hideous Strength* arouses more controversy than his references to the superiority of the "masculine" (as distinct as it might be from biological notion of the "male") and its biblically sanctioned terrestrial implications, which bestow authority (as qualified and tempered as it might be) on the male partner in marriage. Taken together with the insistence on Jane's "obedience" to her husband and the treatment of her conflict between career and childbearing, Lewis's effort to distinguish between "masculine" gender and "male" sex is widely regarded as a subterfuge designed to sanctify the same patriarchal authority it seems to call into question. See Fredrick and McBride (2001) for a recent airing of this problem, and Patterson (1979) and Neuleib (1980) on the more sympathetic elements in Lewis's representation of women and the priority often accorded to "feminine" values in the novel.

36. "If flesh and blood cannot inherit the Kingdom, that is not because they are too solid, too gross, too distinct, too 'illustrious with being.' They are too flimsy, too transitory, too phantasmal" ("Transposition" *WG* 111). Lewis's Platonic reversal of commonplace assumptions finds full expression in *The Great Divorce* (1945) and *The Last Battle,* the final volume of *The Chronicles of Narnia* (1950–1956).

37. "I was not born to be free—I was born to adore and obey" (Como, *Lewis at the Breakfast Table* 29). However controversial his gender politics may be, Lewis was consistent in placing adoration and obedience at the heart of our relationship to God. Closely tied to obedience is his emphasis on our "thinghood," which he treats in the same dialectical manner as the "body" (see note 19). In response to the materialist, Lewis appeals to the union of spirit and flesh entailed in the concept of a "person." By contrast, in response to the elevation of mind over body, he reminds us of our "creatureliness," the fact that one is "a thing designed and invented by Someone Else . . ." (*THS* 315).

38. The descent of the Celestial Intelligences harks back to medieval astrology and its development in Ficino and other Renaissance Platonists. Lewis was certainly attracted to "the discarded image" of medieval cosmology, and

to the various systems of Neoplatonic philosophy from Plotinus to Henry More that preceded the modern dissociation between spirit and nature. But outside of its presence in his imaginary universe, we should hesitate before assuming that the wholesale revival of premodern astrology plays any more of a role in Lewis's call for a "regenerate science" (*AM* 79) than the literal return of Merlin plays in his doctrinal belief in the ultimate triumph of good over evil. As Dimble says of Merlin's "old *magia*," ancient astrology "represents what we've got to get back to in some different way" (*THS* 283).

39. See Patterson (1981) for a detailed analysis of the banquet scene, and Downing (1992, pp. 94–99) for the use of Dante's *Commedia* in this scene and elsewhere in the text.

40. The word "trolls" is missing from many recent paperback editions. See Lake (1989) on the textual differences between the Bodley Head (1945) and Macmillan (1946) editions, and the later paperback editions that derive from each of them.

41. An interesting play on Othello's lines: "It is the very error of the moon,/She comes more near the earth than she was wont/And makes men Mad" (*Othello* V.ii.108–110).

42. In his autopsy of the situation at Bracton College, Dimble refers explicitly (*THS* 370) to the "*Trahison des clercs*" (*The Treason of the Intellectuals*), the title of Julien Benda's classic indictment of the intellectual class (originally published in 1928) for relinquishing its role as guardian of enduring values and acceding to, if not embracing, the dangerous tendencies of the times.

43. The combination of the Director's paternal role, his association with Merlin's magic, and his parting words to Jane before he resigns his position, "You will have no more dreams. Have children instead" (378), calls to mind the figure of Prospero at the end of *The Tempest,* and more generally, the transfer of supernatural magic into the natural enchantment of conjugal love.

CONCLUSION

1. See the individual discussions of these chapters on pages 37–39, 76–79, and 117–121, and the figures on pages 28, 66, and 98. Each of these chapters is also the counterpart to the chapter preceding the central section, and together they make up the inner frame surrounding it. Therefore, we must consider each of these chapters not only as the sequel to the core but also as

the complement to the chapter immediately preceding the core. Unlike the other frames, which feature several chapters on each side of the structural center, the inner frame is comprised of only a single chapter on either side of the central section, and in all three novels the two chapters that make up the inner frame bear considerable thematic weight.

2. Unlike René Girard, whose pioneering work is acknowledged in the title of this chapter, Lewis regards Hobbes's "war of all against all" not as the cause of the institution of the sacred but as the effect of our defection from it. See Milbank (*Theology and Social Theory* 395–402) on Girard and the widespread modern assumption of originary violence.

3. As many people have observed, the Second World War was far more a test case for the pacifist position than for the notion of the "just war." Lewis was hardly a pacifist, but as Ransom's own resistance suggests, it is hard to imagine that the author would not want his readers to remain disturbed by the violent resolution to the crisis on Perelandra. A justifiable course of action is not necessarily the one we would wish to pursue. See "Why I Am Not a Pacifist" (*WG* 64–90) and pages 177–178 n. 12.

4. On Calvary "the degree of accepted Death reaches the utmost bounds of the imaginable and perhaps goes beyond them; not only all natural supports, but the presence of the very Father to whom the sacrifice is made deserts the victim, and surrender to God does not falter though God 'forsakes' it" (*PP* 102). Lewis is not as troubled as many contemporary theologians by the violence at the heart of the Atonement, nor by the "secret of secrets" concealed in "Death of the highest level of all: the mystical slaying of the Lamb 'before the foundation of the world'" (*M* 203). Nevertheless, he acknowledges that the latter is "above our speculations" (*M* 203), and "the ideas of sacrifice, Ransom, Championship (over Death), Substitution etc. are all images to *suggest* the reality (not otherwise comprehensible to us) of the Atonement" (*L* III, 1476, 10/31/63). In the major apologetical works from *The Problem of Pain* to *Miracles,* Lewis's reflections on the Cross focus less on the substitutionary "ransom" of fallen humanity than on "the principle of *Vicariousness*" (*M* 191), with its implications of self-giving and the supreme act of "humility and self-renunciation. . . . [the] blessed spiritual Death to self" (*M* 210) that Christ's followers are called upon to imitate in their own lives. See Boersma (2004) for an overview of the various models of the Atonement and the recent debate that each of them has spawned.

The controversy over Atonement is a subset of the much larger contemporary debate over the relationship between religion and violence. See Girard (1972, 1978), who looms over much recent discussion; de Vries (2001); Keenan's study of sacrifice (2005) and McKenna (1992) on the violence in continental tradition from Kant to Derrida (1992); and Juergensmeyer (2001) and Kimball (2002) among many others on the global resurgence of religious violence.

Bibliography ∽

WORKS BY C. S. LEWIS

The Abolition of Man: or Reflections on Education with Special Reference to the Teaching of English in the Upper Forms of Schools. 1943. New York: HarperCollins, 2001.

The Allegory of Love: A Study in Medieval Tradition. 1936. New York: Oxford University Press, 1995.

All My Road Before Me: The Diary of C. S. Lewis, 1922–1927. Edited by Walter Hooper. San Diego: Harcourt, 1991.

Arthurian Torso: Containing the Posthumous Fragment of the Figure of Arthur by Charles Williams and A Commentary on the Arthurian Poems of Charles Williams by C. S. Lewis. Edited by C. S. Lewis. London: Oxford University Press, 1948.

["Booklists submitted in response to this department's query: 'What books did most to shape your vocational attitude and your philosophy of life?'"], *The Christian Century* 79 no. 23 (1962), p. 719.

Christian Reflections. Edited by Walter Hooper. Grand Rapids: Eerdmans, 1967.

The Chronicles of Narnia. 1950–1956. New York: HarperCollins, 1994.

Collected Letters. 3 vols. Edited by Walter Hooper. San Francisco: Harper, 2000, 2004, 2007.

"The Conditions for a Just War." 1939. In *God in the Dock: Essays on Theology and Ethics.* Grand Rapids: Eerdmans, 1970. pp. 325–327.

The Dark Tower and Other Stories. Edited by Walter Hooper. San Diego: Harcourt, 1977.

"The Decline of Religion." 1946. In *God in the Dock: Essays on Theology and Ethics.* Grand Rapids: Eerdmans, 1970. pp. 218–223.

"De Futilitate." In *Christian Reflections*. Edited by Walter Hooper. Grand Rapids: Eerdmans, 1967. pp. 57–71.

The Discarded Image: An Introduction to Medieval and Renaissance Literature. 1964. Cambridge: Cambridge University Press, 1994.

Dymer. 1926. In *Narrative Poems*. Edited by Walter Hooper. San Diego: Harcourt, 1979. pp. 1–91.

English Literature in the Sixteenth Century Excluding Drama. Oxford: Oxford University Press, 1954.

An Experiment in Criticism. 1961. Cambridge: Cambridge University Press, 1992.

The Four Loves. 1960. San Diego: Harcourt, 1991.

"The Funeral of a Great Myth." In *Christian Reflections*. Edited by Walter Hooper. Grand Rapids: Eerdmans, 1967. pp. 82–93.

George MacDonald: An Anthology. 1947. Edited by C. S. Lewis. New York: Harper-Collins, 2001.

God in the Dock: Essays on Theology and Ethics. Grand Rapids: Eerdmans, 1970.

The Great Divorce. 1945. New York: HarperCollins, 2001.

A Grief Observed. 1961 (under the pseudonym N. W. Clerk). New York: Harper-Collins, 2001.

"Hamlet: The Prince or the Poem?" 1942. In *Selected Literary Essays*. Edited by Walter Hooper. Cambridge: Cambridge University Press, 1969. pp. 88–105.

"The Humanitarian Theory of Punishment," 1949, and "On Punishment: A Reply," 1954. In *God in the Dock: Essays on Theology and Ethics*. Grand Rapids: Eerdmans, 1970. pp. 287–300.

"The Inner Ring." 1944. In *The Weight of Glory and Other Addresses*. 1949. San Francisco: HarperSanFrancisco, 2001. pp. 141–157.

"Is Theology Poetry?" 1945. In *The Weight of Glory and Other Addresses*. 1949. San Francisco: HarperSanFrancisco, 2001. pp. 116–140.

Letters of C. S. Lewis. 1966. Revised edition edited by Walter Hooper. San Diego: Harcourt, 1993.

Letters to Malcolm: Chiefly on Prayer. 1964. San Diego: Harcourt, 1992.

"Meditation in a Toolshed." 1945. In *God in the Dock: Essays on Theology and Ethics*. Grand Rapids: Eerdmans, 1970. pp. 212–215.

Mere Christianity. 1952. New York: HarperCollins, 2001.

Miracles: A Preliminary Study. 1947. New York: HarperCollins, 2001.

"The Novels of Charles Williams." 1949. In *On Stories and Other Essays on Literature*. New York: Harcourt, 1982. pp. 21–28.

Of This and Other Worlds. 1982. Edited by Walter Hooper. London: HarperCollins, 2000.

On Stories and Other Essays on Literature. New York: Harcourt, 1982.

"On Stories." 1947. In *On Stories and Other Essays on Literature*. New York: Harcourt, 1982. pp. 3–20.

Out of the Silent Planet. 1938. New York: Scribner, 2003.

Perelandra: A Novel. 1943. New York: Scribner, 2003.

The Personal Heresy: A Controversy (With E. M. W. Tillyard). London: Oxford University Press, 1939.

The Pilgrim's Regress: An Allegorical Apology for Christianity, Reason and Romanticism. 1933. Grand Rapids: Eerdmans, 1992.

Poems. 1964. San Diego: Harcourt, 1992.

"The Poison of Subjectivism." 1943. In *Christian Reflections*. Edited by Walter Hooper. Grand Rapids: Eerdmans, 1967. pp. 72–81.

A Preface to 'Paradise Lost': Being the Ballard Matthews Lectures Delivered at University College, North Wales, 1941. 1942. London: Oxford University Press, 1960.

The Problem of Pain. 1940. New York: HarperCollins, 2001.

Reflections on the Psalms. San Diego: Harcourt, 1958.

Rehabilitations and Other Essays. London: Oxford University Press, 1939.

"Religion and Rocketry." Originally "Will We Lose God in Outer Space?" *Christian Herald* (Apr. 1958) 19, 74–76. In *The World's Last Night and Other Essays*. 1960. San Diego: Harcourt, 1973. pp. 83–92.

"A Reply to Professor Haldane." In *On Stories and Other Essays on Literature*. New York: Harcourt, 1982. pp. 69–80.

The Screwtape Letters. 1942. New York: HarperCollins, 2001.

"The Seeing Eye." Originally "Onward, Christian Spacemen." *Show* III (Feb. 1963) 57, 117. In *Christian Reflections*. Edited by Walter Hooper. Grand Rapids: Eerdmans, 1967. pp. 167–76.

Selected Literary Essays. Edited by Walter Hooper. Cambridge: Cambridge University Press, 1969.

Studies in Medieval and Renaissance Literature. Edited by Walter Hooper. 1966. Cambridge: Cambridge University Press, 1998.

Studies in Words. 1960. 2nd edition. Cambridge: Cambridge University Press, 1967.

Surprised by Joy: The Shape of My Early Life. 1956. San Diego: Harcourt, 1984.

That Hideous Strength: A Modern Fairy-Tale for Grown-Ups. 1945. New York: Scribner, 2003.

They Stand Together: The Letters of C. S. Lewis to Arthur Greeves (1914–1963). Edited by Walter Hooper. London: Collins, 1979.

Till We Have Faces: A Myth Retold. 1956. San Diego: Harcourt, 1984.

"Transposition." In *The Weight of Glory and Other Addresses*. 1949. Revised and expanded edition, San Francisco: HarperSanFrancisco, 2001. pp. 91–115.

"Unreal Estates." In *On Stories and Other Essays on Literature*. New York: Harcourt, 1982. pp. 143–153.

The Weight of Glory and Other Addresses. 1949. Revised and expanded edition, San Francisco: HarperSanFrancisco, 2001.

"Why I Am Not a Pacifist." In *The Weight of Glory and Other Addresses*. Revised and expanded edition, New York: HarperCollins, 2001. pp. 64–90.

The World's Last Night and Other Essays. 1960. San Diego: Harcourt, 1973.

OTHER WORKS

Abbott, Edwin A. *Flatland: A Romance of Many Dimensions*. 1884. New York: Penguin Books, 1998.

Adey, Lionel. *C. S. Lewis: Writer, Dreamer, and Mentor*. Grand Rapids: Eerdmans, 1998.

Akin, William E. *Technocracy and the American Dream: The Technocratic Movement, 1900–1941*. Berkeley: University of California Press, 1977.

Alexander, Samuel. *Space, Time, and Deity: The Gifford Lectures at Glasgow, 1916–1918*. 2 vols. London: Macmillan, 1920.

Ansell-Pearson, Keith. *Philosophy and the Adventure of the Virtual: Bergson and the Time of Life*. London: Routledge, 2002.

Anstey. F. *Vice Versa, or, A Lesson to Fathers*. 1882. Harmondsworth, Middlesex: Penguin, 1981.

Arendt, Hannah. *The Origins of Totalitarianism*. 1951. New York: Harcourt, 1973.

———. *Essays in Understanding, 1930–1954: Formation, Exile, and Totalitarianism*. Edited by Jerome Kohn. New York: Schocken, 1994.

Ashenden, Gavin. *Charles Williams: Alchemy and Integration*. Kent, Ohio: Kent State University Press, 2008.

St. Athanasius. *On the Incarnation*. Translated by A Religious of C.S.M.V. [Sister Penelope]. 1944. New edition, Crestwood, N.Y.: St. Vladimir's Seminary Press, 1993.

Atterton, Peter, and Matthew Calarco, eds. *Animal Philosophy: Essential Readings in Continental Thought*. London: Continuum International, 2004.

Auden, W. H. *The Complete Works of W. H. Auden: Plays and Other Dramatic Writings, 1928–1938.* Edited by Edward Mendelson. Princeton: Princeton University Press, 1988.

St. Augustine. *Confessions.* Translated by R. S. Pine-Coffin. Harmondsworth, Middlesex: Penguin, 1961.

———. *Concerning the City of God Against the Pagans.* Translated by Henry Bettenson. Harmondsworth, Middlesex: Penguin, 1972.

Baggett, David, Gary R. Habermas, and Jerry L. Walls, eds. *C. S. Lewis as Philosopher: Truth, Goodness and Beauty.* Downers Grove, Ill.: IVP Academic, 2008.

Bakhtin, M. M. *The Dialogic Imagination: Four Essays.* Edited by Michael Holquist. Translated by Caryl Emerson and Michael Holquist. Austin: University of Texas Press, 1981.

Barber, Richard. *The Holy Grail: Imagination and Belief.* Cambridge, Mass.: Harvard University Press, 2004.

Barfield, Owen. *Poetic Diction: A Study in Meaning.* 1928. Third edition, Middletown, Conn.: Wesleyan University Press, 1973.

Barkan, Elazar. *The Retreat of Scientific Racism: Changing Concepts of Race in Britain and the United States between the World Wars.* Cambridge: Cambridge University Press, 1992.

Barzun, Jacques. *Race: A Study in Modern Superstition.* London: Methuen, 1938.

Bataille, Georges. *Theory of Religion.* 1973. Translated by Robert Hurley. New York: Zone, 1992.

Beal, Timothy K. *Religion and Its Monsters.* New York: Routledge, 2002.

Beddoe, Deirdre. *Back to Home and Duty: Women between the Wars 1918–1939.* London: Pandora, 1989.

Benda, Julien. *The Treason of the Intellectuals.* 1928. Translated by Richard Aldington. New York: W. W. Norton, 1969.

Bergonzi, Bernard. *The Early H. G. Wells.* Toronto: University of Toronto Press, 1961.

Bergson, Henri. *Time and Free Will: An Essay on the Immediate Data of Consciousness.* Originally published as *Essai sur les données immédiates de la conscience.* 1889. Translated by F. L. Pogson, 1910. Mineola, N.Y.: Dover, 2001.

———. *Matter and Memory.* 1896. Translated by Nancy Margaret Paul and W. Scott Palmer, 1911. New York: Zone, 1998.

———. *Laughter: An Essay on the Meaning of the Comic.* 1901. Translated by Cloudesley Brereton and Fred Rothwell, 1911. Mineola, N.Y.: Dover, 2005.

―――. *An Introduction to Metaphysics.* 1903. Translated by T. E. Hulme, 1910. Indianapolis: Bobbs Merrill, 1955.

―――. *Creative Evolution.* 1907. Translated by Arthur Mitchell, 1911. Mineola, N.Y.: Dover, 1998.

―――. *Mind-Energy.* 1919. Translated by H. Wilden Carr. New York: H. Holt, 1920.

―――. *The Creative Mind.* Originally published as *La Pénsée et le mouvant: Essais et conférences.* 1934. Translated by Mabelle L. Andison. Mineola, N.Y.: Dover, 2007.

Bernal, J. D. *The World, the Flesh, and the Devil: An Enquiry into the Future of the Three Enemies of the Rational Soul.* 1929. Second edition, Bloomington: Indiana University Press, 1969.

Berry, Edward. *Shakespeare and the Hunt: A Cultural and Social Study.* Cambridge: Cambridge University Press, 2001.

Bevan, Edwyn. *Symbolism and Belief.* London: Allen & Unwin, 1938.

Birkhead, Edith. *The Tale of Terror: A Study of the Gothic Romance.* London: Constable, 1921.

Black, Edwin. *War against the Weak: Eugenics and America's Campaign to Create a Master Race.* New York: Four Walls Eight Windows, 2003.

Blake, William. *The Complete Poetry and Prose of William Blake.* Revised edition edited by David V. Erdman. Berkeley: University of California Press, 1982.

Boersma, Hans. *Violence, Hospitality, and the Cross: Reappropriating the Atonement Tradition.* Grand Rapids: Baker Academic, 2004.

Borges, Jorge Luis. "Time and J. W. Dunne." 1940. In *Selected Non-Fictions.* Edited by Eliot Weinberger. Translated by Esther Allen, Suzanne Jill Levine, and Eliot Weinberger. New York: Viking, 1999. pp. 217–219.

Botting, Fred. *Gothic.* London and New York: Routledge, 1996.

Bowler, Peter. *Reconciling Science and Religion: The Debate in Early-Twentieth-Century Britain.* Chicago: University of Chicago Press, 2001.

Bradbury, Ray. *The Martian Chronicles.* 1950. New York: Bantam, 1979.

Bradley, F. H. *Essays on Truth and Reality.* Oxford: Clarendon, 1914.

Bragdon, Claude. *A Primer of Higher Space (The Fourth Dimension).* 1913. New York: Cosimo Classics, 2005.

Brantlinger, Patrick. *Rule of Darkness: British Literature and Imperialism, 1830–1914.* Ithaca: Cornell University Press, 1988.

Bridgwater, Patrick. *Kafka, Gothic and Fairytale*. Amsterdam: Rodopi, 2003.

Brontë, Charlotte. *Jane Eyre*. 1847. New York: Random House, 2000.

Burleigh, Michael. *The Third Reich: A New History*. New York: Hill and Wang, 2000.

Burnham, James. *The Managerial Revolution*. 1941. Bloomington: Indiana University Press, 1960.

Burton, Dan, and David Grandy. *Magic, Mystery, and Science: The Occult in Western Civilization*. Bloomington: Indiana University Press, 2004.

Burwick, Frederick, and Paul Douglass, eds. *The Crisis in Modernism: Bergson and the Vitalist Controversy*. Cambridge: Cambridge University Press, 1992.

Camus, Albert. *The Rebel: An Essay on Man in Revolt*. 1951. Translated by Anthony Bower. New York: Vintage, 1991.

Carlson, Elof Axel. *The Unfit: A History of a Bad Idea*. Cold Spring Harbor, N.Y.: Cold Spring Harbor Laboratory Press, 2001.

Carpenter, Humphrey. *The Inklings: C. S. Lewis, J. R. R. Tolkien, Charles Williams and Their Friends*. London: Allen & Unwin, 1978.

Carroll, Lewis. *Alice's Adventures in Wonderland*. 1865. In *The Annotated Alice: Alice's Adventures in Wonderland & Through the Looking-Glass*. Edited by Martin Gardner. New York: W. W. Norton, 2000. pp. 17–164.

———. *Through the Looking-Glass*. 1871. In *The Annotated Alice: Alice's Adventures in Wonderland & Through the Looking-Glass*. Edited by Martin Gardner. New York: W. W. Norton, 2000. pp. 167–345.

Cassirer, Ernst. *The Individual and the Cosmos in Renaissance Philosophy*. 1926. Edited by Charles W. Hendel. Translated by Mario Domandi. New York: Barnes & Noble, 1963.

———. *The Myth of the State*. Edited by Charles W. Hendel. New Haven: Yale University Press, 1946.

Castle, Terry. *The Female Thermometer: Eighteenth-Century Culture and the Invention of the Uncanny*. New York: Oxford University Press, 1995.

Cavaliero, Glen. *Charles Williams: Poet of Theology*. Grand Rapids: Eerdmans, 1983.

———. *The Supernatural and English Fiction*. Oxford: Oxford University Press, 1995.

Chesterton, G. K. *Eugenics and Other Evils*. London: Cassell, 1922.

———. *The Everlasting Man*. 1925. San Francisco: Ignatius, 1993.

Chrétien de Troyes. *Perceval, or The Story of the Grail*. Translated by Ruth Harwood Cline. Athens: University of Georgia Press, 1985.

Christopher, Joe R. *C. S. Lewis*. Boston: Twayne, 1987.

Clark, David G. *C. S. Lewis: A Guide to His Theology*. Oxford: Blackwell, 2007.

Clayton, Philip. *Mind and Emergence: From Quantum to Consciousness*. New York: Oxford University Press, 2004.

Como, James T., ed. *C. S. Lewis at the Breakfast Table, and Other Reminiscences*. 1979. San Diego: Harcourt, 1992.

———. *Branches to Heaven: The Geniuses of C. S. Lewis*. Dallas: Spence Publishing Company, 1998.

Cooper, John W. *Panentheism—The Other God of the Philosophers: From Plato to the Present*. Grand Rapids: Baker Academic, 2006.

Crowe, Michael J. *The Extraterrestrial Life Debate, 1750–1900*. Mineola, N.Y.: Dover, 1999.

Cunningham, Valentine. *British Writers of the Thirties*. Oxford: Oxford University Press, 1988.

Currell, Susan, and Christina Cogdell, eds. *Popular Eugenics: National Efficiency and American Mass Culture in the 1930s*. Athens: Ohio University Press, 2006.

Cusanus, Nicholas. *Of Learned Ignorance*. 1440. Translated by Fr. Germain Heron. London: Routledge & Kegan Paul, 1954.

Daniels, David R. "The Branches of Time." *Wonder Stories* (August 1935) 294–303, 366.

Dante. *The Divine Comedy*. 6 vols. Translated, with a commentary, by Charles S. Singleton. Princeton: Princeton University Press, 1970–1975.

Darwin, Charles. *The Origin of Species by Means of Natural Selection; or, The Preservation of Favoured Races in the Struggle for Life*. 1859. Edited by J. W. Burrow. Harmondsworth, Middlesex: Penguin, 1968.

Day, William Patrick. *In the Circles of Fear and Desire: A Study of Gothic Fantasy*. Chicago: University of Chicago Press, 1985.

DeLamotte, Eugenia C. *Perils of the Night: A Feminist Study of Nineteenth-Century Gothic*. New York: Oxford University Press, 1990.

Deleuze, Gilles. *Bergsonism*. 1966. Translated by Hugh Tomlinson and Barbara Habberjam. New York: Zone, 1991.

Dentith, Simon. *Parody*. London: Routledge, 2000.

Derrick, Christopher. *C. S. Lewis and the Church of Rome: A Study in Proto-Ecumenism*. San Francisco: Ignatius Press, 1981.

Derrida, Jacques. *Specters of Marx: The State of the Debt, the Work of Mourning, & the New International*. 1993. Translated by Peggy Kamuf. New York: Routledge, 1994.

———. *The Animal That Therefore I Am.* Edited by Marie-Louise Mallet and translated by David Wills. New York: Fordham University Press, 2008.

De Vries, Hent. *Philosophy and the Turn to Religion.* Baltimore: Johns Hopkins University Press, 1999.

———. *Religion and Violence: Philosophical Perspectives from Kant to Derrida.* Baltimore: Johns Hopkins University Press, 2001.

Dick, Steven J. *Plurality of Worlds: The Origins of the Extraterrestrial Life Debate from Democritus to Kant.* Cambridge: Cambridge University Press, 1982.

———. *The Biological Universe: The Twentieth-Century Extraterrestrial Life Debate and the Limits of Science.* Cambridge: Cambridge University Press, 1996.

Dickerson, Matthew, and David O'Hara. *Narnia and the Fields of Arbol: The Environmental Vision of C. S. Lewis.* Lexington: University Press of Kentucky, 2008.

Donne, John. *Poetical Works.* Edited by Sir Herbert Grierson. London: Oxford University Press, 1933.

Douglas, Mary. *Thinking in Circles: An Essay on Ring Composition.* New Haven: Yale University Press, 2007.

Downing, David C. *Planets in Peril: A Critical Study of C. S. Lewis's Ransom Trilogy.* Amherst: University of Massachusetts Press, 1992.

———. "The Discarded Mage: Lewis the Scholar/Novelist on Merlin's Moral Taint." *Christian Scholar's Review* 27 (1998) 406–15.

———. *Into the Region of Awe: Mysticism in C. S. Lewis.* Downers Grove, Ill.: Intervarsity Press, 2005.

Dryden, Linda. *The Modern Gothic and Literary Doubles: Stevenson, Wilde and Wells.* London: Palgrave, 2003.

Du Maurier, Daphne. *Rebecca.* 1938. New York: HarperCollins, 1997.

Dunne, J. W. *An Experiment with Time.* 1927. Fourth edition, New York: Macmillan, 1938.

Dupré, Louis. *Passage to Modernity: An Essay in the Hermeneutics of Nature and Culture.* New Haven: Yale University Press, 1993.

Eddington, Arthur. *The Nature of the Physical World.* New York: Macmillan, 1928.

Edwards, Bruce L., ed. *The Taste of the Pineapple: Essays on C. S. Lewis as Reader, Critic, and Imaginative Writer.* Bowling Green, Ohio: Bowling Green State University Popular Press, 1988.

Eilberg-Schwartz, Howard, and Wendy Doniger, eds. *Off with Her Head! The Denial of Women's Identity in Myth, Religion, and Culture.* Berkeley: University of California Press, 1995.

Ellis, Kate. *The Contested Castle: Gothic Novels and the Subversion of Domestic Ideology.* Urbana: University of Illinois Press, 1989.

Fairfield, Leslie P. "Fragmentation and Hope: The Healing of the Modern Schisms in *That Hideous Strength.*" In *The Pilgrim's Guide: C. S. Lewis and the Art of Witness.* Edited by David Mills. Grand Rapids: Eerdmans, 1998. pp. 145–160.

Farber, Paul Lawrence. *The Temptations of Evolutionary Ethics.* Berkeley: University of California Press, 1994.

Ficino, Marsilio. *Platonic Theology.* 6 vols. Edited by James Hankins with William Bowen. Translated by Michael J.B. Allen and John Warden. Cambridge, Mass.: Harvard University Press, 2001–2006.

Fiedler, Leslie A. *Love and Death in the American Novel.* 1960. Revised edition, New York: Stein and Day, 1966.

Filmer, Kath. "From Belbury to Bernt-arse: The Rhetoric of the Wasteland in Lewis, Orwell and Hoban." *Mythlore* 52 (14.2; Winter 1987) 18–22.

———. "'Out of the Silent Planet': Reconstructing Wells with a Few Shots at Shaw." *Inklings: Jahrbuch für Literatur und Asthetik* 6 (1988) 43–54.

Flieger, Verlyn. *A Question of Time: J. R. R. Tolkien's Road to Faërie.* Kent, Ohio: Kent State University Press, 1997.

Fontenelle, Bernard le Bovier de. *Conversations on the Plurality of Worlds.* 1686. Translated by H. A. Hargreaves. Berkeley: University of California Press, 1990.

Fowler, Alistair. "C. S. Lewis: Supervisor." *Yale Review* 91.4 (October 2003) 64–80. Reprinted in *C. S. Lewis Remembered: Collected Reflections of Students, Friends and Colleagues.* Edited by Harry Lee Poe and Rebecca Whitten Poe. Grand Rapids: Zondervan, 2006. pp. 98–114.

Fredrick, Candice, and Sam McBride. *Women Among the Inklings: Gender, C. S. Lewis, J. R. R. Tolkien, and Charles Williams.* Westport, Conn.: Greenwood Press, 2001.

Freud, Sigmund. "The Uncanny." 1919. In *The Uncanny.* Translated by David McLintock. New York: Penguin, 2003. pp. 121–162.

Frye, Northrop. *Anatomy of Criticism: Four Essays.* Princeton: Princeton University Press, 1957.

———. *The Secular Scripture: A Study of the Structure of Romance.* Cambridge, Mass.: Harvard University Press, 1976.

Geoffrey of Monmouth. *The History of the Kings of Britain.* Translated by Lewis Thorpe. London: Penguin, 1966.

———. *Life of Merlin: Vita Merlini.* Edited and translated by Basil Clarke. Cardiff: University of Wales Press, 1973.

Gibson, Evan K. *C. S. Lewis, Spinner of Tales: A Guide to His Fiction.* Grand Rapids and Washington, D.C.: Christian University Press, 1980.

Girard, René. *Violence and the Sacred.* 1972. Translated by Patrick Gregory. Baltimore: Johns Hopkins University Press, 1977.

———. *Things Hidden Since the Foundation of the World.* 1978. Translated by Stephen Bann and Michael Metteer. Stanford: Stanford University Press, 1987.

Glover, Donald E. *C. S. Lewis: The Art of Enchantment.* Athens: Ohio University Press, 1981.

Glyer, Diana Pavlac. *The Company They Keep: C. S. Lewis and J. R. R. Tolkien as Writers in Community.* Kent, Ohio: Kent State University Press, 2007.

Goffar, Janine. *The C. S. Lewis Index: A Comprehensive Guide to Lewis's Writings and Ideas.* Wheaton, Ill.: Crossway Books, 1995.

Gollnick, James, ed. *Comparative Studies in Merlin from the Vedas to C. G. Jung.* Lewiston, N.Y.: Edwin Mellen, 1991.

Goodrich, Peter, and Raymond H. Thompson, eds. *Merlin: A Casebook.* New York: Routledge, 2003.

Grahame, Kenneth. *The Wind in the Willows.* 1908. Harmondsworth, Middlesex: Penguin, 1983.

Green, Roger Lancelyn, and Walter Hooper. *C. S. Lewis: A Biography.* 1974. Revised edition, London: HarperCollins, 2002.

Griffin, David Ray. *Reenchantment without Supernaturalism: A Process Philosophy of Religion.* Ithaca: Cornell University Press, 2001.

Grimstad, Kirsten J. *The Modern Revival of Gnosticism and Thomas Mann's* Doktor Faustus. Rochester, N.Y.: Camden House, 2002.

Grogin, R. C. *The Bergsonian Controversy in France, 1900–1914.* Calgary: University of Calgary Press, 1988.

Grosz, Elizabeth. *The Nick of Time: Politics, Evolution, and the Untimely.* Durham, N.C.: Duke University Press, 2004.

Guerlac, Suzanne. *Literary Polemics: Bataille, Sartre, Valéry, Breton.* Stanford: Stanford University Press, 1997.

———. *Thinking in Time: An Introduction to Henri Bergson.* Ithaca: Cornell University Press, 2006.

Guthke, Karl S. *The Last Frontier: Imagining Other Worlds, from the Copernican Revolution to Modern Science Fiction.* 1983. Translated by Helen Atkins. Ithaca: Cornell University Press, 1990.

Habermas, Jürgen. *The Future of Human Nature.* Cambridge: Polity Press, 2003.

Haggard, H. Rider. *King Solomon's Mines*. 1885. Oxford: Oxford University Press, 1989.

Haldane, J. B. S. *Dædalus; or, Science and the Future. A Paper Read to the Heretics, Cambridge, on February 4, 1923*. New York: Dutton, 1924.

———. *Possible Worlds and Other Essays*. 1927. New Brunswick, N.J.: Transaction, 2000.

Hannay, Margaret P. "A Preface to *Perelandra*." In *The Longing for a Form: Essays on the Fiction of C. S. Lewis*. Edited by Peter J. Schakel. Kent, Ohio: Kent State University Press, 1977. pp. 73–90.

Hart, Dabney Adams. *Through the Open Door: A New Look at C. S. Lewis*. University: University of Alabama Press, 1984.

Hastings, Adrian. *A History of English Christianity, 1920–1985*. London: Collins, 1986.

Hawes, Clement, ed. *Jonathan Swift: Gulliver's Travels and Other Writings*. Boston: Houghton Mifflin, 2004.

Hazelgrove, Jenny. *Spiritualism and British Society between the Wars*. Manchester: Manchester University Press, 2000.

Henderson, Linda Dalrymple. *The Fourth Dimension and Non-Euclidean Geometry in Modern Art*. Princeton: Princeton University Press, 1983.

Hillegas, Mark R. "*Out of the Silent Planet* as Cosmic Voyage." In *Shadows of Imagination: The Fantasies of C. S. Lewis, J. R. R. Tolkien, and Charles Williams*. Edited by Mark R. Hillegas. Carbondale: Southern Illinois University Press, 1969. pp. 41–58.

Hinton, C. Howard. *The Fourth Dimension*. 1904. Kila, Mont.: Kessinger Publishing, 1997.

Hodgkins, Christopher. *Reforming Empire: Protestant Colonialism and Conscience in British Literature*. Columbia: University of Missouri Press, 2002.

Hoeveler, Diane Long. *Gothic Feminism: The Professionalization of Gender from Charlotte Smith to the Brontës*. University Park: Pennsylvania State University Press, 1998.

Hogle, Jerrold E. *The Cambridge Companion to Gothic Fiction*. Cambridge: Cambridge University Press, 2002.

Holt, Victoria. *Mistress of Mellyn*. Garden City, N.Y.: Doubleday, 1960.

Hooper, Walter. *C. S. Lewis: A Companion & Guide*. San Francisco: HarperSanFrancisco, 1996.

Horkheimer, Max, and Theodor W. Adorno. *Dialectic of Enlightenment: Philosophical Fragments*. 1947. Edited by Gunzelin Schmid Noerr. Translated by Edmund Jephcott. Stanford: Stanford University Press, 2002.

Horsley, Lee. *Fictions of Power in English Literature: 1900–1950*. London: Longman, 1995.

Howard, Thomas. *C. S. Lewis, Man of Letters: A Reading of his Fiction*. San Francisco: Ignatius Press, 1987.

———. "The Triumphant Vindication of the Body: The End of Gnosticism in *That Hideous Strength*." In *The Pilgrim's Guide: C. S. Lewis and the Art of Witness*. Edited by David Mills. Grand Rapids: Eerdmans, 1998. pp. 133–144.

Hughes, H. Stuart. *The Obstructed Path: French Social Thought in the Years of Desperation, 1930–1960*. New York: Harper, 1966.

Hulme, T. E. *Speculations: Essays on Humanism and the Philosophy of Art*. 1924. London: Routledge & Kegan Paul, 1936.

Hurley, Kelly. *The Gothic Body: Sexuality, Materialism, and Degeneration at the Fin de Siècle*. Cambridge: Cambridge University Press, 1996.

Huttar, Charles A. "Milton." In *Reading the Classics with C. S. Lewis*. Edited by Thomas L. Martin. Grand Rapids: Baker Academic, 2000. pp. 161–186.

Huttar, Charles A., and Peter J. Schakel, eds. *The Rhetoric of Vision: Essays on Charles Williams*. Lewisburg: Bucknell University Press, 1996.

Huxley, Aldous. *Brave New World*. 1932. New York: HarperCollins, 2006.

Huxley, Julian S., and A. C. Haddon. *We Europeans: A Survey of 'Racial' Problems*. New York: Harper, 1936.

Huygens, Christiaan. *The Celestial Worlds Discover'd*. 1698. Translated by Timothy Childe. London: Cass, 1968.

Hynes, Samuel. *The Auden Generation: Literature and Politics in England in the 1930s*. London: Bodley Head, 1976.

Inglis, Brian. *Science and Parascience: A History of the Paranormal, 1914–1939*. London: Hodder and Stoughton, 1984.

Jackson, Rosemary. *Fantasy: The Literature of Subversion*. London and New York: Methuen, 1981.

Jacobs, Alan. *The Narnian: The Life and Imagination of C. S. Lewis*. San Francisco: HarperSanFrancisco, 2005.

James, Edward. *Science Fiction in the Twentieth Century*. Oxford: Oxford University Press, 1994.

Jameson, Fredric. *Archaeologies of the Future*. London: Verso, 2005.

Jeans, James. *The Mysterious Universe*. 1930. Revised edition, Cambridge: Cambridge University Press, 2008.

Jonas, Hans. *The Gnostic Religion: The Message of the Alien God and the Beginnings of Christianity*. 1958 (based on his *Gnosis und spätantiker Geist*, 1934; 1954). Third edition, Boston: Beacon Press, 2001.

Jones, Greta. *Social Darwinism and English Thought: The Interaction between Biological and Social Theory.* Brighton: Harvester; Atlantic Highlands, N.J.: Humanities Press, 1980.

Juergensmeyer, Mark. *Terror in the Mind of God: The Global Rise of Religious Violence.* Berkeley: University of California Press, 2000.

Kafka, Franz. *The Trial.* 1925. Translated by Breon Mitchell. New York: Schocken, 1998.

————. *The Castle.* 1926. Translated by Mark Harman. New York: Schocken, 1998.

Kant, Immanuel. *Universal Natural History and Theory of the Heavens.* 1755. Translated by Stanley L. Jaki. Edinburgh: Scottish Academic Press, 1981.

————. *Critique of the Power of Judgment.* 1790. Edited by Paul Gyer. Translated by Paul Gyer and Eric Matthews. Cambridge: Cambridge University Press, 2000.

Keenan, Dennis King. *The Question of Sacrifice.* Bloomington: Indiana University Press, 2005.

Kevles, Daniel J. *In the Name of Eugenics: Genetics and the Uses of Human Heredity.* New York: Knopf, 1985.

Kiely, Robert. *The Romantic Novel in England.* Cambridge, Mass.: Harvard University Press, 1972.

Kierkegaard, Soren. *Fear and Trembling/Repetition.* 1843. Edited and translated by Howard V. Hong and Edna H. Hong. Princeton: Princeton University Press, 1983.

Kimball, Charles. *When Religion Becomes Evil.* San Francisco: HarperSanFrancisco, 2002.

King, Alec, and Martin Ketley. *The Control of Language: A Critical Approach to Reading and Writing.* London: Longmans, Green, 1939.

King, Don W. *C. S. Lewis, Poet: The Legacy of His Poetic Impulse.* Kent, Ohio: Kent State University Press, 2001.

King, Karen L. *What is Gnosticism?* Cambridge, Mass.: Harvard University Press, 2003.

Kollar, Rene. *Searching for Raymond: Anglicanism, Spiritualism, and Bereavement between the Two World Wars.* Lanham, Md.: Lexington Books, 2000.

Kort, Wesley A. *C. S. Lewis Then and Now.* Oxford: Oxford University Press, 2001.

Koyré, Alexandre. *From the Closed World to the Infinite Universe.* Baltimore: Johns Hopkins University Press, 1957.

Krauss, Lawrence M. *Hiding in the Mirror: The Mysterious Allure of Extra Dimensions, from Plato to String Theory and Beyond.* New York: Viking, 2005.

Kuhn, Thomas S. *The Structure of Scientific Revolutions.* Chicago: University of Chicago Press, 1962.

Kumar, Krishan. *Utopia and Anti-Utopia in Modern Times.* Oxford: Blackwell, 1987.

Lake, David. "The Variant Texts of *That Hideous Strength.*" *The Ring Bearer* 7.1 (Winter 1989) 52–58.

———. "Wells, *The First Men in the Moon,* and Lewis's Ransom Trilogy." In *Twentieth-Century Fantasists: Essays on Culture, Society, and Belief in Twentieth-Century Mythopoeic Literature.* Edited by Kath Filmer. New York: St. Martin's, 1992. pp. 23–33.

Laurent, John. "C. S. Lewis and Animal Rights." *Mythlore* 71 (19.1; Winter 1993) 46–51.

Lawlor, Leonard. *The Challenge of Bergsonism: Phenomenology, Ontology, Ethics.* London: Continuum, 2003.

———. *This Is Not Sufficient: An Essay on Animality and Human Nature in Derrida.* New York: Columbia University Press, 2007.

Lear, John. *Kepler's Dream.* Originally *Somnium, Sive Astronomia Lunaris, Joannis Kepleri.* 1634. Translated by Patricia Frueh Kirkwood. Berkeley: University of California Press, 1965.

Leinster, Murray. "Sidewise in Time." *Astounding Stories* (June 1934). Reprinted in *Before the Golden Age: A Science Fiction Anthology of the 1930's. Book 2.* Edited by Isaac Asimov. Greenwich, Conn.: Doubleday, 1974. pp. 229–279.

L'Engle, Madeleine. *A Wrinkle in Time.* New York: Farrar, Straus, and Giroux, 1962.

Lewis, Jane. *Women in England, 1870–1950: Sexual Divisions and Social Change.* Bloomington: Indiana University Press, 1984.

Light, Alison. *Forever England: Femininity, Literature and Conservatism between the Wars.* London: Routledge, 1991.

Lindsay, David. *A Voyage to Arcturus.* 1920. Mineola, N.Y.: Dover, 2005.

Lindskoog, Kathryn. *The C. S. Lewis Hoax.* Portland, Ore.: Multnomah Press, 1988.

Lippmann, Walter. *A Preface to Politics.* 1913. Reprint, New York: Henry Holt, 1917.

Lobdell, Jared. "The Caroline Vision and Detective-Fiction Rhetoric: The Evidence of the Reviews." In *The Rhetoric of Vision: Essays on Charles Williams.* Edited by Charles A. Huttar and Peter J. Schakel. Lewisburg, Penn.: Bucknell University Press, 1996. pp. 290–308.

———. "Prolegomena to a Study of Lewis's Arcadian Science-Fiction: How Would 'The Dark Tower' Have Come Out?" *Extrapolation* 41 (2000) 175–196.

———. *The Detective Fiction Reviews of Charles Williams, 1930–1935.* Jefferson, N.C.: McFarland, 2003.

———. *The Scientifiction Novels of C. S. Lewis: Space and Time in the Ransom Stories.* Jefferson, N.C.: McFarland, 2004.

Lovejoy, Arthur O. *The Great Chain of Being: A Study of the History of an Idea.* Cambridge, Mass.: Harvard University Press, 1936.

Luckhurst, Roger. *Science Fiction.* Cambridge: Polity Press, 2005.

Lutton, Jeannette Hume. "Wasteland Myth in C. S. Lewis's *That Hideous Strength.*" In *Forms of the Fantastic.* Edited by Jan Hokenson and Howard D. Pearce. Westport, Conn.: Greenwood Press, 1986. pp. 69–86.

Macdonald, George. *The Princess and the Goblin.* 1872. Reprint, Whitethorn, Calif.: Johannesen, 1993.

———. *The Princess and Curdie.* 1883. Reprint, Whitethorn, Calif.: Johannesen, 1993.

Mancoff, Debra N., ed. *King Arthur's Modern Return.* New York: Garland, 1998.

Mann, Thomas. *Doctor Faustus: The Life of the German Composer Adrian Leverkühn as Told by a Friend.* 1947. Translated by John E. Woods. New York: Vintage, 1999.

Maritain, Jacques. *Bergsonian Philosophy and Thomism.* 1913. Translated by Mabelle L. Andison in collaboration with J. Gordon Andison. South Bend, Ind.: University of Notre Dame Press, 2007.

Markale, Jean. *Merlin: Priest of Nature.* 1981. Translated by Belle N. Burke. Rochester, Vt.: Inner Traditions International, 1995.

Markley, Robert. *Dying Planet: Mars in Science and the Imagination.* Durham, N.C.: Duke University Press, 2005.

Martin, Thomas L., ed. *Reading the Classics with C. S. Lewis.* Grand Rapids: Baker Academic, 2000.

Mascall, E. L. "The Christian and the Next War." *Theology* 38 (1939) 53–58.

Massé, Michelle A. *In the Name of Love: Women, Masochism, and the Gothic.* Ithaca: Cornell University Press, 1992.

McKenna, Andrew J. *Violence and Difference: Girard, Derrida, and Deconstruction.* Urbana: University of Illinois Press, 1992.

Meilaender, Gilbert. *The Taste for the Other: The Social and Ethical Thought of C. S. Lewis.* Grand Rapids: Eerdmans, 1978.

Merleau-Ponty, Maurice. *Phenomenology of Perception.* 1945. Translated by Colin Smith. London: Routledge, 2002.

Midgley, Mary. *Animals and Why They Matter.* Athens: University of Georgia Press, 1984.

Milbank, John. *Theology and Social Theory: Beyond Secular Reason.* 1990. Second edition, Oxford: Blackwell, 2006.

Millin, Sarah Gertrude. *Rhodes.* London: Chatto & Windus, 1933.

Milton, John. *Complete Poems and Major Prose.* Edited by Merritt Y. Hughes. Indianapolis: Bobbs-Merrill, 1957.

Moberly, C. A. E. and E. F. Jourdain. *An Adventure.* 1911. Fourth edition, London: Faber and Faber, 1931.

Moore, C. L. "Tryst in Time." *Astounding Stories* (December 1936). Reprinted within *The Best of C. L. Moore.* Edited by Lester del Rey. New York: Ballantine, 1975. pp. 114–136.

More, Henry. *Henry More's Manual of Metaphysics: A Translation of the Enchiridium Metaphysicum (1679) with an Introduction and Notes.* 2 vols. Translated by Alexander Jacob. Hildesheim; New York: G. Olms, Verlag, 1995.

———. *A Platonick Song of the Soul.* 1642. Second edition edited by Alexander Jacob. Lewisburg, Penn.: Bucknell University Press, 1998.

Morgan, C. Lloyd. *Emergent Evolution: The Gifford Lectures, Delivered in the University of St. Andrews in the Year 1922.* New York: Henry Holt, 1923.

Morrisson, Mark. *Modern Alchemy: Occultism and the Emergence of Atomic Theory.* New York: Oxford University Press, 2007.

Mullarkey, John, ed. *The New Bergson.* Manchester: Manchester University Press, 1999.

Myers, Doris T. "Law and Disorder: Two Settings in *That Hideous Strength.*" *Mythlore* 71 (19.1; Winter 1993) 9–14.

———. *C. S. Lewis in Context.* Kent, Ohio: Kent State University Press, 1994.

———. "Hrossa, Pigs, and Teddy Bears: The Animal Kingdom According to C. S. Lewis." *Mythlore* 84 (22.2; Summer 1998) 4–9.

Nahin, Paul J. *Time Machines: Time Travel in Physics, Metaphysics, and Science Fiction.* 1993. Second edition, New York: Springer, 1999.

Nelson, Dale J. "C. S. Lewis on Weird Fantasy." *CSL: The Bulletin of the New York C. S. Lewis Society* 31.10–11 (Oct/Nov 2000) 1–13.

Neuhouser, David L. "Higher Dimensions: C. S. Lewis and Mathematics." *Seven* 13 (1996) 45–63.

Neuleib, Janice. "Love's Alchemy: Jane in *That Hideous Strength.*" *Mythlore* 23 (7.1; March 1980) 16–17.

———. "Comic Grotesques: The Means of Revelation in *Wise Blood* and *That Hideous Strength.*" *Christianity and Literature* 30.4 (1981) 27–36.

Nicholson, Mervyn. "Bram Stoker and C. S. Lewis: Dracula as a Source for *That Hideous Strength.*" *Mythlore* 73 (19.3; Summer 1993) 16–22.

Nicolson, Marjorie Hope. *Voyages to the Moon.* New York: Macmillan, 1948.

O'Neill, Joseph. *Land under England.* 1935. Woodstock, N.Y.: Overlook Press, 1985.

Oppenheim, Janet. *The Other World: Spiritualism and Psychical Research in England, 1850–1914.* Cambridge: Cambridge University Press, 1985.

O'Regan, Cyril. *Gnostic Return in Modernity.* Albany: SUNY Press, 2001.

Orwell, George. *Nineteen Eighty-Four: A Novel.* 1949. New York: Plume, 2003.

Osborn, Marijane, "Deeper Realms: C. S. Lewis' Re-Visions of Joseph O'Neill's *Land under England.*" *Journal of Modern Literature* 25 (2001) 115–120.

Otto, Rudolf. *The Idea of the Holy: An Inquiry into the Non-Rational Factor in the Idea of the Divine and Its Relation to the Rational.* 1917. Translated by John W. Harvey. New York: Oxford University Press, 1958.

Ouspensky, P. D. *Tertium Organum, or the Third Canon of Thought and a Key to the Enigmas of the World.* 1912. Kila, Mt: Kessinger, 2005.

———. *A New Model of the Universe: Principles of the Psychological method in its Application to Problems of Science, Religion, and Art.* 1931. New edition, Mineola, N.Y.: Dover, 1997.

Owen, Alex. *The Place of Enchantment: British Occultism and the Culture of the Modern.* Chicago: University of Chicago Press, 2004.

Patrick, James, "C. S. Lewis and Idealism." In *Rumours of Heaven: Essays in Celebration of C. S. Lewis.* Edited by Andrew Walker and James Patrick. Guildford, Surrey: Eagle, 1998. pp. 156–173.

Patterson, Nancy-Lou. "*Guardaci Ben:* The Visionary Woman in C. S. Lewis' Chronicles of Narnia and *That Hideous Strength.*" *Mythlore* 21 (6.3; Summer 1979) 6–10; 22 (6.4; Fall 1979) 20–24.

———. "Banquet at Belbury: Festival and Horror in *That Hideous Strength.*" *Mythlore* 29 (8.3; Autumn 1981) 7–14, 42.

———. "'Some Kind of Company': The Sacred Community in *That Hideous Strength.*" *Mythlore* 47 (13.1; Autumn 1986) 8–19.

Peters, Thomas C. "The War of the Worldviews: H. G. Wells and Scientism versus C. S. Lewis and Christianity." In *The Pilgrim's Guide: C. S. Lewis and the Art of Witness.* Edited by David Mills. Grand Rapids: Eerdmans, 1998. pp. 203–220.

Phillips, Justin. *C. S. Lewis at the BBC: Messages of Hope in the Darkness of War.* London: HarperCollins, 2002.

Plato. *The Collected Dialogues of Plato.* Edited by Edith Hamilton and Huntington Cairns. Princeton: Princeton University Press, 1963.

Plotinus. *The Enneads.* Translated by Stephen MacKenna. Fourth edition revised by B. S. Page. London: Faber, 1969.

Poe, Harry Lee, and Rebecca Whitten Poe, eds. *C. S. Lewis Remembered: Collected Reflections of Students, Friends & Colleagues.* Grand Rapids: Zondervan, 2006.

Proctor, Robert. *Racial Hygiene: Medicine under the Nazis.* Cambridge, Mass.: Harvard University Press, 1988.

Pugh, Martin. *Women and the Women's Movement in Britain: 1914–1959.* London: Macmillan, 1992.

Punter, David. *The Literature of Terror: A History of Gothic Fictions from 1765 to the Present Day.* London: Longman, 1980.

———, ed. *A Companion to the Gothic.* Oxford: Blackwell, 2000.

Purtill, Richard L. "*That Hideous Strength:* A Double Story." In *The Longing for a Form: Essays on the Fiction of C. S. Lewis.* Edited by Peter J. Schakel. Kent, Ohio: Kent State University Press, 1977. pp. 91–102.

Quirk, Tom. *Bergson and American Culture: The Worlds of Willa Cather and Wallace Stevens.* Chapel Hill: University of North Carolina Press, 1990.

Radcliffe, Ann. *The Mysteries of Udolpho.* 1794. London: Penguin, 2001.

Railo, Eino. *The Haunted Castle: A Study of the Elements of English Romanticism.* London: Routledge, 1927.

Rateliff, John D. "*The Lost Road, The Dark Tower* and *The Notion Club Papers:* Tolkien and Lewis's Time Travel Triad." In *Tolkien's "Legendarium": Essays on "The History of Middle-earth."* Edited by Verlyn Flieger and Carl F. Hostetter. Westport, Conn.: Greenwood, 2000. pp. 199–218.

Rawson, Ellen. "The Fisher King in *That Hideous Strength.*" *Mythlore* 34 (9.4; Winter 1983) 30–32.

Redgrove, H. Stanley. *Alchemy: Ancient and Modern.* 1911. Second edition, London: William Rider, 1922.

Reilly, John R. "The Torture Tutorial: Finding out the Awful Truth in *That Hideous Strength* and *1984.*" *Mythlore* 82 (21.4; Winter 1997) 39–41.

Relihan, Joel C. *Ancient Menippean Satire.* Baltimore: Johns Hopkins University Press, 1993.

Richter, David H. *The Progress of Romance: Literary Historiography and the Gothic Novel.* Columbus: Ohio State University Press, 1996.

Roberts, Marie. *Gothic Immortals: The Fiction of the Brotherhood of the Rosy Cross.* London: Routledge, 1990.

Rousseau, Jean-Jacques. *The First and Second Discourses.* Edited by Roger D. Masters. Translated by Roger D. and Judith R. Masters. New York: St. Martin's, 1964.

Sammons, Martha C. *A Guide through C. S. Lewis' Space Trilogy.* Westchester, Ill.: Cornerstone, 1980.

Sartre, Jean-Paul. *Being and Nothingness: An Essay on Phenomenological Ontology.* 1943. Translated by Hazel E. Barnes. London: Routledge, 2003.

Sayer, George. *Jack: C. S. Lewis and His Times.* New York: Harper & Row, 1988.

Schakel, Peter J., ed. *The Longing for a Form: Essays on the Fiction of C. S. Lewis.* Kent, Ohio: Kent State University Press, 1977.

———. "That 'Hideous Strength' in Lewis and Orwell: A Comparison and Contrast." *Mythlore* 50 (13.4; Summer 1987) 36–40.

———. "The Satiric Imagination of C. S. Lewis." *Studies in the Literary Imagination* 22 (1989) 129–148.

———. *Imagination and the Arts in C. S. Lewis: Journeying to Narnia and Other Worlds.* Columbia: University of Missouri Press, 2002.

Schakel, Peter J., and Charles A. Huttar, eds. *Word and Story in C. S. Lewis.* Columbia: University of Missouri Press, 1991.

Schultz, Jeffrey D., and John G. West, Jr., eds. *The C. S. Lewis Readers' Encyclopedia.* Grand Rapids: Zondervan, 1988.

Schwartz, Sanford. "Bergson and the Politics of Vitalism." In *The Crisis in Modernism: Bergson and the Vitalist Controversy.* Edited by Frederick Burwick and Paul Douglass. Cambridge: Cambridge University Press, 1992. pp. 277–305.

———. "Paradise Reframed: Lewis, Bergson, and Changing Times on Perelandra." *Christianity and Literature* 51 (2002) 569–602.

———. "Cosmic Anthropology: Race and Reason in *Out of the Silent Planet.*" *Christianity and Literature* 52 (2003) 523–556.

———. "Why Wells Is from Mars, Bergson from Venus: Mapping Evolution in the *Space Trilogy.*" In *C. S. Lewis: Views from Wake Forest.* Edited by Michael Travers. Wayne, Penn.: Zossima Press, 2008. pp. 201–222.

Schweizer, Bernard. *Radicals on the Road: The Politics of English Travel Writing in the 1930s.* Charlottesville: University of Virginia Press, 2001.

Sell, W. "Other Tracks." *Astounding Science Fiction* (October 1938). Reprinted in *Science-Fiction Adventures in Dimension.* Edited by Groff Conklin. New York: Vanguard, 1953. pp. 98–117.

Shaw, George Bernard. *Back to Methuselah: A Metabiological Pentateuch.* 1921. Harmondsworth, Middlesex: Penguin, 1988.

Shelley, Mary. *Frankenstein, or, The Modern Prometheus.* 1818. New York: Penguin, 2003.

Shelley, Percy Bysshe. *Shelley's Poetry and Prose.* Second edition edited by Donald H. Reiman and Neil Fraistat. New York: W. W. Norton, 2002.

Shideler, Mary McDermott. *The Theology of Romantic Love: A Study in the Writings of Charles Williams.* Grand Rapids: Eerdmans, 1962.

Silvestris, Bernardus. *Cosmographia.* Translated by Winthrop Wetherbee. New York: Columbia University Press, 1973.

Spencer, Kathleen. *Charles Williams.* Mercer Island, Wash.: Starmont House, 1986.

———. "Naturalizing the Fantastic: Narrative Technique in the Novels of Charles Williams." *Extrapolation: A Journal of Science Fiction and Fantasy* 28 (1987) 62–74.

Spenser, Edmund. *The Faerie Queene.* 1590; 1596. Edited by A. C. Hamilton. Harlow, England: Longman, 2001.

Squier, Susan. *Babies in Bottles: Twentieth-Century Visions of Reproductive Technology.* New Brunswick, N.J.: Rutgers University Press, 1994.

Stableford, Brian. *Scientific Romance in Britain, 1890–1950.* London: Fourth Estate, 1985.

Stapledon, Olaf. *Last and First Men.* 1930. Mineola, N.Y.: Dover, 2008.

———. *Star-Maker.* 1937. Middletown, Conn.: Wesleyan University Press, 2004.

Starr, Nathan. *King Arthur Today: The Arthurian Legend in English and American Literature, 1901–1953.* Gainesville: University of Florida Press, 1954.

Steiner, Rudolf. *The Fourth Dimension: Sacred Geometry, Alchemy, and Mathematics.* Great Barrington, Mass.: Anthroposophic Press, 2001. (A collection of lectures and other related pieces, 1905–1922).

Stern, Alexandra. *Eugenic Nation: Faults and Frontiers of Better Breeding in Modern America.* Berkeley: University of California Press, 2005.

Stewart, R. J. *The Mystic Life of Merlin.* London: Arkana, 1986.

Stocking, George W., Jr. *Victorian Anthropology.* New York: Macmillan, 1987.

———. *After Tylor: British Social Anthropology, 1888–1951.* Madison: University of Wisconsin Press, 1995.

Stoker, Bram. *The New Annotated Dracula.* 1897. Edited by Leslie S. Klinger. New York: W. W. Norton, 2008.

Summers, Montague. *The Gothic Quest: A History of the Gothic Novel.* London: Fortune Press, 1938.

Swift, Jonathan. *Gulliver's Travels.* 1726. *The Prose Works of Jonathan Swift. Vol. 11.* Edited by Herbert Davis. Oxford: Blackwell, 1941.

Taylor, Beverly, and Elisabeth Brewer. *The Return of King Arthur: British and American Arthurian Literature since 1900.* Cambridge: D.S. Brewer, 1983.

Teilhard de Chardin, Pierre. *The Phenomenon of Man.* 1955. Translated by Bernard Wall. New York: Harper, 1975.

Thiébaux, Marcelle. *The Stag of Love: The Chase in Medieval Literature.* Ithaca: Cornell University Press, 1974.

Thompson, Raymond H. *The Return from Avalon: A Study of the Arthurian Legend in Modern Fiction.* Westport, Conn.: Greenwood Press, 1985.

Todorov, Tzvetan. *The Fantastic: A Structural Approach to a Literary Genre.* 1970. Translated by Richard Howard. Ithaca: Cornell University Press, 1975.

Tolkien, J. R. R. *The Hobbit, or, There and Back Again.* 1937. Boston: Houghton Mifflin, 2002.

———. *The Lord of the Rings.* 1954–1955. Boston: Houghton Mifflin, 2004.

———. *The Letters of J. R. R. Tolkien: A Selection.* Edited by Humphrey Carpenter. 1981. Boston: Houghton Mifflin, 2000.

———. "The Notion Club Papers." In *Sauron Defeated.* Edited by Christopher Tolkien. In *The History of Middle Earth,* Vol. IX. Boston: Houghton Mifflin, 1992. pp. 143–327.

Tolstoy, Nikolai. *The Quest for Merlin.* London: H. Hamilton, 1985.

Tompkins, J. M. S. *The Popular Novel in England 1770–1800.* London: Constable, 1932.

Travers, Michael, ed. *C. S. Lewis: Views from Wake Forest.* Wayne, Penn.: Zossima Press, 2008.

Urang, Gunnar. *Shadows of Heaven: Religion and Fantasy in the Writing of C. S. Lewis, Charles Williams, and J. R. R. Tolkien.* Philadelphia: Pilgrim Press, 1971.

Varma, Devendra P. *The Gothic Flame: Being a History of the Gothic Novel in England.* London: A. Barker, 1957.

Varnado, S. L. *Haunted Presence: The Numinous in Gothic Fiction.* Tuscaloosa: University of Alabama Press, 1987.

Voegelin, Eric. *The History of the Race Idea: From Ray to Carus.* 1933. Edited by Klaus Vondung. Translated by Ruth Hein. Baton Rouge: Louisiana State University Press, 1998.

———. *Race and State.* 1933. Edited by Klaus Vondung. Translated by Ruth Hein. Baton Rouge: Louisiana State University Press, 1997.

———. *The New Science of Politics: An Introduction.* Chicago: University of Chicago Press, 1952.

Waddington, C. H. *Science and Ethics: An Essay.* London: Allen & Unwin, 1942.

Walker, Andrew, and James Patrick, eds. *Rumours of Heaven: Essays in Celebration of C. S. Lewis.* Guildford, Surrey: Eagle, 1998.

Walker, D. P. *Spiritual and Demonic Magic: From Ficino to Campanella.* 1958. University Park: Pennsylvania State University Press, 2000.

Wallace, Diana. "Revising the Marriage Plot in Women's Fiction of the 1930s." In *Women Writers of the 1930s: Gender, Politics and History.* Edited by Maroula Joannou. Edinburgh: Edinburgh University Press, 1999. pp. 63–75.

Walpole, Horace. *The Castle of Otranto.* 1764. London: Penguin, 2001.

Ward, Michael. *Planet Narnia: The Seven Heavens in the Imagination of C. S. Lewis.* New York: Oxford University Press, 2008.

Warner, Marina. *From the Beast to the Blonde: On Fairy Tales and Their Tellers.* 1994. London: Vintage, 1995.

Warner, Rex. *The Aerodrome: A Love Story.* 1941. Chicago: Ivan R. Dee, 1993.

Weikart, Richard. *From Darwin to Hitler: Evolutionary Ethics, Eugenics, and Racism in Germany.* New York: Palgrave, 2004.

Weinbrot, Howard D. *Menippean Satire Reconsidered: From Antiquity to the Eighteenth Century.* Baltimore: Johns Hopkins University Press, 2005.

Wells, H. G. *The Wonderful Visit.* London: J. M. Dent, 1895.

———. "The Crystal Egg." 1897. *The Complete Short Stories.* New York: St. Martin's, 1971. pp. 626–643.

———. *The Outline of History: Being a Plain History of Life and Mankind.* New York: Macmillan, 1920.

———. *Men Like Gods: A Novel.* New York: Macmillan, 1923.

———. *The Island of Doctor Moreau: A Critical Text of the 1896 London First Edition.* Edited by Leon Stover. Jefferson, N.C.: McFarland, 1996.

———. *The Time Machine: An Invention: A Critical Text of the 1895 London First Edition.* Edited by Leon Stover. Jefferson, N.C.: McFarland, 1996.

———. *The First Men in the Moon: A Critical Text of the 1901 London First Edition.* Edited by Leon Stover. Jefferson, N.C.: McFarland, 1998.

———. *The War of the Worlds: A Critical Text of the 1898 London First Edition.* Edited by Leon Stover. Jefferson, N.C.: McFarland, 2001.

Werskey, Gary. *The Visible College: The Collective Biography of British Scientific Socialists of the 1930's.* New York: Holt, Rinehart, and Winston, 1979.

Whitehead, Alfred North. *Science and the Modern World.* 1925. New York: Free Press, 1997.

———. *Process and Reality: An Essay in Cosmology.* 1929. Corrected edition by David Ray Griffin and Donal W. Sherburne. New York: Free Press, 1979.

Wilkins, John. *The Discovery of a World in the Moone.* 1638. Delmar, New York: Scholars' Facsimiles & Reprints, 1973.

Williams, Anne. *Art of Darkness: A Poetics of Gothic.* Chicago: University of Chicago Press, 1995.

Williams, Charles. *War in Heaven.* 1930. Grand Rapids: Eerdmans, 1994.

———. *Many Dimensions.* 1931. Grand Rapids: Eerdmans, 1993.

———. *The Place of the Lion.* 1931. Grand Rapids: Eerdmans, 1991

———. *The Greater Trumps.* 1932. Grand Rapids: Eerdmans, 1976.

———. *Shadows of Ecstasy.* 1933. Vancouver: Regent College Publishing, 2003.

———. *Descent into Hell.* 1937. Grand Rapids: Eerdmans, 1996.

———. *He Came Down From Heaven.* 1938. Berkeley, Calif.: Apocryphile Press, 2005.

———. *Taliessin through Logres.* 1938. *Taliessin through Logres [and] The Region of the Summer Stars.* Grand Rapids: Eerdmans, 1974. pp. 15–112.

———. *The Descent of the Dove: A Short History of the Holy Spirit in the Church.* 1939. Vancouver: Regent College Publishing, 2002.

———. *The Figure of Beatrice: A Study in Dante.* 1943. Berkeley, Calif.: Apocryphile Press, 2005.

———. *The Region of the Summer Stars.* 1944. *Taliessin through Logres [and] The Region of the Summer Stars.* Grand Rapids: Eerdmans, 1974. pp. 113–179.

———. *All Hallows' Eve.* 1945. Grand Rapids: Eerdmans, 1981.

Williamson, Jack. *The Legion of Time.* 1938. New York: Pyramid Books, 1952.

Wilson, A.N. *C. S. Lewis: A Biography.* New York: W. W. Norton, 1990.

Wilt, Judith. "The Imperial Mouth: Imperialism, the Gothic and Science Fiction." *Journal of Popular Culture* 14 (1981) 618–628.

Wolfe, Cary. *Animal Rites: American Culture, the Discourse of Species, and Posthumanist Theory.* Chicago: University of Chicago Press, 2003.

———, ed. *Zootologies. The Question of the Animal.* Minneapolis: University of Minnesota Press, 2003.

Wright, Patrick. *The Village That Died for England: The Strange Story of Tyneham.* 1995. London: Faber, 2002.

Zgorzelski, Andrzej. "Is Science Fiction a Genre of Fantastic Literature?" *Science-Fiction Studies* 6 (1979) 296–303.

Index

Abbott, Edwin: *Flatland*, and the fourth
    dimension 162n5, 180n19.
    See also higher dimensions
Adorno, Theodor: *Dialectic of Enlightenment*
    (co-author), and *Abolition of Man*
    192–193n28
An Adventure (Moberly and Jourdain): and
    DT 152–153. *See also* occult
    alchemy 99, 186n10. *See also* occult
Aldiss, Brian: round-table with CSL ("Unreal
    Estates") 173n23
Alexander, Samuel. *See also* creative evolution
    contemplation/enjoyment 174n1
    CSL on 174n1, 176–177n9
    emergent evolution 73
    and idea of *nisus* 176n8
    as "indispensable tool of thought" 176n9
    related to "stepping out of life into the
        Alongside" (*P*) 176n9
    in *Space, Time and Deity* 174n1
Alighieri, Dante: *Divine Comedy, contrapasso* and
    retributive justice (*THS*) 135, 196n39
Amis, Kingsley: round-table with CSL ("Unreal
    Estates") 173n23
andwards/eckwards. *See also* higher dimensions
    as movement between levels of Being 162n5
    as transit between worlds (*DT*) 155
"The Animal That Therefore I Am (More to
    Follow)" (Derrida): as play on
    cogito, ergo sum 172n20
animals. *See also* body
    the *animale rationale* ("rational animal") 63,
        83–85
    cohabitation with 170–171n14
    "creatureliness" 189–190n19, 195n37
    cruelty to 21–22, 24, 32
    distinguishing human/nonhuman 21–22, 48,
        165–166n2, 172n21
    elemental fear of 31–32
    emancipation of (*THS*) 134–137

human kinship to 37–39, 43–44, 189n19
humans as 21–22, 43–44, 80, 165–166n2,
    172n20
humans as union of spirit and flesh 121–122,
    124–125, 139, 143, 147, 148, 189n19,
    195n37
hunting (*OSP*) 13, 20, 37–39, 45, 66, 141–149
mating of the beasts (*THS*) 137
Merlin associated with (*THS*) 125
(mis)recognition of other rational (*OSP*)
    14, 19–20, 38–39, 40–41, 50–52,
    165–166n2, 170–171n14,
    171–172n19
as more than mere matter (*THS*) 121–122
Mr. Bultitude (*THS*) 115, 121–122, 124, 135,
    191n24
rational aliens resemble (*OSP*) 40–41, 69
recent discourse on 172nn20–21
scientific sacrifice of 27
sentience, consciousness, intelligence in 21,
    124, 165–166n2
stewardship of 165–166n2
vivisection of 104
Animals and Why They Matter (Midgley): on
    human/animal cohabitation
    170–171n14. *See also* animals
Anstey, F.
    and Mr. Bultitude (*THS*) 115
    as "the only truthful school story" 191n24
    Vice Versa, and criss-cross plot (*THS*) 114,
        191n24
anthropology. *See also* evolution; evolutionary
    model
    Chesterton as critic of evolutionary 51–52
    "cosmic" or "corrective" 52
    evolutionary 20–21, 29–30, 36–37
    Midgley on human/animal cohabitation
        170–171n14
    ("old stone age") 168n9
    Rousseau's 50–52, 173n25

223

Apocolocyntosis [Seneca]: as ancestor of modern "fantastic" satire 185n7
apophatic discourse: in mystical tradition 163n5
Apuleius: and the "method" of *THS* 185n7
archetype/copy. *See* original/copy
Art of Darkness (Anne Williams): on "female" Gothic 185n8, 190n21. *See also* Gothic fiction
Arthurian romance. *See* romance
astrology 196–197n38. *See also* occult
Atonement. *See also* Cross
   CSL on 197–198n4
   modern controversy over 197–198n4
Auden, W. H.: *The Ascent of F6*, scholar Ransom protagonist of 169n11
Augustine. *See* St. Augustine

Back to Methuselah (Shaw): myth of creative rebellion 74. *See also* evolutionary model
Barfield, Owen
   "ancient unities" of (*THS*) 124
   debate with CSL 189–190n19
   Poetic Diction 193–194n31
Beauty and the Beast: and "female" Gothic 107–108, 185–186n8, 190n21. *See also* fairy tales; Gothic fiction
becoming. *See also* Being
   as originary principle 54–59
   P as Christian vision of 15, 54–55, 68, 90
   on Perelandra 68
Beethoven, Ludwig von: associated with "energy, fertility, and urgency" of "life" 63
Being and Becoming 15, 54–59, 68. *See also* Augustine; becoming; Bergson; creative evolution
   and Nothing(ness) 63–65, 72, 76
Being and Nothingness (Sartre): and time in *P* 176n7
Benda, Julien: *The Treason of the Intellectuals* (*Trahison des clercs*), in *THS* 196n42
Benson, R. H.: supernatural fiction of 92, 181n2
Bergson, Henri 54–62. *See also* creative evolution; material/organic/spiritual realms; *Perelandra*; vitalism
   Creative Evolution 10–11, 59–62, 64–65, 89, 174n1, 175n4
   The Creative Mind 65
   CSL's response to 10–13, 62–64, 73, 89, 155 (DT), 175n4, 175n5, 180n20
   departure from Darwinism 10–11, 59–62, 89, 174n1
   durée réelle (real duration) 57–59
   early twentieth-century response to 57–62, 89, 162n5, 175n3
   élan vital (vital impetus) 56–57, 60–61, 61–62, 117
   and French existentialism 176n7
   intellect/intuition 59–60

Introduction to Metaphysics 59
   "inversion of Platonism" in 15, 59
   Laughter ("Le Rire") 177n10
   Matter and Memory 57, 175n4
   Mind-Energy (*L'Énergie spirituelle*) 175n4 and *P* 10–13, 53–90
   recent revival of 175n3
   Time and Free Will 57–59, 177n10
   transfigured in *P* 12–13, 54, 90
Bernal, J. D.: *The World, the Flesh, and the Devil,* and evolution into bodiless species 190–191n22
biocentrism. *See* material/organic/spiritual realms
biological philosophy. *See* creative evolution
Blackwood, Algernon: CSL reading 184n6
Blake, William
   on Milton's Satan (*The Marriage of Heaven and Hell*) 55, 174n2
   promethean vision of 73–74
Bluebeard: Alcasan as (*THS*) 99, 112. *See also* fairy tales
body. *See also* animals
   "creatureliness" 189–190n19, 195n37
   CSL on 189–190n19
   desire to transcend (*THS*) 94, 100, 111–112, 119, 123, 190n19, 190–191n22
   human as union of spirit and flesh 121–122, 124–125, 139, 148, 189–190n19, 195n37
   humans as animals 21–22, 43–44, 80, 165–166n2, 172n20
   as more than mere matter 121–122, 125–126, 147
   as seat of affections and sentiments 124–125, 126
   women as reducible to (*THS*) 100
Borges, Jorge Luis: review of Dunne 153
Bowler, Peter: *Reconciling Science and Religion,* on emergent evolution 174n1
Bradbury, Ray: *The Martian Chronicles,* and CSL's influence on science fiction 173n24
Bradley, F. H.: *Essays on Truth and Reality* 3 (epigraph)
Brave New World (Huxley) 188n17
British Empire. *See also* imperialism
   CSL's hatred of 167n8
   Swift as critic of 171n16
   twentieth-century critics of 167n8
Brontë, Charlotte: *Jane Eyre,* and "female" Gothic 137, 185n8, 190n21. *See also* Gothic fiction
Bulwer-Lytton, Edward. *See also* Gothic fiction
   A Strange Story 182n3
   Zanoni 182n3
Burnham, James: *The Managerial Revolution,* and technocracy movement 193n29

Campbell, John W.: influence of technocracy on science fiction of 193n29

Derrida, Jacques
  on animality 172nn20–21
  on "negative theology" 163n5
  Specters of Marx 91(epigraph)
  "The Animal That Therefore I Am (More to
    Follow)", as play on *cogito, ergo sum*
    172n20
Descartes, René. *See also* scientific revolution
  cogito, ergo sum 43, 172n20
  debate with Henry More 180n18
  dissociation of mind and body 44, 189n19
  developmental model. *See* evolutionary model
Dialectic of Enlightenment (Horkheimer and
    Adorno): and *Abolition of Man*
    192–193n28
Dilthey, Wilhelm: and *Lebensphilosophie* 56
  "discarded image." *See* medieval model
*Discourse on the Origin and Foundations of
    Inequality* (Rousseau) 19 (epigraph)
  on attributes of human nature 50–51
  on European ethnocentrism 50–51
Divine Comedy (Dante): contrapasso and
    retributive justice (*THS*) 135, 196n39
Doctor Faustus (Mann): and the "dialectic of
    Enlightenment" 192–193n28
Donne, John: "women" in Love's Alchymie (*THS*)
    99–101
Downing, David: study of Trilogy 7
Dr. Jekyll and Mr. Hyde [Stevenson] 183n5.
  See also Gothic fiction
Dracula (Stoker)
  Jonathan Harker 102, 110
  Mina Harker 118
  as source of *THS* 184n6, 188n15
DuMaurier, Daphne: *Rebecca*, and "female" Gothic
    185n8, 190n21. *See also* Gothic fiction
Dunbar, William: associated with "energy, fertility,
    and urgency" of "life" 63
Dunne, J. W. *See also* higher dimensions
  An Experiment with Time, and *DT* 153, 155
  influence on thirties literature 153
durée réelle (Bergson) 57–59

Eddington, Arthur: *The Nature of the Physical
    World*, on "Becoming" 174n1. *See also*
    becoming; Being
Eddison, E. R.: Dunne's influence on 153
élan vital (Bergson) 57, 60–61, 61–62, 117
Eliot, T. S.: Hulme's influence on 162n5
emergent evolution. *See* creative evolution
Enlightenment
  Adorno and Horkheimer on 192–193n28
  Rousseau on 50–52
Essays on Truth and Reality (Bradley) 3 (epigraph)
eugenics 101, 168–169n10
  Chesterton as critic of 168–169n10, 187n13
  early twentieth-century development of 30,
    168–169n10
  Galton as founder of 168n10

Haldane as proponent of 168n10, 187n13
  and Mental Deficiency Act 30
  in opening chapters of *OSP* 30, 187n13
  in the Third Reich 7, 30, 101, 168n10
  in *THS* 11("self–transformation of man"),
    101, 187n13
  in twenty-first century 7, 168–169n10
  in the United States 30, 168n10
Eugenics and Other Evils (Chesterton)
    168–169n10, 187n13
Evans, I. O.: CSL's letters to 192n25, 194n33
The Everlasting Man (Chesterton): on Wells's
    Outline of History 51–52
evolution. *See also* creative evolution; Darwinism;
    eugenics; evolutionary model; material/
    organic/spiritual realms
  CSL on Darwinism as "genuine scientific
    hypothesis" 6, 168n9
  evolutionary anthropology 6, 20–21, 29–30,
    36 ("old stone age"), 52, 167–168n9
  evolutionary ethics 6–7, 27, 29, 47,
    172–173n 22, 193n 29
  material/organic/spiritual views of 7–14,
    138–139, 141–149
  as model of human relations 6–7, 10, 12,
    17, 47, 73
evolutionary (developmental) model. *See also*
    Bergson; Darwin; eugenics; evolution;
    material/organic/spiritual realms
  Chesterton as critic of 51–52
  Darwin symptom not cause of 6, 168n9
  in *The Discarded Image* 164n8
  material/organic/spiritual views of 7–14,
    138–139, 141–149
  Ransom shares assumptions of (*OSP*) 36–37,
    41, 170n13
  and sequence of Trilogy 7–8, 10–12
  as successor to "medieval model" 6, 12,
    16–17, 29, 53, 73
  transfigured in Trilogy 8, 12–18, 138–139,
    148–149
existentialism. *See also* becoming; Being
  Bergson's anticipation of 176n7
  and time in *P* 176n7, 178n13
An Experiment with Time (Dunne). *See also*
    higher dimensions
  and *DT* 153, 155
  influence on thirties literature 153

The Faerie Queene (Spenser): and Scudamour in
    DT 152, 154–155
fairy tales
  Beauty and the Beast 107, 185–186n8, 190n21
  Bluebeard: Alcasan as (*THS*) 99, 112
  CSL on "realistic" character of 183n5
  Fairy Hardcastle as ogress of 110
  George Macdonald's 108–109
  Jane and Mark (*THS*) as couple 101–102
  and subtitle of (*THS*) 92, 183n5

"fantastic fiction" (Spencer, Zgorzelski). *See also*
  "supernatural fiction"
Charles Williams and 92
CSL on "fantastic" satire 185n7
distinguished from "fantasy" 181–182n2
Fantasy (Jackson): CSL as escapist 183n5
fascism. *See* Third Reich
Faust
  and Charles Williams's necromancers 16
  final chance to repent 135
  as prototype for "male" Gothic 113
Ficino, Marsilio
  and Neoplatonism 196–197n38
  and revival of "magia" 195–196n34
The First Men in the Moon (Wells)
  CSL on fear in 34
  as source of *OSP* 23, 25, 92, 161n3, 166n4
First World War
  and Bergson's philosophy 62
  CSL wounded in 33
  Ransom's participation in 5, 32–33
Flatland (Abbott): and the fourth dimension
  162n5, 180n19. *See also* higher
  dimensions
Flieger, Verlyn: on Dunne and Tolkien 153
Fontenelle, Bernard le Bovier de [*Conversations on
  the Plurality of Worlds*] 165n1. *See also*
  "plurality of worlds"
Forster, E. M.: as critic of Empire 167n8
Foucault, Michel: and CSL on punishment
  193n30
fourth dimension. *See* higher dimensions
Fowler, Alistair: on authenticity of *DT* 152
Frankenstein (Shelley) 101, 182n3
  "hideous progeny" 137
  Victor Frankenstein, and "male" Gothic 95,
  101, 137
free will (free agency)
  Bergson on 58, 65
  and the hunting scene (*OSP*) 142–144,
  147–149
  in *P* 65, 71–79, 86, 89, 176n7
  and predestination 79, 163n5
  and Ransom's call to battle Un-man (*P*)
  143–146, 147–149
  and the Studdocks' reckoning with death
  (*THS*) 145–149
French Revolution: echoes of (*THS*) 188n15
Freud, Sigmund
  "Gothic" model of the mind 185n7
  and interpretation of dreams and visions
  (*THS*) 103, 105–106, 127, 188n16
Frogs and Mice [*Battle of Frogs and Mice*, anon.
  Greek parody]: as ancestor of modern
  "fantastic" satire 185n7
Frye, Northrop: on Christian apologetics 17

Galton, Francis: as founder of eugenics 168n10.
  See also eugenics

Geoffrey of Monmouth: as source of CSL's Merlin
  194n33
Gernsback, Hugo: influence of technocracy on
  science fiction of 193n29
Gilman, Charlotte Perkins ("The Yellow
  Wallpaper"): and "female" Gothic
  185n8. *See also* Gothic fiction
Girard, René: assumption of primordial violence
  in 197n2
Gnosticism
  denigration of the body in 44, 189–190n19
  in *THS* 139, 172n21
Godwin, William: *St. Leon* 182n3. *See also* Gothic
  fiction
Goethe, Johann Wolfgang von: associated with
  "energy, fertility, and urgency" of "life" 63
Gothic fiction 92–97, 181–186nn2–8
  conventions of 16, 93, 101
  CSL on 181–184nn2–6
  as dark double of traditional romance (*THS*)
  16, 96, 117, 130–131
  doubles in 16, 96, 152–156 (DT)
  and *Dracula* 102, 110, 118, 184n6, 188n15
  "female" 97, 107–108, 112–113, 118, 137,
  184n6, 185–186n8, 190n21
  and *Frankenstein* 95, 101, 137, 182n3
  and Kafka 104
  "male" 95, 102, 113, 185–186n8, 187n12
  as mixture of the Probable and the Marvelous
  18, 92–97, 182–183n5
  and Otto's *mysterium tremendum* 182n4, 185n7
  romance origins of 95–96, 185n7
  and Rosicrucianism 182n3
  and science fiction 184n6
  and Shakespeare's *Hamlet* 183n6
  studies of 184n6
  transfigured in Williams and Lewis 16–18,
  93, 107–108, 182n2, 182n4
Grail legend 190n20. *See also* romance
Great War. *See* First World War
Greene, Graham: as critic of Empire 167n8
Greeves, Arthur: CSL's letter to 175n4
Gulliver's Travels (Swift) 28, 171n16
  Brobdingnag 109
  Houyhnhnms 37, 40

Haggard, H. Rider
  and British imperial anxieties 167n5
  CSL reading 184n6
  King Solomon's Mines, echoes in *OSP* 171n15
Haldane, J. B. S.
  Dædalus, and eugenics 168n10, 187n13
  Possible Worlds, and origins of the Trilogy
  190–191n22
  and "scientific hope of defeating death" 29,
  187n13
Hamlet (Shakespeare)
  CSL essay on 183n6
  as Ur-Gothic 183n6

Layamon: as source for CSL's Merlin 194n33
Lebensphilosophie. See creative evolution
Leinster, Murray: thirties time-travel fiction 154
L'Engle, Madeleine: *A Wrinkle in Time,* linked to
    DT 151
Lewis, C. Day: and thirties literature 169n11
Lewis, C. S.
    The Abolition of Man 4
      and "dialectic of Enlightenment"
        192–193n28
      eugenics 168–169n10
      modern dissociation of subject/object
        122–123, 125, 192–193n28, 194n32
      Natural Law (*Tao*) 193n29
      a "new Natural Philosophy" 180n18
      "post-humanity" 93
      and *THS* 192–193n28
    All My Road Before Me
      friendship with Jane McNeill 186n9
      reading Bergson 175n4
      reading Chesterton on eugenics 169n10
      "shocker play" as germ of *THS* 184n6
    The Allegory of Love 4
    Beyond Personality 4
    Broadcast Talks 4
    Christian Behaviour 4
    The Chronicles of Narnia 3, 4, 156, 163n6,
      172n21
      The Last Battle 195n36
      The Lion, the Witch and the Wardrobe 4
    Collected Letters
      Bergson 175n4
      Kafka 189n18
      Merlin 194n33
      Nazism and the occult 192n25
      "Westonism" 29
    "The Conditions for a Just War" (*GID*): as
      response to E.L. Mascall's "The
      Christian and the Next War" 169n12
    The Dark Tower 151–156
      controversy over 151–152
      publication of 7, 151
      totalitarian regime in 153–154, 156
    "The Decline of Religion" (*GID*): "middle
      things are gone" 187n14
    The Discarded Image: medieval model in 164n8
    Dymer
      and the occult 191n23
      and totalitarianism 188–189n17
    English Literature in the Sixteenth Century
      179–80n17
    The Four Loves: three views of the body in
      189n19
    George MacDonald: An Anthology: Kafka as
      "mythopoeic" artist in Preface to
      189n18
    The Great Divorce 4, 195n36
    "Hamlet: The Prince or the Poem" (*SLE*): as
      Ur-Gothic 183n6

    "The Humanitarian Theory of Punishment"
      (*GID*): and *THS* 193n30
    "The Inner Ring" (*WG*): and Mark Studdock
      (*THS*) 187n12
    "Is Theology Poetry?" (*WG*): and Darwinism
      168n 9
    "Meditation in a Toolshed" (*GID*): and
      Alexander's contemplation/
      enjoyment 177n9
    Mere Christianity 4
    Miracles 4
      on "principle of Vicariousness" 197n4
    "The Novels of Charles Williams" (*OS*):
      between "classical novel" and "pure
      fantasy" 183n5
    Out of the Silent Planet. See under *Out of the
      Silent Planet*
    Perelandra. See under *Perelandra*
    "The Poison of Subjectivism" (*CR*): Natural
      Law 193n29
    A Preface to 'Paradise Lost' 4
      temporal process in Homer/Virgil
      175–176n6
    The Problem of Pain 4, 141 (epigraph)
      animal suffering 172n21
      atonement 197n4
      first apologetical work 197n4
      necessity of "matter" 189–190n19
      Otto's *The Idea of the Holy* 182n4
    "Religion and Rocketry" (*WLN*): extraterrestrial
      encounter 50, 173n23
    The Screwtape Letters 4
    "The Seeing Eye" (*CR*): meeting other rational
      species 49–50, 173n23
    Surprised by Joy
      Bergson 63, 175n4
      the occult 191n23
      Vice Versa (Anstey) 191n24
    That Hideous Strength. See under *That Hideous
      Strength*
    Till We Have Faces: Cupid and Psyche 107,
      190n21
    "Transposition" (*WG*): movement between
      material/organic/spiritual realms 162n5
    "Unreal Estates" (*OS*)
      CSL's contribution to science fiction
      173n24
      extraterrestrial encounter 49–51, 173n23
    "Why I Am Not a Pacifist" (WG) 169n12
Lewis, Warren (brother of CSL)
    and *DT* 151
    as expert on seventeenth-century France
      187n14
"Life-Force philosophy." *See* creative evolution
Lindsay, David
    as "the real father of my planet books" 161n3
    A Voyage to Arcturus, as model for Trilogy 12, 92
Lindskoog, Kathryn: *The C. S. Lewis Hoax,* on
    authorship of *DT* 151

naturalism of 22, 92–95, 103, 115
time reconceived in 89–90
Moore, C. L.: thirties time-travel fiction 154
More, Henry. *See also* higher dimensions;
    Neoplatonism
    debate with Descartes 180n18
    and modern multi-tiered universe 180n18
    and Neoplatonism 196–197n38
    and "plurality of worlds" 164–165n1
    as subject of CSL's unwritten thesis 85
Morgan, C. Lloyd: emergent evolution 73, 174n1
Morris, William 63
    CSL's discovery of 181n1
Morrisson, Mark: on alchemy and atomic science
    186n10, 192n26
Müller, Max: Barfield on 193–194n31
Munich Agreement 4. *See also* World War II
Mutabilitie Cantos (Spenser): and Hymn of
    Praise 84
Myers, Doris: study of CSL's modern contexts
    161n1
The Mysteries of Udolpho (Radcliffe): and "female"
    Gothic 110, 137, 185n8, 190n21
mysterium tremendum 139
Otto's 182n4, 185n7
mysticism 163n5

Nagasaki 5. *See also* World War II
Nahin, Paul J.: *Time Machines,* and thirties
    time-travel fiction 154
naturalism
    evolutionary 11, 14, 22–26, 32, 138
    of modern thought 22, 92–95, 103, 115
    rationality reduced to naturalistic function 25,
        42, 51–52
    religious vs. naturalistic viewpoints 17, 49, 54,
        56, 60–61, 116
    scientific 81
    vitalistic 55–56, 60–61, 89–90
nature
    beyond our sense of regularities (*THS*) 136
    energy and fertility of 63–64
    and grace 179n17
    indwelling of the divine in 85–86
    the meaning of beyond Man 81, 85
    multidimensional 87
    and Natural Law 125, 193n29
    "New Man" free from (*THS*) 11
    "red in tooth and claw" 13
    and "regenerate science" 126
    revolt of (*THS*) 136, 188n15
    as spoiled copy of "original" 13, 162n4,
        167n6
The Nature of the Physical World (Eddington): on
    "Becoming" 174n1. *See also* becoming;
    Being
Nazism. *See* Third Reich
negative theology: in mystical tradition and
    contemporary philosophy 163n5

Neoplatonism
    CSL's attraction to 196–197n38
    hierarchical levels of Being in 162n5
    in Hymn of Praise (*P*) 85
    More's debate with Descartes 180n18
Nicholas of Cusa
    CSL's poems on 179–180n17
    De Docta Ignorantia, and the new cosmology
        179n17
Nicholson, Mervyn: Dracula and *THS* 184n6,
    188n15
Nietzsche, Friedrich
    as forebear of existentialism 176n7
    and *Lebensphilosophie* 56
    Promethean vision of 73–74
Nineteen Eighty-Four (Orwell)
    and *THS* 188–189n17
    and totalitarianism 192–193n28
Notion Club Papers (Tolkien): and *DT* 151
Novalis 161n3, 189n18

obedience
    "bare willing of" 145
    Christ's "pure will to obey" 145, 197–198n4
    to God 129, 195n37
    Jane's vow to Director (*THS*) 117, 146
    Mark's redemptive disobedience (*THS*) 134
    in marriage (*THS*) 108, 129, 195n35,
        195n37
    Ransom's acceptance of mission (*P*) 145
    Ransom's tragic disobedience (*OSP*) 39, 143
occult. *See also* magic
    alchemy 99, 186n10
    astrology 196–197n38
    Charles Williams as student of 92
    CSL's antipathy toward 191n23
    Dunne on 153
    fused with "scientific" (*THS*) 15, 95, 99,
        186n10, 192n26
    the "Inner Ring" (*THS*) 187n12
    in Moberley and Jourdain, *An Adventure*
        152–153
    Nazism and 192n25
    N.I.C.E. steeped in (*THS*) 95–96
    second sight (*THS*) 96, 99–101, 102–103,
        105, 113, 191n23
    specters (*THS*) 91 (epigraph), 114
    spiritualism 116, 122, 191n23
    telepathic surveillance (*THS*) 106, 117, 120
The Odyssey (Homer)
    Odysseus's ruse in 133
    reunion of Odysseus and Penelope in 137
O'Neill, Joseph (*Land under England*)
    CSL reading 188n17
    totalitarian dystopia in 153
organic ("vital") realm. *See* material/organic/
    spiritual realms
Origin of Species (Darwin) 6, 29, 89, 167–168n9.
    See also Darwinism

original/copy. *See also* Neoplatonism; Plato;
St. Augustine; transfiguration
deriving "original" from "copy" 13, 16–17
as informing principle of Trilogy 16
Nature as 12, 55, 162n4
in *OSP* 20
Romance/Gothic as (*THS*) 16, 96–97, 117,
130–131
St. Anne's/Belbury (*THS*) as 7–8, 16, 96, 117,
121–122, 131, 133
Orwell, George
as critic of Empire 167n8
and modern "fantastic" satire 185n7
Nineteen Eighty-Four, and *THS* 188–189n17
and totalitarianism 192–193n28
Othello (Shakespeare) 196n41
other(ness)
as aim of space travel fiction 12
apprehension of self as 44
aptitude for misrecognition of 49–52
CSL's uses of term 166n3
receptivity to (*OSP*) 34
troubled relations to animal, human,
extraterrestrial (*OSP*) 22
"Othertime" 152–156 (*DT*)
Otto, Rudolf
The Idea of the Holy, the Divine as "wholly
Other" in 166n3, 185n7
and Gothic "terror" 182n4
mysterium tremendum in 182n4
Out of the Silent Planet 19–52
animals in
distinguishing human/nonhuman 21–22,
48, 165–166n2, 172n21
elemental fear of 31–32
human kinship to 37–39, 43–44, 189n19
humans as 21–22, 43–44, 165–166n2,
172n20
hunting 13, 20, 37–39, 45, 66, 141–146
(mis)recognition of other rational 14,
19–20, 38–39, 40–41, 50–52,
165–166n2, 170–71n14,
171–172n19
Wells and 23–24
compared to
other literature of the thirties 169n11
other volumes of Trilogy 10–18, 53–54,
138–139, 141–149, 163n6
Devine and Weston in
captivity of 28, 46–47
hross killed by 38–39
imperialism (racism) of 10, 13, 19, 21–22,
29–32, 46–48, 50
Wells's Bedford and Cavor (*The First
Men in the Moon*) as source of 25
young Harry treated as disposable by
26–27, 29–30
eugenics in 30, 168–169n10
evolution in

material (mechanistic) view of 7, 10–12,
20, 41, 138–139, 141–149
Ransom shares assumptions of 36–37, 41,
170n13, 171n15
as rationale for exploitation, domination,
conquest 6, 7–8, 20, 24–25, 29, 37,
40–41, 47, 51–52, 168n9,
172–173n22, 193n29
transfiguration of 7–8, 13–14, 17, 20, 26,
54, 93, 138–139, 142–149
fear in
impending war and 4–6, 22, 32
Malacandrans free from 12, 20, 38–39,
48, 148
Oyarsa's reflections on 45–50
pacifism and 5, 33, 169n12, 177n10,
197n3
Ransom besieged by 26–27, 31–36
Ransom overcoming 37–40, 142–143
H. G. Wells in 10, 22–26
critics on 166n4
CSL's response to 23, 25–26, 34, 161n3
evolutionary naturalism of 10–15, 23–26,
32, 50–52, 54, 138
The First Men in the Moon as CSL's main
debt to 23, 25, 34, 92, 161n3, 166n4
Ransom's imagination shaped by 19, 22,
26, 31–34, 40, 170n13
imperialism, jingoism, racism ("blood") in 13,
19 (epigraph), 22, 26, 29, 32, 46–51
literary influences on
Lindsay 12, 92, 161n3
Swift 28, 37, 40, 171n16
tradition of "scientific romance" 161n1
Wells 10, 19, 22–26, 31–32, 34, 92,
161n3, 166n4, 170n13
Malacandra in
ancient invasion of 13, 45, 48
earthlings misconceive inhabitants of 14,
19–20, 26–27, 31–32, 40–41, 46,
49–51, 170n13
eldila on 37–38, 45
Mars (planet) and 4–5, 12–13, 33, 163n6
three rational species of 14, 19–22, 40–44,
171–172n19
topography of 20, 36
origins and contexts of
CSL on "scientific hope of defeating death"
29, 167n7
CSL's career 3–4
impending war 4–6
modern debate over human origins 6
Oyarsa in 19 (epigraph), 28, 39, 41, 45–50,
163n6
Ransom in
abduction of 19, 26–27, 28
courage renewed in 37–40, 142–143, 148
evolutionary assumptions shared by 14,
36–37, 41, 50, 169–170n13

fear besets 26–27, 31–36
hrossa befriends 35–39
Oyarsa judges and admonishes 45–50
sorns enlighten 40–44
transformation of 33–40
Wells's fiction shapes imagination of 19, 22,
26, 31–34, 34, 40, 170n13
rationality in
biocentrism and 20, 25, 42
biology ("blood") transcended by 14, 21,
42–43, 46, 54, 138–139, 147–148
"cosmic" or "corrective" 21, 52
CSL's post-Sputnik essays and 49–51,
165–166n2, 173nn23–24
hnau and 37
natural order reflects divine 22–23, 35, 42
Rousseau and CSL on 51–52
Swift's "universal" 37
three Malacandran species possess 14,
19–22, 40–44
space/heavens in 33–34, 50
structure of 9–10, 28 (illustration), 40,
171n17
The Outline of History (Wells): Chesterton as
critic of 51–52
Oxford
Charles Williams moves to 181n1
Lewis at 4, 167n8
proximity to Harwell 188n17

pacifism. *See also* Just War; violence
CSL's opposition to 33, 169n12, 177n12,
197n3
in the thirties 5
panentheism: distinguished from pantheism
174n1
Paradise Lost (Milton)
CSL on Romantic view of Satan 55
hints of evolving Eden in 15, 53, 164n7,
176n6
meeting of Adam and Eve in 35–36
as source of *P* 161n3
Paradise Regained (Milton): and temptation
scenes in *P* 5, 161n3
parallel worlds: in *DT* 152–156. *See also* higher
dimensions
Parody. *See also* satire; St. Augustine
in *OSP* 20
in *P* 55, 74, 144
in *THS* 96, 120–121, 124, 133, 185n7,
192n26
in Trilogy 12, 17, 138–139
Pascal, Blaise: "silence of the eternal spaces" 34
Péguy, Charles: and Catholic response to
Bergson 61–62
Penelope (wife of Odysseus) 137
Perceval (Chrétien de Troyes): and Jane at
St. Anne's (*THS*) 107
Perelandra 53–90

animale rationale in 63, 83–85
compared to other volumes 4–18, 53–54, 67,
69, 73, 111, 138–139, 141–149, 156,
163n6, 196–97n1
creative/emergent evolution in
"biological philosophy" as expression for
10, 54, 73
critique of 73–74
transfiguration of 13–15, 17, 54–55,
89–90, 144, 149
Weston's conversion to 10–11, 14–15,
53–54, 73
Fixed Land in
prohibition to settle on 15, 54, 68
Ransom explains ban on 86
temptation to settle on 72–74
free will in
Bergson and 56–59
fragility of 71–73, 78–79, 88
obedience and 75, 86
openness of time and 65, 79, 86, 89
predestination and 79
Green Lady (Queen, Tinidril) in
free will comprehended by 71–73
King (Tor) with 83, 88
Ransom meets 69–73
Weston/Un-man tempts 74–77
Henri Bergson in 10–18, 54–65, 70, 79,
89–90
Hymn of Praise and 85–87
idea of Nothing(ness) and 63–65, 70,
73, 76
Holy Mountain in 82–88
Great Dance on 84, 87
Hymn of Praise and 84–87
King of Perelandra (Tor) in 53 (epigraph),
82, 83, 87
"Lewis" as narrator of 65, 67
Milton in
CSL's *Preface to 'Paradise Lost'* and 4, 55,
174–175n2, 176n6
origins and contexts of: CSL's career 3–4
Paradise Lost and 15, 53 (epigraph), 161n3,
163–164n7, 176n6
Paradise Regained and 5, 161n3
modern debate over naturalism 6
Second World War 5–6, 177–178n12
Venus's "floating islands" 15, 68, 81,
163–164n7
Perelandra in
fertility of 63, 163n6
Fixed Land of 15, 54, 68, 72–74, 86
Holy Mountain of 66, 82–88
paradisal state of becoming on 15, 17,
54–55, 68–73, 84–88, 90, 164n7,
176n6
surface/depths of 66, 80, 81
Venus (planet) and 12–13, 15, 68,
163–64nn6–7

Wells, H. G. (*continued*)
influence on Ransom's imagination (*OSP*) 19,
22, 26, 31–34, 40, 170n13
The Island of Dr. Moreau 23
and material view of evolution 10–14, 15, 23,
32, 138
Men Like Gods and *OSP* 166n4
and *OSP* 10, 11, 22–26
The Outline of History, and Chesterton's
Everlasting Man 51–52
as source for Director of N.I.C.E.
(*THS*) 134
"The Crystal Egg," and *DT* 154
The Time Machine 23, 41(*OSP*), 152–154
(*DT*)
transfigured in *OSP* 12–14, 54
The War of the Worlds 10, 23–25, 165n1
The Wonderful Visit and *DT* 154
"Wellsianity." *See* evolutionary model
"Westonism." *See also* eugenics; imperialism
as "dream of interplanetary colonization"
27, 29
and eugenics 169n10
and imperialism 50
Whitehead, Alfred North
as "our greatest natural philosopher" 174n1
Process and Reality and *Science and the Modern
World,* and dynamic conception of
nature 174n1
Wilkins, John [*The Discovery of a World in the
Moone*] 165n1. *See also* "plurality of
worlds"
Williams, Anne: *Art of Darkness,* on "female"
Gothic 185n8, 190n21
Williams, Charles 16–18, 92–96
CSL's "The Novels of Charles Williams"
183n5

debt to Benson, Underhill, and Machen
181n2
detective fiction reviews 182n3
friendship with CSL 180–181n1
Gothic elements in 92–96, 182nn2–3
influence on *THS* 16–18, 92–96, 117, 136,
161n3, 180–181n1
novels and poems 180–181n1
occult influences on 92
on parallel universes (*Many Dimensions*) 156
on St. Athanasius 163n5
transfiguration of Gothic in 16, 92–93, 182n2
War in Heaven 92–93
Williamson, Jack: thirties time-travel fiction 154
The Wonderful Visit (Wells): and parallel universes
(*DT*) 154
"working-up." *See* transfiguration
The World, the Flesh, and the Devil (Bernal):
and evolution into bodiless species
190–191n22
World War I. *See* First World War
World War II. *See* Second World War
Wren, Christopher: associated with "energy,
fertility, and urgency" of "life" 63
Wright, Patrick: *The Village that Died for England,*
and government expropriation 188n17

Yeats, William Butler 63
"The Yellow Wallpaper" (Gilman): and "female"
Gothic 185n8

Zanoni (Bulwer-Lytton) 182n3. *See also* Gothic
fiction
Zgorzelski, Andrzej: "fantastic fiction"
(distinguished from "fantasy")
181–182n2. *See also* "supernatural
fiction"